# The Wolves of Denali

The University of Minnesota Press gratefully acknowledges the generous assistance for the publication of this book by the Hamilton P. Traub University Fund.

# The Wolves of Denali

L. DAVID MECH

LAYNE G. ADAMS • THOMAS J. MEIER

JOHN W. BURCH • BRUCE W. DALE

*University of Minnesota Press*

*Minneapolis*

*London*

Published by the University of Minnesota Press
111 Third Avenue South, Suite 290
Minneapolis, MN 55401-2520
http://www.upress.umn.edu

Printed in the United States of America on acid-free paper

Library of Congress Cataloging-in-Publication Data

The wolves of Denali / L. David Mech . . . [et al.].
       p.     cm.
    Includes bibliographical references and index.
    ISBN 0-8166-2958-7 (hc : alk. paper)
    1. Wolves—Alaska—Denali National Park and Preserve.    I. Mech, L. David.
  QL737.C22W648   1998
  599.773'09798'3—dc21                                                    97-34687

The University of Minnesota is an equal-opportunity educator and employer.

10 09 08 07 06 05 04 03 02 01 00 99 98      10 9 8 7 6 5 4 3 2 1

*We dedicate this book to Allan L. Lovaas and John Dalle-Molle. "Big Al" was the National Park Service's Regional Chief Scientist for Alaska from 1981 to 1993. He was a strong advocate of long-term research and fought hard, always against the bureaucratic inertia, to keep this research afloat. We are deeply and forever in his debt.*

*John Dalle-Molle, Denali Resource Manager from 1978 to 1989, conceived of the study and pushed to get it funded. Once we were up and running, John continued to assist and encourage us in every way he could. We all felt the loss when John left Denali in 1989 at the beginning of his battle with cancer, and we mourned his untimely death in 1990.*

# Contents

# *Acknowledgments*

The authors conducted the research for and prepared this book under the following auspices: L. David Mech, Patuxent Wildlife Research Center, Biological Resources Division, U.S. Geological Survey; Layne G. Adams, Alaska Science Center, Biological Resources Division, U.S. Geological Survey; Thomas J. Meier and John W. Burch, Denali National Park and Preserve, U.S. National Park Service; and Bruce W. Dale, Alaska Region, U.S. National Park Service.

This research was funded primarily by the U.S. National Park Service (NPS) through the Natural Resources Preservation and Protection Program and the Alaska Regional Office. Denali National Park, the U.S. Fish and Wildlife Service, the U.S. Forest Service North Central Forest Experiment Station, and the National Biological Survey also contributed to the project.

Joe Van Horn, John Dalle-Molle's assistant when the study began and currently the "institutional memory" for resource management at Denali, has always been there when we needed him. He has helped with everything from fieldwork to continually arranging housing for our small air force.

We received excellent support from the resource management staff throughout our studies. Following in John Dalle-Molle's footsteps, Jim Benedict, Gordon Olson, and Ken Stahlnecker maintained the enthusiasm for our research and have provided endless assistance.

The entire staff of Denali National Park has regularly furnished support, field assistance, and facilities. We are especially indebted to superintendents Clay Cunningham and Russ Berry, and assistant superintendent Linda Buswell.

To complete the fieldwork and associated activities described here, we have relied on a large number of people for their assistance with radiocollaring, monitoring, kill investigations, and specimen processing. In particular, we thank Andrea Blakesley, Jane Bryant, Robyn Burch, Laurie Daniel, Patty Del Vecchio, Nick Demma, Mark Masteller, Brad Shults, Doug Waring, Jeff Keay, Jennifer Wolk, Neil Barten, Gary Koy, Bud Krause, Pat Owen, and Miki and Julie Collins.

We are also indebted to the dozens of pilots who have flown us for thousands of safe hours, particularly Ken Butters, Don Glaser, Sandy Hamilton, Bill Lentsch, Dennis Miller, Ron Purdum, Bill Roberts, Hollis Twitchell, Jim Unruh, and Ron Warbelow. For stand-up comedy and regularly baring his soul, Glaser deserves special mention.

Our research has benefited from continued interchange with many biologists throughout Alaska. Thanks to Rod Boertje, Jim Davis, Danny Grangaard, Dale Hagstrom, Mark McNay, Bob Stephenson, Pat Valkenburg, and Ken Whitten, all of the Alaska Department of Fish and Game, and to John Blake and Jim Woolington.

Production of this book has been a substantial task, and we have called on many people for help. Patty Del Vecchio and Liz Harper produced the many maps we needed, and Paul Wolf made many of the other illustrations. Nancy Anderson and Liz Harper assisted with the literature cited and other subsidiary tasks. Two anonymous reviewers helped us improve the book.

We thank all of the people mentioned here, and hope they are as pleased as we are with the outcome.

# Introduction

Wolf 5051 was having trouble keeping the old Dall sheep still. Even though the ram was dead and partly eaten, its precarious position on a gravel bar in the Toklat River kept the wolf from tearing much off the carcass without tugging it into the swift current.

The wolf paid me no heed as I sat nearby; he was too intent on trying to contend with his quarry. And, after all, this was in the center of Alaska's Denali National Park (formerly Mount McKinley National Park), where wolves had nothing to fear from human beings. Some wolves, however, were not so sure. Lying in the open brush 150 yards behind radio-collared wolf 5051, the younger pack animals apparently did not yet trust humans quite like their father did.

As I sat at the base of Polychrome Mountain, which the old sheep had been trying to reach when it was killed, I could not help but acknowledge to myself just how glad I was to be studying the wolves in this park. The crisp September air bathed the crimson and gold tundra foliage all around me while presaging the annual white carpet about to come. Already the tops of the sur-rounding mountains far in the background bore the beginning of their annual coat.

## Denali's Wolf Study Pioneer

To one who has studied wolves for most of his career, the National Park Service's project to study wolves in Denali was the frosting on the cake. On hearing about it, I immediately conjured up the image of Adolph Murie, the legendary pioneer of wolf studies who sat in these very mountains (plate 1) and watched the predecessors of these very animals some four decades before. Not only had "Ade" watched the wolves hunt and the sheep defy the wolves, but he had also written about it in such a way as to reveal to the world their many secrets that he had uncovered.

Murie's (1944) study came at a time when wildlife science was relatively new. The only previous work of any consequence on wolves was Sigurd Olson's (1938a,b) general look at wolves and deer in the Superior National Forest of northern Minnesota. Most previous literature on wolves involved historical accounts and naturalists' notes made incidental to other activities. Murie actually observed a pack of wolves around its den, a rare

*Figure 0.1. Members of the East Fork wolf pack feed on a Dall sheep they killed on the park road. (Photo by Thomas J. Meier.)*

feat even to this day, and watched individually recognizable pack members interact with each other. He also recorded their interactions with prey, and with other community fauna, collected and analyzed their scats, and examined remains of their kills.

Murie's primary contributions to our understanding of wolf biology were threefold. First, by making detailed observations of the East Fork pack members interacting around their den, Murie laid the foundation for understanding the wolf pack as basically a family (figure 0.1). He described each individual in the pack and its personality, behavior, and role in the group. Although Murie may have overinterpreted the precise relationships among the pack members, his conclusion that most of the members were related has been borne out by other research (Joslin 1967; Mech 1973, 1974a, 1977a; Carbyn 1974; Van Ballenberghe et al. 1975; Fritts and Mech 1981).

Since Murie's time, we have learned many more details about the life cycle of the wolf pack. Basically, lone male and female wolves find each other, mate, and produce pups in a den during spring (Rothman and Mech 1979). The adults radiate out, hunt, and bring food back to the pups. The wolves abandon the den after about 8 weeks and live at "rendezvous sites" above ground until early autumn. The whole pack then roams nomadically around a large territory for the rest of the year.

Most wolves disperse when they are 1 to 2 years old (Fritts and Mech 1981; Mech and Hertel 1983; Gese and Mech 1991), and those that remain usually help feed and care for the new pups each year (Murie 1944; Haber 1977; Mech 1988a). Wolves rarely remain in their natal pack after 3 years of age (Gese and Mech 1991), but past-prime breeders may remain with the pack (Mech 1995a). Murie's (1944) observations of the East Fork pack would have involved watching parents, young offspring, the new pups, and possibly an old former breeder.

The second important finding of Murie's was that wolves must make many attempts at catching prey for each time they succeed. He described numerous unsuccessful hunts by wolves seeking Dall sheep and caribou. It was one to two decades before anyone made similar observations of wolves hunting other prey (Crisler 1956; Mech 1966a,b; Pimlott et al. 1969; Mech and Frenzel 1971).

Murie's third main contribution to knowledge about wolves was his discovery that Denali wolves were preying primarily on the most vulnerable classes of Dall sheep: the lambs and the old or debilitated individuals. Of 221 skulls he found of sheep perishing between 1937 and 1941, most of which were probably wolf-killed, only 4% were 2 to 8 years old and showing no sign of disease. This finding was the first quantification of Olson's (1938a,b) claim that wolves tended to take "old, diseased, or crippled" animals. Murie's findings have been confirmed many times over with several prey species (Mech 1970).

When Murie published his results as a National Park Service (NPS) monograph, he put the Denali wolves on the world biological map. *The Wolves of Mount McKinley* became one of the first wildlife classics, remaining in print even to this day. Murie was such an idol to me that I dedicated my 1970 book, *The Wolf: Ecology and Behavior of an Endangered Species*, to him.

## The Denali Wolf Project

When the NPS asked if I was interested in studying Denali's wolves, I leaped at the chance. Murie had done an excellent job with the tools available to him—binoculars, sled dogs, and a notebook. However, a new era had dawned for wolf research with the advent of the technique of aerial radio-tracking (Mech and Frenzel 1971; Mech 1974b, 1983). This advance meant that far more could be learned about Denali's wolves, not just about an individual pack or two but about the entire population.

As one who had applied this technique to hundreds of wolves in Minnesota, I was primed to use it on Denali's wolf population. The Denali population differs from the Minnesota wolves in that its packs are generally larger (figure 0.1), and they prey upon moose, caribou, and Dall sheep.

Minnesota wolves prey primarily on white-tailed deer, although some do take moose also. No doubt the Denali wolf pack territories would be much larger than those of the wolves in Minnesota. Thus, this was a chance for me to study an entirely different type of wolf-prey system. That was my personal reason for wanting to do the study.

From a scientific standpoint, I wanted to conduct this study because it needed to be done. Denali National Park contains the world's least disturbed mainland wolf population. The old Mount McKinley National Park, now the "Old Park" or the "Wilderness Area," of Denali National Park and Preserve, encompasses approximately 3,294 square miles (8,433 square kilometers). Wolves have been legally protected from human exploitation in the old park since the early 1950s. Expansion of the park in 1980 added 4,088 square miles (10,468 square kilometers) of park and 2,086 square miles (5,340 square kilometers) of "preserve" around the old park where wolf harvest is allowed but is a very minor influence on the wolf's population dynamics. The park and preserve encompass more area than the entire state of Massachusetts. As will be detailed later, annual harvests in Denali National Park and Preserve take about 1% of the wolf population, and another 1% are harvested outside Denali.

Only in the High Arctic, where wolves live far from any human beings who might exploit them, are there other such large natural populations (Mech 1988a, 1995a; Miller 1995). Minnesota's wolves have been protected only since 1974. Other national parks in both the United States and Canada as well as in other parts of the world also contain protected wolf populations, but the protection has been more recent or the populations are relatively small, such as the one on Isle Royale (Peterson 1995).

Thus, scientifically, a thorough study of the Denali wolf population would yield a wealth of information about wolf natural history, ecology,

*Figure 0.2. In 1981, aerial poachers killed wolves in Denali park, took their skins, and left their carcasses. (Photo by NPS.)*

prey relations, and population dynamics unattainable elsewhere in the world. What was needed, and what now could be done, was an investigation of all the Denali wolf packs and their interactions with each other and their prey.

Murie's (1944) study was classic as far as it went, but it focused primarily on one pack of wolves. Several years later graduate student Gordon Haber (1977) concentrated primarily on two packs of wolves. Even though Haber used aircraft to follow the wolves and track them in the snow and studied the packs for several years (1966–74), he did not attempt to investigate the entire population.

Therefore, although years of study had been done on the Denali wolves, no information was available about the number of packs in the park and preserve, about the way these packs were organized in the Denali wolf community, or about the genetic structure of the population, the population trend, survival rate, mortality factors, or dispersal characteristics. In addition, little information was available about how the Denali wolves as

a population interacted with their major prey species.

## Reasons for the Study

Similar types of information were available from studies elsewhere. However, there had been no comprehensive, long-term wolf-prey study in a relatively pristine system in Alaska. Bob Stephenson and David James (1982) had radio-tracked a population of wolves in the western Brooks range, 350 miles (560 kilometers) northwest of Denali, from 1977 to 1979 and learned that some members of the population migrated to caribou wintering grounds each year about 124 miles (200 kilometers) to the south and returned again in spring to their denning areas, where caribou also summered.

On the Kenai Peninsula from 1976 to 1981, Rolf Peterson, Jim Woolington, and Ted Bailey studied an exploited population of wolves preying primarily on moose (Peterson et al. 1984). They obtained considerable information about wolf pack territoriality, dispersal, and interactions with moose. Because theirs was an exploited population, these workers were able to obtain an estimate of the effect of various levels of harvesting on the wolf population.

In interior Alaska just east of Denali, biologists from the Alaska Department of Fish and Game (ADFG) demonstrated the role of wolves in limiting prey populations, especially moose (Gasaway et al. 1983). Another major ADFG study, southeast of Denali, showed that wolves quickly repopulated areas with adequate prey after most of the wolf population had been removed (Ballard et al. 1987). The study also described conditions under which wolves did not limit moose numbers.

The reason the NPS wanted the Denali wolf study done was more practical. Aerial poachers had been swooping into the park occasionally and taking wolves (figure 0.2). In 1985, poachers killed five wolves 40 miles (65 kilometers) inside the park boundary. Park officials realized then that they really knew very little about their wolf population and the possible effect on it of such factors as poaching. Also, the research activities themselves (i.e., regular monitoring of wolf packs) would help deter poaching.

Thus, in 1986 we launched the study. It soon became apparent that poaching was not a significant problem for the Denali wolf population. Nevertheless, the information that was being produced was of such basic value both to science and to the park that the investigation was repeatedly extended.

### The Wolf and the Public

The mid-1980s was a period of unprecedented public awareness about wolves, which made the study timely. Wolves had been extinct since 1960 in all of the lower 48 states except Minnesota and Isle Royale, Michigan. The federal Endangered Species Act of 1973 protected wolves in those areas, and they were beginning to recover in Minnesota, Michigan, and Wisconsin. Canadian wolves had also begun recolonizing Montana. Considerable public interest was generating increased support for a proposal to reintroduce wolves into Yellowstone National Park. Furthermore, work was just beginning with the remarkable pack of arctic wolves on Ellesmere Island, which brought about a spate of articles, books, and television specials that furthered public interest in the wolf (Mech 1988a).

Meanwhile, in Alaska the wolf situation was quite different. Alaska's wolf population had never been endangered and was thriving. Its 6,000 to 7,000 wolves were far more secure than they had been since settlement (Stephenson et al. 1995). Before Alaska's statehood in 1959, the federal government had intensively poisoned and hunted wolves from the air throughout much of the state (Rausch and Hinman 1977; Harbo and Dean 1983). After Alaska gained its statehood, wolf control was increasingly restricted. In 1960, formal poisoning was discontinued. Robert Rausch and Robert Hinman (1977, 149) characterized the changes statehood brought to wolf management in Alaska as follows:

> In just over a decade wolf management had changed from rampant exploitation with no closed seasons or bag limits, few restrictions on methods and means of take, year-round hunting and trapping, formal control using poison, aircraft, traps, and snares, to a progressive management and research effort that formed the basis for a program that recognized the positive and negative aspects of wolf populations. In other words, a comprehensive statewide management program that, while not perfect, insured the well-being of the wolf.

On the other hand, the ADFG continued to conduct wolf control by aerial shooting in limited areas. They found that under certain conditions, intensive wolf control would result in higher recruitment and survival of both moose and caribou populations (Gasaway et al. 1983). Because some prey herds had been reduced by various combina-

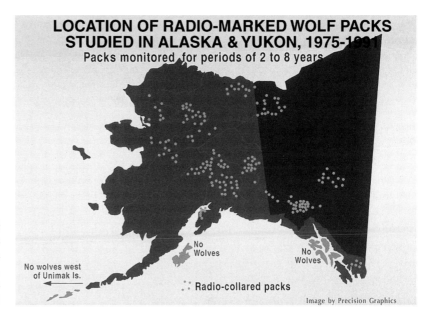

**LOCATION OF RADIO-MARKED WOLF PACKS STUDIED IN ALASKA & YUKON, 1975-1991**
Packs monitored for periods of 2 to 8 years

No wolves west of Unimak Is.

No Wolves

No Wolves

∴ Radio-collared packs

Image by Precision Graphics

*Figure 0.3. Wolf pack territories studied in Alaska and the nearby Yukon Territory of Canada. (Adapted from Stephenson et al. 1995.)*

tions of severe winters, predation, and over-harvesting, Alaska proposed limited wolf control in those areas.

How Alaska could seek to control wolves while other states were promoting their recovery was more than the national public could understand. Various animal-rights organizations seized the opportunity and publicized this apparent contradiction. Their propaganda led the public to believe that Alaska was exterminating its wolves.

### Denali's Wolves and the Alaska Population

Some perspective is necessary to understand how the public's concern could be so seriously misplaced yet force Alaska public officials to promote wolf research to provide answers to issues being raised. Alaska's wolf population is contiguous with the Canadian population of 50,000 to 60,000 wolves (Hayes and Gunson 1995). Hundreds of wolf packs in this population have been radio-tagged and studied (figure 0.3).

Wolves are harvested in both Canada and Alaska. The harvesting is highly regulated and monitored, and some 675 to 1,100 wolves are taken in Alaska each year (Alaska's wolves, 1992). These numbers amount to 11% to 14% of the population. Various studies have shown that up to 40% (Ballard et al. 1987) of wolf numbers can be harvested without reducing the population. Furthermore, to really suppress a subpopulation within a larger one, an annual take of about 70% is necessary (Hayes et al. 1991). Therefore, the Alaska wolf population has not been in danger of overharvesting since statehood.

Nevertheless, the concerned public in the lower 48 states maintained the misconception that Alaska was exterminating its wolves. Claims were also made that some Denali wolf packs had long genetic lines that were being disrupted. Along the eastern border of the park, the so-called Headquarters Pack lives partly inside the protected part of the park and partly outside, where it is subject to public hunting and trapping. Other park packs also share this dual status, and nearly all Denali packs occasionally stray into areas where they could legally be killed.

Thus, animal-rights advocates claimed that Denali's wolves were threatened by harvesting. A

*Figure 0.4.* *The effect of wolves on caribou herds had not been studied before in a wolf-prey system with minimal human disturbance. (Photo by L. David Mech.)*

wolf survey had never been done for the entire park and preserve, so NPS officials did not know how many wolves and packs actually inhabited the area and which lived partly in and outside the park. Without this basic knowledge, it was difficult to answer the concerns of the public who opposed wolf control or harvesting. This concern about Denali packs further fueled the basic controversy over wolf control in general.

### The Wolf's Effect on Caribou

Another issue that prompted the NPS to undertake a wolf study was the question of the wolf's effect on prey. This was, of course, the same question Murie (1944) had been assigned to answer. However, the basis for concern this time was a more considered one.

During the 1970s and 1980s, biologists had found that under some conditions wolves can strongly limit their prey populations (Mech and Karns 1977; Bergerud 1980, 1983; Gasaway et al. 1983). This finding formed one of the main reasons for the wolf-control programs both in Alaska and Canada.

Nevertheless, the effect of wolves on caribou numbers had not been studied in any wolf-caribou system where human hunting was insignificant (figure 0.4). Elsewhere it had been demonstrated that although wolves sometimes hold down both moose and white-tailed deer populations, they do not always do so (Mech 1970; Peterson 1977; Mech and Karns 1977; Nelson and Mech 1986a; Ballard et al. 1987).

Denali's caribou herd had declined from perhaps 20,000 in 1941 (Murie 1944) to about 1,000 in the mid-1970s and had failed to recover (Adams et al. 1989). Thus, the NPS had launched a caribou study in 1984 that was well under way when we began the wolf project.

The park's caribou study provided highly intriguing data of its own that would dovetail nicely with those derived from the wolf study. The caribou project closely examined caribou calf mortality and caribou population dynamics. Because wolves prey regularly on caribou, it was clear from the beginning that much of what the caribou study learned would be of high import to understanding Denali wolf biology, and vice versa. Only after several years of work, however, did we begin to realize the true significance of the interaction between the caribou and the wolves in Denali.

## Caribou Survival

As we will detail in later chapters, the caribou is one of the wolf's more interesting prey animals. Caribou weigh about three times as much as deer and live year-round in herds. In addition to relying on keen senses, extra alertness, and sheer bursts of speed to escape wolves like deer do, the caribou depends greatly on several other traits. The creature's social nature, for example, helps spread the risk, increases sensory input, and sows confusion in predators (Triesman 1975).

Caribou also minimize their risk to wolf predation through their nomadic tendencies. By moving constantly over large areas, caribou increase the difficulty and time it takes for wolves to find them. This characteristic makes it harder for wolves to rely solely on caribou as their primary food supply and may minimize a wolf's opportunities to learn how to hunt them.

I have many times been highly impressed when flying over Denali at how difficult it is to find the Denali Caribou Herd or any of the scattered peripheral groups. It is easy to see that for a wolf without the benefit of an aerial view, finding caribou would be time consuming. Besides being scarce and always on the move, caribou are cryptically colored in a way that allows them to blend in very well with their tundra background.

Caribou calves, like young of most other animals, are easily caught and killed when newborn, so they are particularly vulnerable to wolf predation. However, caribou herds are able to minimize the risk to their newborn calves in two main ways. First, about 85% of the calves are born over a period of about 2 weeks (Adams and Dale 1998). This synchronous birthing minimizes the amount of time over which the calves are vulnerable, and swamps the wolf population with a great amount of easy prey for a relatively short period. As we will

show, a high percentage of newborn caribou deaths to wolves occur during only a 1- to 2-week period of the calving season in any given year (Adams, Dale, and Mech 1995).

A second way in which caribou minimize wolf predation on their newborn calves is to continue long movements right up until the day of birth and then select a difficult-to-find location to bear their calves. Generally these locations are also as far from local wolf packs as possible. In Denali, caribou birthing locations are often on the peaks of the knifelike ridges at the base of Mount McKinley or in extensive spruce bogs far from any other prey animals and from areas commonly used by wolves.

These many anti-predator traits of caribou, along with the common suspicion that wolves severely limit caribou populations, made wolf predation on caribou another especially interesting aspect of the wolf study. To the NPS, such an emphasis was natural both for its intrinsic value and because of its parallel study on Denali's caribou population.

## Wolf-Caribou Research

By wedding the wolf and caribou studies over the years, we were able to facilitate both. As will be clear in chapter 2, each study depended greatly on the use of fixed-wing aircraft, helicopters, and radio-tracking. Sharing of equipment, flying time, and personnel was a natural way to operate. Furthermore, I had long ago learned from my Minnesota wolf-deer work that intensively studying both wolf and prey was much more productive and enlightening than emphasizing one animal and studying the other only incidentally (Hoskinson and Mech 1976; Nelson and Mech 1981).

The close collaboration between the wolf and caribou projects of course led to a greater emphasis on caribou as a wolf prey species than on moose or Dall sheep. We studied wolf interactions with all three prey species but learned far more about interactions with caribou than with the other two.

The conduct of such an extensive project as

**Figure 0.5.** *Tom Meier* (right) *and John Burch conducted most of the fieldwork, including radio-tagging and tracking the wolves. (Photo by Thomas J. Meier.)*

the wolf-prey study in Denali's large area required a great deal of personpower, cooperation, and collaboration among scientists. Fortunately, we were able to effect that. At the onset, I oversaw the Denali wolf research with the aid of collaborators John Dalle-Molle, Denali's resource manager, and Layne Adams, a wildlife researcher from the NPS regional office in Anchorage and the leader of the caribou project. To carry out the day-to-day research activities, I turned to two biologists who had served me well in Minnesota and were highly experienced (figure 0.5). Tom Meier had 10 years, and John Burch 5 years, of experience with live-trapping, drugging, handling, and radio-tracking wolves; examining wolf-killed prey; and collecting and preserving specimens. I ventured to Denali for a few weeks each year, but through 1993, Meier and Burch gathered most of the wolf data.

Adams and his colleague Bruce Dale (figure 0.6), along with an assortment of wildlife technicians, periodically visited Denali to capture, count, and radio-track caribou, and to assist with wolf research activities. Over the years, personnel from the two projects worked more and more closely together, and our collaborations strengthened.

In 1993, with reductions in funding, Meier and Burch left the park to pursue graduate degrees utilizing the Denali wolf research, and the responsibilities for conducting the wolf research fell to Adams with my continued collaboration. The wolf and caribou research continues today with substantial assistance from the park resources-management staff.

This book describes our wolf research from March 1986 through April 1994. Because of changes in funding, project objectives, and research opportunities, as well as the timing of scientific papers we produced, we provide results on different aspects of the study for different periods. Thus, when discussing various results, we indicate which years of the study they cover.

## Overview

Although it would have been best to have intensively studied the caribou, moose, and sheep along with the wolves, funding constraints prevented that. However, Murie's (1944) strong emphasis

*Figure 0.6. Layne Adams and Bruce Dale collected most of the data for the caribou study; determining cause of death for caribou calves was one of the most important aspects of the study. (Photo by L. David Mech.)*

on wolf-sheep interactions had already provided excellent background on that subject; our wolf-sheep work tended to support his findings. Wolf-moose interactions in a caribou-moose-sheep system still remain to be thoroughly studied, and we hope to begin such work soon. The role of the grizzly bear in this interesting system also deserves much emphasis, especially its predatory habits.

Meanwhile, we concentrated on the wolves and the caribou and collected what data we could on the other pertinent species. This book, based on data from 147 radio-collared wolves and 653 radio-collared caribou (173 adult cows and 480 calves), is an attempt to synthesize those findings. To round out the presentation, we call upon some material that has been presented elsewhere (Lehman et al. 1992; Adams, Dale, and Mech 1995; Mech et al. 1995; Meier et al. 1995; Smith et al. 1997) and weave our new material around it.

We begin in chapter 1 by describing our study area, which is the most beautiful and scenic area I have ever worked in. Denali's subarctic setting, its 60-million-year-old ochre and ferruginous up-thrusts, its raw and rugged glaciers, all dominated

by incredible ice- and snow-swathed Mount McKinley, set Denali off from the rest of the world. Thus, in 1917 when concern was high about the market hunting of wildlife, Congress established Mount McKinley National Park as a game preserve. This designation insured that both the scenery and the area's animals would be preserved, thus eventually allowing us the opportunity to study some of the most prominent ones.

Chapter 2 covers the methods we used to conduct this study and some of the basic results. The magnitude of the area, the peripatetic nature of our subjects—both predator and prey—and the type of information we sought all dictated a high-tech, state-of-the-art approach. We believe readers will better appreciate both our findings and their limitations if they understand the methods we used.

In Chapter 3, we introduce Denali's wolf packs and our best approximation of their natural history during our study. These wolf packs—some 12 to 18 of them at any one time—and their territories can be viewed as a spatial overlay on Denali's vast expanse. Chapter 3 provides a close look at the most prominent packs that comprise the Denali wolf population.

Chapter 4, on the other hand, examines both the spatial and temporal organization of the Denali wolf population. This is no random assortment of individuals but rather a highly structured community whose members patrol their own parts of the mountains and valleys, the spruce swamps, and glacial outwashes. We describe here the genetic relationships among the various packs as well as the behavioral interactions among them. The pulsing, dynamic nature of the population will become apparent as the competitive striving of each member to survive and reproduce is described.

The next chapter (chapter 5) outlines the basic ways Denali wolf packs function and details the role of wolf movements in this functioning. The behavior, hunting habits, reproduction and denning, seasonal travel, and dispersal of Denali wolves are examined. We describe the defenses of the wolf's prey and how the wolf attempts to overcome the challenges each species poses. The constant contest between predator and prey will leap out and help explain the interesting end results in which both predator and prey populations survive despite the eternal struggle between the two.

Chapter 6 treats the results of predation by the Denali wolves. We analyze the classes of prey that Denali wolves kill and how those classes change throughout the year as well as between years. Moose, caribou, and sheep, young, old, male, and female are each killed in differing proportions at different times. The common factor helping to determine vulnerability, poor condition, is discussed in detail.

The special relationship between the Denali caribou and the wolf population is the subject of chapter 7. Caribou herds roam Denali park among the wolves, constantly striving to scarf up what food they can while simultaneously attempting to avoid and evade predation. During their momentous spring calving season, the caribou employ especially canny methods to survive.

In chapter 8, we discuss the numerical relationships between the Denali wolves and their prey, particularly the caribou. The tenures of individual wolves in their natal packs are covered, along with various mortality factors. Both Denali wolf and caribou numbers increased during our study and then declined, all without influence from human factors. Which was the cause and which the effect? What were the roles of moose, caribou, and sheep in this relationship? What about weather? This chapter addresses these issues.

Chapter 9 wraps up the earlier material presented and synthesizes it. Denali National Park can be seen as a complex ecosystem vibrating with many layers of life. To the human viewer, the wolf and prey layer dominates the ecosystem and provides the most obvious and dramatic reason to savor Denali National Park and insure its continued preservation. This layer is also a reminder of the other interesting layers on several other scales that are automatically preserved when the more prominent wolf-prey system is protected.

Throughout this extensive investigation we were constantly aware of how privileged we were to be pursuing these studies in the shadow of Mount McKinley. We regularly wished that everyone who appreciates Denali National Park and its wilderness could share our experiences. Since they could not, the next best thing would be for us to allow them to read about our experiences. This book is our attempt to do so.

L. David Mech

1

# In the Shadow
# of the Mountain

Nuuk, Reykjavik, Nome, Barrow, Murmansk—all are frozen outposts toward the northern end of the earth that evoke images of snowbound, wind-swept winters and fleeting, urgent summers. Much farther south on the earth rise huge mountain peaks like K2, Annapurna, and Everest. All higher than 20,000 feet (6,000 meters), these massifs of ice, snow, and rock are so huge they make their own frigid weather.

The effects of both northern latitude and sheer elevation combine around central Alaska's own massif, Mount McKinley (plate 2). There it can snow any time of the year, yet perpetual summer daylight promotes a flush of flowers, as well as a myriad of mosquitoes.

At 64° N latitude and 150° W longitude, in the shadow of Mount McKinley ("the Mountain"), lies a land where wildlife and their habitat persist in as natural a state as any found on earth. Throughout this great wilderness live the wolves of Denali National Park and Preserve, a 6.1-million-acre (24,000-square-kilometer) area south-west of Fairbanks and north of Anchorage, where human influence is minimal.

Only by realizing the extreme geophysical set-ting, the combination of latitude and topography, can one begin to understand the wolves and other wildlife of Denali. Latitude determines the sun's angle of incidence and the pattern of daylight hours. These basic physical factors in turn help set the weather and climate, the plant communities, and the wildlife that depend on them.

The widely divergent patterns of daylight in the Denali area seem alien and unfamiliar. A Fair-banks, Alaska, teacher once asked a student to fill in the blanks for "The sun rises in the——(what direction?) and sets in the——(what direction?)." The student, not about to fall for a trick question, responded "summer or winter?" That far north, the sun rises in the northeast in summer, hangs high all day, and briefly dips below the horizon in the northwest at "night." In the dead of winter, however, the sun creeps above the horizon from the south for only a few hours in midday.

In autumn, the days rapidly shorten, and the sun hits the earth at a lower and lower angle. It heats the ground and atmosphere only a little, even during the day (figure 1.1). At night, much heat is lost through radiation and conduction.

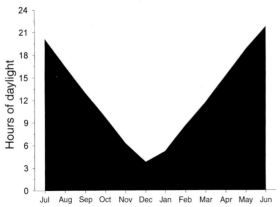

*Figure 1.1.* *Amount of light in Denali National Park and Preserve*

Moisture in soils freezes so deep that in many areas it never thaws, forming permafrost.

As winter tightens its grip, lakes and rivers freeze. In distant coastal areas, the ocean acts like a giant hot-water bottle, its thermal mass buffering winter heat losses. Moisture-laden air, blowing from oceanic areas, crosses into the colder interior, dropping its water load as snow. Ultimately, the Arctic Ocean, Chukchi Sea, and the northern reaches of the Bering Sea are capped with ice, removing this source of moisture for interior Alaska. With little moisture now available to the north and west, clear winter skies, frigid temperatures, and shortening days finish the job, locking the Denali region into the cold and dark of winter.

## "The Mountain"

This combination of high latitude and continental climate is not unique to interior Alaska but reaches across vast expanses of Canada and Siberia as well. Setting the Denali region apart, however, is the Mount McKinley massif with a base of over 1,000 square miles (2,500 square kilometers) of granite and ice projecting abruptly up to 20,320 feet (6,100 meters) above sea level from a piedmont plateau at 2,000 feet (600 meters) above sea level.

Many peaks in the park range from 5,000 to 7,000 feet (1,500–2,100 meters) high and are characterized by alpine tundra vegetation, rock and scree slopes, and small headwater glaciers. However, the peaks of Mount McKinley and its sister Mount Foraker (17,400 feet, or 5,220 meters) soar thousands of feet higher. Composites of rock, snow, and ice, they are devoid of soil and vegetation, and of any life save the few hardy humans who clamber up their sides in valiant, death-defying attempts to meet some personal challenge.

The McKinley massif was born of the collision of gargantuan tectonic plates. Gigantic glaciers gradually cascaded from the high peaks and eventually shaped the surrounding region. Movement of the glaciers crushed underlying rock into a fine silt loam, or loess, that, transported by wind and water, filled in large basins creating the Tanana Flats far to the north. Receding glaciers left U-shaped valleys, and eons of meltwater runoff carved jagged canyons through hills and rocks. Few large lakes lie in the study area, although thousands of ponds dot the landscape.

Our study area lies primarily north of Mount McKinley. Its only road is the gravel "park road" that begins near park headquarters at the east end of the park. It curves and stretches some 90 miles (144 kilometers) to Wonder Lake and Kantishna due north of the Mountain in the center of the park.

## Denali Weather

The huge mountains of the Alaska Range, including Mount McKinley, set the stage for an array of life more diverse, abundant, and visible than found on the flats of the interior just to the north or on the snow-buried slopes of the south side. It is often said that The Mountain makes its own weather, and that is true. Southerly and westerly flows of moist air masses from the Pacific Ocean and Bering Sea predominate much of the year. These warm fronts dump large quantities of snow on the south side due to adiabatic cooling, where moist ocean air masses cool as they lift over the steep terrain.

**Table 1.1.** Cumulative September to May snowfall (cm) at Headquarters, Denali National Park and Preserve, Alaska

| Winter | Cumulative snowfall |
|---|---|
| 1983–84 | 155 |
| 1984–85 | 336 |
| 1985–86 | 86 |
| 1986–87 | 103 |
| 1987–88 | 121 |
| 1988–89 | 244 |
| 1989–90 | 217 |
| 1990–91 | 391 |
| 1991–92 | 286 |
| 1992–93 | 394 |
| 1993–94 | 280 |

*Note: 63-year mean is 190.5 cm.*

On the north side and in the mountain passes, high winds, due to the gradients between low-pressure systems in the Gulf of Alaska and high pressure in the Arctic, scour snow from the ridges and hills, leaving relatively shallow snowpacks and exposed vegetation. These breaks in the snow provide wintering habitat for caribou, Dall sheep, and other wildlife.

Nevertheless, the 80-inch (200-centimeter) average annual snowfall leaves a knee- to waist-deep snowpack in areas not wind-scoured that persists from late September to early May (table 1.1). Although 80 inches is a great deal of snow and strongly influences the area, it amounts to only 15 inches (38 centimeters) of water.

Denali's rugged mountains and foothills can receive dustings of snow in any month. By October, even the lowlands are blanketed with snow and ice, which remains into May (figure 1.2).

*Figure 1.2. Snow cover in Denali usually lasts from October through May. (Photo by L. David Mech.)*

*Figure 1.3. Extensive spruce flats dominate the western half of Denali. (Photo by Thomas J. Meier.)*

These conditions result in 8 months of insignificant photosynthesis; 8 months of snowpack; icy, overflowing rivers; and frozen ground. Temperatures range from 90°F (32°C) in summer to -53°F (-47°C) in winter, highly dependent on elevation.

Not only are conditions harsh, but like the Toklat-colored grizzly bear, they are unpredictable. In mid-September 1992, 2 to 4 feet (60–120 cm) of heavy, wet snow fell in the Tanana and upper Kuskokwim regions. The early snowstorm caused hardwoods, still leafed, to bend under the weight of the wet snow, in some cases until the tops touched the ground. Cold weather then froze the trees, and in many places they remain forever in that condition. All this followed a late spring; consequently the summer of 1992 was the shortest on record, with ramifications we will discuss later.

These variations on the main theme of very long winters in Denali play a pivotal role in the functioning of the ecosystem. One of the most significant aspects of the variations involves the total annual snowfall. During our study, that

figure varied fourfold (table 1.1), a natural "experiment" that yielded great dividends to our investigations.

## Soils and Vegetation

Soils in Denali, where present, are poorly drained because of the silt and permafrost. Standing water often becomes acidic due to tannic acids from slowly decaying organic materials. Plant communities on the flats of the northwest edge of the park and preserve consist of black spruce (*Picea*) and tamarack (*Larix*) bogs and wet tussock tundra with sedge (*Carex*), moss (*Sphagnum*), and heath (*Ericaceae*) understories. Cotton grass (*Eriophorum*) is a common component of wet tussock tundra and is seasonally important to caribou.

More-productive high ground and riparian areas hold white spruce (*Picea*), birch (*Betula*), aspen (*Populus*), and alder (*Alnus*) with understories of berries and willow (*Salix*) (figure 1.3). Foothills below roughly 3,500 feet (1,050 meters) support woodlands of white spruce, aspen, and birch. Willows and alder at the tree line give way to alpine tundra and bare ground at higher elevations. The alpine tundra is dominated by *Dryas* mats and prostrate willows. Lichens, particularly *Cetraria* and *Cladonia*, are locally abundant in many vegetative communities, especially woodlands and alpine tundra.

Rivers in Denali are heavily laden with glacial silt. These rivers rise during the heat of the day as snowfields and glaciers melt under the summer sun. Clear-water streams and tundra ponds host a variety of aquatic and riparian plants important to moose and other wildlife. In winter, many water bodies freeze to the bottom. Rivers freeze to the substrate, and flowing groundwater seeks new routes adjacent and atop the ice, creating treacherous overflow and patches of "aufeis" that persist well into summer. The action of ice and water erosion along river courses creates a continually renewing ecotone of pioneering willows and other colonizing plants, which are important forage for moose, caribou, and numerous small animals.

Wildfires caused by lightning strikes are common in the northwest flats of the park, and in a dry year, thousands of acres will burn (plate 3). Willows, forbs, birches, and aspen frequently recolonize after fire, creating mosaics of productive patches of ungulate forage.

## Wildlife Populations

Denali was made a national park largely because of its wildlife resources. The park hosts herds of Dall sheep, caribou, and moose, along with their primary predators, wolves and grizzly bears, as well as wolverines, foxes, coyotes, black bears, many smaller mammals, and a wide variety of raptors, waterfowl, ptarmigan, and other birds (Sheldon 1930).

### Dall Sheep

Dall sheep, the species that has figured so prominently in the history of the park, are stout, medium-size ungulates adapted to utilizing steep and rocky terrain (plate 4). In Denali, they are the smallest ungulate available as wolf prey. Adult rams sport large horns that curl in a tight spiral, while ewes carry smaller sickle-shaped horns. Rams weigh around 200 pounds (90 kilograms) but can exceed 250 pounds (110 kilograms). Adult ewes are much smaller, weighing only about 120 pounds (55 kilograms) on average (Bunnell and Olsen 1976; Nichols 1978).

Dall sheep are currently common throughout the Alaska Range at densities similar to those found in Denali. We will never know whether sheep were more abundant in Denali than adjacent areas when the park was designated because so few records exist from outside the park.

Denali's sheep were hunted by native Alaskans, big-game hunters, miners, and market hunters (Walker 1992). Concerns for overharvest of this species helped lead to the creation of the park. Sheep populations have fluctuated markedly in Denali, with highs in the late 1920s of at least 5,000, and perhaps many more (Murie 1944). Their numbers declined severely to 1,000 to 1,500 after the big-snow winters of the early 1930s. Sheep numbered about 2,000 in the park just before our study (Singer et al. 1981; Taylor et al. 1987).

Dall sheep habitat consists of scree and alpine-tundra-dominated mountain slopes. The animals are rarely found far from steep, rocky slopes, which provide refuge from their predators, primarily wolves, grizzly bears, golden eagles, coyotes, and wolverines (Murie 1944). Sheep venture away from escape terrain in search of forbs, grasses, and willows, but if caught there, are easily killed.

In winter, sheep frequent windblown slopes and ridges where favored forages like fescue grasses are more accessible. In some parts of Alaska, sheep winter range overlaps summer range, while elsewhere seasonal migrations of 6 to 12 miles (10–20 kilometers) have been documented (Ayres 1986). In Denali, sheep sometimes move between the taller Alaska Range peaks and the lower "Outer Range" ridges to the north. However, they are present in both areas regardless of the season. Denali's sheep breed in November, and ewes give birth to a single lamb in mid-May (Geist 1971).

## Caribou

Caribou numbers have also fluctuated dramatically in Denali, as indicated earlier. The staple meat animal for the region (Rawson 1994), caribou were much more numerous before 1945, likely exceeding 20,000 animals (Murie 1935; Singer 1986). During the late 1940s to the early 1960s, herd estimates ranged from 8,000 to 10,000 caribou (Adams et al. 1989). In the 1960s, several caribou herds throughout Alaska and Canada declined dramatically. The Denali herd was no exception, reaching a low of around 1,000 caribou by 1975 (Troyer 1977, 1978). Since the mid-1970s, the Denali herd has fluctuated between 1,000 and 3,200 animals.

It is important to note that early caribou estimates were confounded by the limitations on the methods available. Many of these estimates were made during seasonal migrations or were based on gross numbers seen by travelers. The highly variable distribution of caribou made it extremely difficult to even determine to which herd a group of caribou may have belonged. With the increasing use of aerial surveys and radiotelemetry in the past couple of decades, the accuracy of herd-size estimates has greatly improved.

About 30 caribou herds inhabit Alaska, ranging in size from hundreds to hundreds of thousands of animals. They total about a million (Davis and Valkenburg 1991). Most are of the "Alaskan" ecotype (Davis and Valkenburg 1991). This is an arbitrary class of caribou herds that fit behaviorally between the large migratory barren-ground herds of the Arctic and the dispersed low-density woodland populations of the boreal forest.

Alaskan ecotype caribou commonly inhabit mountainous terrain, migrate en masse seasonally (but on a lesser scale than barren-ground herds), and share ranges with grizzly bears and wolves, as well as with other ungulate prey. Although they commonly frequent spruce forests, these caribou usually live above the tree line and on the open tundra.

Denali caribou, as well as other Alaskan ecotype herds, are larger than their barren-ground counterparts, and adult bulls carry large ornate antlers in fall (plate 5). Mature bulls average 490 pounds (220 kilograms) but can weigh up to 590 pounds (270 kilograms) (L. Adams, unpublished data). Cows are about half as big, weighing 255 pounds (115 kilograms) on average, and range from 185 pounds (85 kilograms) to 325 pounds (145 kilograms) (L. Adams, unpublished data).

Denali's caribou undertake migrations of about 50 miles (80 kilometers) between summer and winter ranges, rather short compared to the hundreds of miles covered seasonally by barren-ground herds. Their movements cover a wide elevation range from below 2,000 feet (610 meters) in winter to above 6,000 feet (1,830 meters) in summer in search of the lichens, shrubs (particularly willows), graminoids, forbs, and mushrooms on which they subsist (Boertje 1984).

In interior Alaska, caribou breed in late September and early October while migrating from mountain summer ranges to tundra and woodland plains for the winter. Then, in late April and early May, caribou cows return to their calving grounds as the calving season begins.

As we will show in chapter 7, caribou calving is highly synchronous and takes place in mid-May. Most females bear their single calves high in the mountains near glaciers and snowfields, concentrated in a relatively small area. Others will calve scattered in the mountains or spruce woodlands. Although quite precocious, walking and feeding a few hours after birth, caribou calves are extremely vulnerable to predators during their first 2 weeks of life.

Cows try to avoid detection by calving in areas hard for predators to search, such as mottled snowfields high in the mountains. If the cow detects a predator, she tries to move away unde-tected. If detected, the cow will not usually try to defend the calf against a wolf or bear but, rather, will make a run for it. Young calves that are small and slow quickly fall behind and are easily caught.

Later, caribou frequent areas near high moun-tain snowfields and glaciers to escape the mosqui-toes, warble flies, and botflies of June. On a calm, warm day in late June, nearly the entire herd can be found huddled and still on snowfields and glaciers, seeking relief. Finally, the weather becomes cool and rainy in late July and early August, and the caribou move about freely and feed voraciously on the lush new vegetation.

### Moose

Moose (plate 6) occur at moderate to low densi-ties typical of the interior, approximately 6 moose per 10 square miles (2 per 10 square kilometers) (Meier et al. 1991). They were considered plenti-ful in Denali before about 1920, when market hunters greatly reduced them (Murie 1944). By the late 1930s, however, they had regained "satis-factory" numbers (Murie 1944), which then re-mained relatively stable through the next several decades (Haber 1977) but may have declined in the late 1970s and early 1980s. Since then, park-wide estimates of 1,400 to 1,900 moose have been made using various types of aerial censuses (Meier et al. 1991).

Moose are the largest wolf prey in Denali, weighing two or three times as much as caribou. Alaskan cow moose average about 880 pounds (400 kilograms), whereas adult bulls average about 120 pounds (55 kilograms) heavier (Franz-mann et al. 1978). However, bulls greater than 1,200 pounds (545 kilograms) have been reported (Franzmann et al. 1978; Gasaway and Coady 1974).

Moose, an important food for wolves, are widely distributed in Denali and are locally abun-dant wherever willow are common (Miquelle et al. 1992). These animals eat a large variety of willows,

especially *Salix alexensis*, *S. planifolia*, *S. arbuscu-loides*, and *S. glauca* (Risenhoover 1989). Moose also feed on birch and aspen seedlings and blow-downs, and occasionally on the bark of aspens. Al-though similar in appearance to the preferred shrubs, the abundant stands of dwarf birch, resin birch, and alder are avoided by moose. In summer, moose feed also on aquatic vegetation.

Moose in interior Alaska, including Denali, are an overlapping mixture of migrating and lo-cally resident animals (Gasaway et al. 1983; Bal-lard et al. 1987). Some travel to foothills for win-ter and to swamps and lowlands for summer, while others remain in one area year-round, typically in foothills at the tree line, riparian areas, and swamps.

Moose are well adapted to snow and cold; however, snow depths greater than about 20 inches (53 centimeters) decrease their foraging efficiency and increase energetic costs of movement, result-ing in greater vulnerability to predators (Stephen-son 1995). Aside from population surveys (Meier 1987; Dalle-Molle 1987; Meier et al. 1991), only a small segment of resident moose have been stud-ied in Denali (Miquelle et al. 1992).

### Smaller Prey

Other prey for wolves include beavers (figure 1.4), which are common wherever stands of deciduous trees or shrubs border streams, rivers, deep ponds, and lakes; and hares, which can be abundant dur-ing population highs. Marmots, ground squirrels, numerous microtine rodents, and other small mammals and birds are also occasional food items (Murie 1944). Packs whose territories include salmon rivers feed heavily on salmon at times, es-pecially in autumn and early winter.

### Bears and Other Competitors

Grizzly bears (plate 7) in upland habitats and black bears in woodlands compete with wolves for prey in Denali (Murie 1944). Bears of both species in interior Alaska do not have as much access to pro-

*Figure 1.4. During summer, beavers are one of the primary alternate prey animals for wolves, especially in Denali's western half. (Photo by L. David Mech.)*

tein-rich salmon as coastal bears and are much smaller. Adult grizzlies average about 550 pounds (115 kilograms) and 450 pounds (205 kilograms) for females and males, respectively, in spring (J. Keay, unpublished data); black bears average about 40% lighter (J. Hechtel, unpublished data). Both grizzlies and black bears emerge from dens around May and search for winter kills, newborn ungulate calves, and accessible vegetation. They breed during summer. By August, berries, and in some Denali rivers, salmon, become important food resources. Both bear species occasionally prey upon adult ungulates (Dean et al. 1986; Boertje et al. 1988; L. Adams, unpublished). By autumn, they have gained about 30% over their spring weights.

In October, Denali bears enter dens, where from one to three cubs are born in February. Grizzly bear cubs stay with their mother until they are 2 to 3 years of age (Reynolds and Hechtel 1983), while black bear cubs are generally weaned at 1 to 2 years of age (Hechtel 1991). Grizzlies in Denali den in holes typically located on snow-covered hillsides at 3,000 to 4,000 feet (900–1,200 me-

ters) (Darling 1987). Black bears den in all types of habitats in holes, brush piles, or simply under a blanket of snow (Smith 1994).

Bears have been censused only in portions of Denali (Dean 1987; J. Keay, unpublished), but density data for those parts suggest a minimum population of 300 grizzlies and conceivably as many as 450, plus an unknown number of black bears.

Wolves and bears tend to avoid each other, but altercations between the two species are not unusual, especially at kills and around dens. Murie (1944) described several wolf-bear incidents in Denali, and our observations tend to parallel his.

During one interaction, the East Fork wolves (see chapter 3) attacked a sow grizzly and 3 yearlings. On July 23, 1989, at about 8:40 A.M., 12 members of the East Fork pack were paralleling the park road, when they headed up a willow drainage in which the 4 bears were rummaging around. Neither the bears nor the wolves seemed aware of each other until the wolves came to within 50 feet (15 meters) of the bears.

The 3 yearlings immediately rushed up the

drainage, with the sow right behind. As the wolves caught up, the sow turned to fight them off. The yearlings split, however, and the sow could not defend them all. Two of the yearlings continued on. Five or 6 wolves harassed the sow, while the rest chased the yearlings. The wolves quickly caught up and killed them both. The remaining wolves then rushed over to join in the feast. In this case, the attack was one of sheer predation rather than the usual skirmish between competitors.

Also competing with wolves to various degrees are wolverines, lynx, coyotes, red foxes, and golden eagles. None of these compete with wolves to anywhere near the extent that bears do, however.

Most often wolves interact with their competitors around kill remains because kills are magnets for all the meat-eaters. Wolves usually chase away their smaller competitors, sometimes catching and killing them (Mech 1970). The same is true when they encounter a competitor by chance.

Tom Meier recalled an encounter one of our wolf packs had with a wolverine that impressively demonstrates how tough this particular competitor is:

> In January 1987, pilot Jim Cline and I were radio-tracking the East Fork pack when we spied seven wolves running up a creek bed near the Teklanika River. The wolves overtook and attacked a fleeing wolverine, forming a ring around the animal, lifting it off the ground and shaking it. Making a low pass, we saw that the wolverine was on its back with one wolf continuing the attack. On the next pass, some of the wolves were rolling on the ground, and the others were resting. Several ravens had also arrived. However, we could not find the wolverine.
>
> For 10 minutes we searched. The seven wolves eventually arose and moved on up the creek. Finally, after another 20 minutes, we spotted the wolverine running rapidly down the creek the way it and the wolves

had come. The creature appeared unhurt, and no blood was visible at the attack site.

> I visited the scene on the ground the next day. Approaching on the wolves' exit trail, I saw drops of blood in their tracks. At the attack site were a few small tufts of wolverine hair and a few drops of blood. It appeared that the wolverine had escaped under a shelf of ice until the wolves left. I saw no blood in the wolverine's exit trail, and I believe it escaped unharmed.

## Wolves

Wolves are not unusually abundant in Denali, but the population is both vigorous and viable. The animals have been legally protected in the original park area since 1952 (Harbo and Dean 1983). However, only fragmentary information about their numbers is available from 1952 through 1965. From 1966 through 1974, Gordon Haber (1977) estimated that five wolf packs lived primarily in the old (pre-1980) park, although he was able to define the approximate territories of only two of them. His maximum winter estimates for each of the five packs from 1966 through 1974 total 76 wolves living primarily in the 3,294 square miles (8,432 square kilometers) of the old park, or about 9.0 wolves per 1,000 square kilometers.

Our estimates of late-winter wolf density varied from 3.1 wolves per 1,000 square kilometers in 1987 to 7.8 wolves per 1,000 square kilometers in 1991 (figure 1.5). Roughly a third of the park and preserve is high-altitude rock and ice, not suitable habitat for wolves or their prey, so these numbers translate to an estimated 50 to 125 wolves over the 6,312 square miles (16,160 square kilometers) of available wolf habitat in the park and preserve. In early winter, after pup production and before much dispersal, wolf density is at its highest. Our highest estimate of wolf density at that time was 9.8 wolves per 1,000 square kilometers, or a parkwide estimate of 158 wolves.

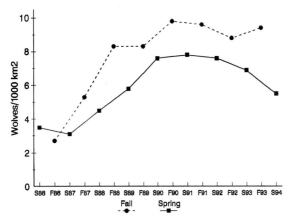

*Figure 1.5. During the study, Denali wolf numbers almost doubled.*

Between 1988 and 1993, pups made up 35% to 44% of all wolves observed in fall counts. Combined with parkwide estimates of fall wolf numbers and estimated over-summer mortality of 9% (see chapter 8), these figures yield annual estimates of 65 to 79 pups produced in the park.

## Humans in Denali

Before European contact, native Alaskans hunted and trapped throughout the region, and wolves were a part of their harvest. Wolves were respected as hunters and competitors, and were an integral part of the native spiritual culture. In the Denali region, wolves were probably taken primarily by deadfall traps, although pit traps, torsion traps, and puncturing shards frozen in bait may also have been used (Scarff 1972; Rawson 1994). The hides of wolves made warm clothing that enabled survival in the cold winters.

The Athabascan Indians that hunted in the Denali region lived primarily along the major waterways north of the park where salmon were available (Brown 1991). They made hunting trips to the foothills during spring through autumn. Some clans may have spent entire summers in the foothills, pursuing caribou and sheep and gathering berries.

With European contact came firearms, steel traps, and a market for fur. The hides of wolves and

other furbearers became important components of the local economy. Explorations of the Denali area by Alfred Brooks, James Wickersham, and Frederick Cook in 1902 and 1903 resulted in writings about the abundant game herds. These in turn attracted big-game hunters and museum collectors like Charles Sheldon and Belmore Browne.

At the same time, growing gold camps along the Yukon and Tanana drainages created a great demand for game meat. Market hunters frequented the north slope of the Alaska Range, including Denali, to provide caribou, moose, and sheep for mining camps in Fairbanks, Kantishna, and elsewhere (Loftus 1967; Rawson 1994).

## Park Establishment and the First Wolf Controversy

Charles Sheldon's concerns over the future of Dall Sheep and other game led him to promote the region as a national park. Through the clout of the Boone and Crockett Club and the Camp Fire Club of America, Mount McKinley was designated a national park in 1917. Mount McKinley Park, it turns out, quickly spawned the world's first wolf controversy, a dispute that lasted more than three decades and split the ranks of park personnel, sportsmen, and even scientists.

The controversy began in California. Zoologists Joseph Grinnell and Tracy Storer (1916) published one of the first pleas for protecting predators in general. Grinnell's students spread the philosophy, and in 1924, the American Society of Mammalogists held a symposium on mammalian predators. Charles Adams, one of Grinnell's students, then declared that national parks should be "our main sanctuaries for predaceous animals" (Adams 1925, 90). The New York Zoological Society and the Boone and Crockett Club passed resolutions in 1929 supporting predator protection in national parks (Rawson 1994).

Sanctuaries were needed because by this time official government predator control was in full swing, and the wolf was a main target. Bounties and special predator controllers with the U.S. Biological Survey wreaked havoc in an attempt "to eradicate the wolves and coyotes of Alaska" and elsewhere (Rawson 1994, 92).

On the other side of the issue, Grinnell spoke to a conference of National Park Service (NPS) superintendents about the value of predators. His audience was sympathetic, and NPS director Horace Albright (1931, 185–86) proclaimed that "predatory animals are to be considered an integral part of the wildlife protected within national parks, and no widespread campaigns of destruction are to be countenanced." This was just after the government had exterminated the last wolves in Yellowstone.

The plot thickened, however, when prominent members of the Camp Fire Club of America began a campaign to promote extermination of wolves in Mount McKinley Park. Because the Camp Fire Club had been instrumental in establishing the park, the club's influence was strong. Its view was that wolves would exterminate the Dall sheep and spill out to all other areas of Alaska.

## Murie's Studies and Wolf Protection

Thus began a seesawing of official attitude and action in Denali. From 1930 to 1934, rangers killed 23 wolves; in 1935, acting park director Arno Cammerer forbade rangers from killing wolves; the next year, assistant director Arthur Demaray approved killing wolves "for food habits studies," and rangers shot 14 from 1936 to 1938 (Rawson 1994). Damned if they killed wolves, and damned if they did not, the NPS ended up recommending a scientific study. The scientist was to be Adolph Murie.

Murie's charge was to determine whether the park's sheep faced extermination by the wolves and whether wolf control was necessary. He spent 15 months in the field in 1940 and 1941 and learned much new information, as discussed earlier (figure 1.6). He concluded that while wolves were the primary factor limiting the sheep, the

sheep and wolves were currently in proper balance. Furthermore, management should be directed at maintaining that balance, and wolf control should be applied only when absolutely necessary (Murie 1944).

Murie's book was widely acclaimed as objective and highly informative. However, it was roundly criticized by the anti-wolf forces, who, while becoming increasingly marginalized, still held great power in Alaska. Murie was sent back to the park in August 1945 for a month and found that the sheep population had declined from about 2,700 in 1941 to about 500. He recommended killing 10 to 15 wolves in sheep range and continuing wolf control until the sheep increased.

The Camp Fire Club decided to seek legislation to force wolf control, and in late 1945 a bill was introduced into the U.S. House of Representatives. The NPS, however, successfully resisted the legislation.

Nevertheless, NPS rangers did begin controlling wolves. From 1946 through 1948, some 18 wolves were taken (Rawson 1994). Murie agreed that wolf control should continue until the sheep population reached 2,500, and he personally began snaring wolves. Eleven more wolves were killed from 1949 to 1952. By 1953, sheep numbers had reached 1,500.

With the sheep herd increasing, the older members of the Camp Fire Club dying off, and wolves being controlled by federal efforts outside the park, the anti-wolf pressure on the NPS began dissipating. At the same time, a signal request was made of the park that evolved into a historic decision.

Walt Disney Studios wished to produce a "True Life Adventure" film about wolves in Denali (Rawson 1994). To do so, undisturbed wolves would be needed, so the studio requested a temporary cessation of wolf control. NPS director Conrad Wirth agreed, and Disney produced the film *White Wilderness*. It portrayed the wolf sympathetically to a wide audience. Public protest

*The Dandy*

*Grandpa*

*Black Male*

*Black Female*

*Gray Female*

*Robber Mask*

*Figure 1.6. Adolph Murie (1944) named and observed individual members of the park's East Fork wolf pack from 1939 to 1941 and learned much new information about wolf social behavior. (Drawing by Olaus Murie.)*

against wolf protection was by that time minimal, so the NPS never rescinded their ruling. As a result, wolf protection in Denali has continued uninterrupted since 1952 (Harbo and Dean 1983), and the NPS enjoys considerable public support for that stand.

## Wolf-Taking Restrictions

Even today, however, protection of Denali's wolves is not without controversy. Today's laws, while protecting wolves in the original 2.1 million acres (8,400 square kilometers) of the park, provide for a limited harvest of wolves in the park expansion and preserve around the park (figure 1.7).

In 1980, the federal Alaska National Interest Lands Conservation Act (ANILCA) greatly ex-

panded existing national parks and refuges and created expansive new parks and refuges as well. Mount McKinley National Park, renamed Denali National Park and Preserve, swelled from about 3,294 to 9,468 square miles (8,432 to 24,238 square kilometers). However, ANILCA provided for the customary and traditional use of wildlife on federal lands created by the act, even in national parks. The act recognized subsistence lifestyles and the importance of wildlife and other natural resources to the livelihood of local residents. Thus, ANILCA allows the taking of wolves and other wildlife in the 1980 additions to the park by qualified rural residents (figure 1.7). Rural residents qualify if they reside in rural villages that historically used the park lands or if they can demon-

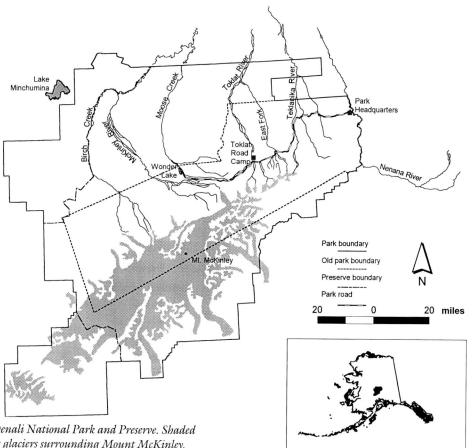

*Figure 1.7. Denali National Park and Preserve. Shaded area represents glaciers surrounding Mount McKinley.*

strate that they or their families traditionally used the areas. The regulations are liberal and nearly identical in seasons, methods, and means of taking to areas outside the new park expansions. In addition to rural subsistence, sport hunting and trapping are permitted in the preserve (figure 1.7).

Hunting of wolves is allowed from mid-August through April. During this time an individual may take up to 10 wolves. Trapping is legal from November through March, and there is no limit. While these seasons may seem extreme for a national park, they result in very little wolf harvest (about 2% of the park and preserve wolf population annually) (see chapter 2). This is because few residents qualify and actually reside where they have access to the new park.

For the same reasons, the harvest of other wildlife in the park is extremely limited. The Denali Caribou Herd is closed to hunting under both state and federal regulations. The taking of wolves and other animals remains prohibited in the original "wilderness" portion of the park.

## The Denali Ecosystem

For Denali National Park and Preserve, truly the whole is more valuable than the sum of its parts. Plant and animal populations, virtually all trophic levels, occur in natural and pristine assemblages.

25

Human influences are minimal and have been for decades. Although some small areas have been altered by humans, they seem trivial when compared to the magnificent scale of the entire area.

Denali encompasses a broad ecotonal belt ranging from high and severe mountains of rock and ice, through the mountain and river valley complexes, to the spruce woodlands. This assemblage of habitats supports a diverse array of wildlife communities. Wildfire, a naturally occurring disturbance important for maintaining productive and diverse habitats, has been allowed to run its course since the early 1980s.

Another, often overlooked factor distinguishing the Denali ecosystem from other natural areas is that Denali is not an island. Rather, it is part of continuous habitats and populations throughout Alaska and into Canada. Moose, wolves, sheep—virtually all plants and animals—are members of larger, continuous populations that are also relatively undisturbed. This means that population fluctuations, gene flow, and persistence of populations are not affected by the insular qualities of most natural areas caused by the massive alteration of adjacent habitats and wildlife communities.

The presence of metapopulations sharing ecosystems external to the park provides an important added benefit: comparisons can be drawn between systems to help further understanding of the influence of humans on wildlife resources.

For all these reasons—species richness, protected nature, surrounding buffer areas, and the long-term integrity of the ecosystem—Denali National Park and Preserve was an ideal location for a long-term study of wolves and their prey.

# Technology Yields the Data

"Haw," the frosted figure yelled as his dog team approached the fork in the snow-covered trail. The yelps grew louder, and the sled lurched to the left and up a gradual rise. A few minutes later, the whole entourage halted, and the figure pulled binoculars from under his parka. He scanned the river bar below, and suddenly spotted nine wolves heading single file up the bar. Elated, he recorded his observation in a small pocket notebook and watched as the wolves disappeared around a bend.

Such a scene may well have taken place in Denali many decades ago as Adolph Murie did his seminal studies. It does not characterize our techniques, however. In areas as extensive as Denali National Park and Preserve, the only way one can study an entire population of wolves and their prey is to use the latest technologies available. Dogsleds, binoculars, and snowshoes, while still important, now only complement such techniques as radio-tracking, aerial darting, and molecular genetic analyses.

Our project in Denali, like most current wolf research, depended on catching two or three wolves from each pack to be studied, attaching radio collars to them, and locating them from aircraft. Once the signal source was pinpointed, the location and behavior of the radio-collared wolves and their packmates were recorded, counts were made of the number of wolves seen, and information on any prey they may have killed was noted. This was not always as easily done as said, of course.

## Binoculars and Notepads

To appreciate the advantages as well as the problems of modern wolf research, it is useful to look back again at Adolph Murie's (1944) efforts before the advent of radio-tracking. From 1939 to 1941, when Murie conducted his study of wolf–Dall sheep relationships, his methods were primarily observational. His most technical piece of equipment was his spotting scope, and he spent long hours observing wolves from the ground. This was not easy.

However, Murie had two advantages. Denali's open terrain and sparse vegetation allowed spotting and observing all kinds of wildlife from distances of several miles. Just as important, however, was that Murie had found a wolf den in vast open terrain, which allowed him to watch the wolves not only at the den but as they traveled to and from it. Murie was able to watch wolves consistently while they were around the den, gathering valuable new information on wolf social organization, behavior, and summer activities.

As often happens when doing pioneering research, all that Murie learned led to more questions: How far from the den did the wolves travel? How many animals did they kill while away? What were their interactions with neighboring packs? But most important, where did the wolves go and what did they do during the 8-month winter period when not tied to a den with a litter of small pups?

Although Murie did get out during winter by dog team and snowshoes, he was very limited in how far he could travel and how long he could make observations in the short daylight and bitter cold. Most of a person's time traveling by dog team is spent breaking trail, caring for the dogs, and merely surviving; there is little way one could keep up with a pack of wolves.

Even following wolf tracks from the ground is difficult because of the terrain the wolves cross, with wind and snow obliterating their trails in just a few days, sometimes in hours. The one thing Murie did learn about wolves traveling during winter was that they covered a vast area with amazing efficiency. But where they went and what they did remained unknown—thus, the advantage of using aircraft.

## Use of Aircraft

From the early 1940s to the late 1960s, Murie and others continued to record wolf observations and denning activity, but no formal wolf research was done in Denali. Meanwhile, south of the park and in the lower 48 states, light aircraft were being used successfully to track wolves around in the snow and collect new information (Stenlund 1955; Burkholder 1959; Mech 1966a).

One of the first serious efforts to conduct an aerial survey of wolves in Denali was by park employee Richard Prasil in 1967 and 1968 (Singer 1986). With an aircraft, the vast area occupied by multiple wolf packs could be covered in a single day. Because Denali is covered with snow for 8 months of the year, all one has to do is fly around until wolf tracks are found and follow them to the wolves. This too is easier said than done, but under the right conditions, it greatly beats dog-sledding for following wolves.

From 1969 through 1974, Gordon Haber (1977) used aircraft to study two packs of wolves in Denali. Thus, he could record counts and locations of his study packs no matter where they roamed, as well as a rough estimate of their territory sizes. Even when the wolves could not be found, tracks showed where they had traveled, what kills they had made, and how many wolves were in the pack. Clearly the use of aircraft vastly improved the ability of biologists to study wolves, as well as their prey.

### Aerial Snow-Tracking of Wolves

Snow-tracking wolves from light aircraft is easy in sparse vegetation and open terrain under the right snow and weather conditions. We seldom experienced such conditions, however.

The first prerequisite for success is a powerful aircraft that flies slowly and has great maneuverability and good visibility for both pilot and passenger. The Piper PA-18 Super Cub has become the first choice among bush pilots and biologists alike for this type of work (figure 2.1). Its narrow fuselage and tandem seating allow good visibility from both sides of the aircraft. Its 160-horsepower engine, 40-mph stalling speed, light but strong airframe, and large fuel capacity round out the more important features of this aircraft. Flying it, preferably, is a former wolf hunter or other expert tracker. We used some of the best.

Our usual technique to find wolves before they were radio-tagged was to fly river drainages,

*Figure 2.1. The Super Cub was the most suitable aircraft for snow-tracking or radio-tracking wolves and other wildlife. (Photo by Thomas J. Meier.)*

mountain ridges and passes, and open slopes, looking for the long, thin furrow that is the trademark of a line of traveling wolves in fresh snow. Of course, wolves are not the only animals traveling in Denali, and the ability to distinguish wolf tracks from all the others is the first test of a wolf tracker.

It is amazing how much Dall sheep tracks or wolverine trails can resemble a wolf track at first; indeed, the list goes on and on of the wildlife in Denali that can leave tracks that at times look like those of wolves. Coyotes, lynx, fox, and even moose or caribou can sometimes fool wolf trackers. It all depends on the snow conditions, available light, and flying conditions, all of which can severely hamper one's efforts.

Occasionally we came across a set of tracks that seemed unexplainable. One day John Burch was shivering in the back of a Super Cub, when he and pilot Bill Lentsch spotted some very unusual tracks. The snow was fresh, fluffy, and deep, and the tracks were narrowly spaced, very large, and almost round, unlike any animal tracks.

Bill thought the imprints looked almost like snowshoe tracks, which was possible as they were near park headquarters and the road. However, the tracks were so small and deep that the men decided against that explanation. Besides, interspersed along the tracks were large areas of disturbed snow, almost as though some kind of fight had taken place.

Bill banked the plane sharply, concentrating on the tracks, and John spotted a large, dark figure not far off. Bill had been right—it was someone on snowshoes: a large, roundish man on tiny snowshoes sinking up to his crotch in snow. He waved to the plane, his face and beard adorned with hoarfrost and his clothes covered with snow. He looked like the abominable snowman. The disturbed areas along his trail were areas where he had fallen and struggled to get up.

A few minutes later the plane was miles away and following a fresh set of wolf tracks. It would have taken the men days by snowshoe or dog team just to get to where they first picked up the tracks.

Once wolf tracks were found, our next problem was determining which way the tracks were heading, either by distinguishing the heel pad from the toe pads, or more often, looking for a

*Figure 2.2. After the radio-collared wolves were tracked from the air a few times, they got used to the aircraft. (Photo by L. David Mech.)*

small shadow cast by a ridge of snow that forms at the front of most tracks.

Probably the biggest problems we encountered in snow-tracking wolves in Denali were the weather and snow conditions. Good flying weather a day or two after 6 or more inches (15 centimeters) of fresh snow is preferable. This combination is rare on the north side of the Alaska range, where most of the park's wolf population resides. Wolves can be tracked in old snow, but the task is much more difficult. This was when our use of former wolf hunters as pilots really paid off.

## The Aerial Radio-Tracking Technique

If the use of airplanes improved wolf research, then the advent of aerial radiotelemetry revolu-

tionized it (Mech and Frenzel 1971; Mech 1974b, 1979, 1983). The two main advantages of radio-tracking are that it allows researchers, first, to locate radio-tagged animals anytime weather and resources allow and, second, to identify each and learn their individual histories.

For wolves, we attached small radio transmitters and batteries in collars weighing about 1.3 pounds (580 grams). Each transmitter emits a radio signal on a unique frequency (like a radio station), which can then be traced to the wolf by a special receiver and directional antennas.

On level ground, the biologist can detect the "beep-beep-beep" of the signal from 1 to 2 miles (2–3 kilometers) away, although if either wolf or biologist is on a mountainside, the signal can be

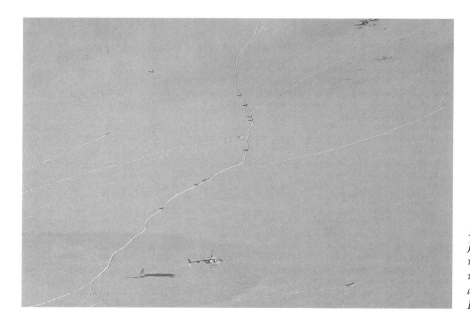

*Figure 2.3.* A Bell 206 JetRanger helicopter was used to approach the wolves for drugging with anesthetic darts. (Photo by L. David Mech.)

received for many miles. On the back of the mountain, however, the signal is obscured. Wolves travel so far and wide that most biologists routinely use aircraft to radio-track them.

From the air, we regularly detected the signal from 10 to 20 miles (16–32 kilometers) and sometimes from as far as 50 to 60 miles (80–95 kilometers), depending on our altitude. We then flew to its location and counted, observed, and mapped the location of the wolves. After the wolves are found this way two or three times, they get used to the airplane and seem to ignore it (figure 2.2).

## The Wolf-Darting Routine

Before any of this could happen, we had to capture the wolves to radio-collar them. We captured most of them by shooting them from a helicopter with darts containing drugs. From March 1986 to May 1994, we caught only four wolves in snares and one in a foothold trap, and we darted the rest.

Darting wolves from a helicopter involves a great deal of advance planning, organizing, and coordination. Because use of helicopters is expensive, we chartered them for short periods and planned as much work for them as possible when they were available.

Our general darting procedure was as follows. A Super Cub (or two or three if there were wolves from many noncollared packs to be captured) begins searching for and snow-tracking wolves. The helicopter (we used a Bell 206 JetRanger) stands by in the general area, where it can remain in radio contact with the Super Cubs.

When the Super Cub finds a pack of wolves, the helicopter approaches them (figure 2.3). Once the helicopter pilot and darter spot the wolves, the pilot maneuvers the helicopter in close to one of them. The fixed-wing craft continues circling high above the helicopter and relays the wolves' location. Ideally the wolf is in open terrain (with no or very few trees) and runs from the helicopter.

The helicopter follows about 12 feet (3 meters) above the wolf, matching its speed, and then closes in. When 10 to 15 yards (meters) away, the biologist, strapped in the back seat of the helicopter, lowers the shooting window, aims at the wolf's rump, and tries to dart the animal. If it is hit, the Super Cub pilot and passenger, with their broad overview, continue to keep track of the wolf.

As long as the wolf is in a safe area (no open water, cliffs, or steep slopes), the helicopter immediately leaves so as not to further frighten it, and lands. The fixed-wing plane continues to monitor the creature. Within 5 to 10 minutes the wolf usually drops. The helicopter then flies the biologist back (with the Super Cub directing it) to begin radio-collaring and examining the wolf.

This procedure is really easier than it would appear as long as the pilot is highly competent and experienced. Probably 95% of the success in darting lies with the pilot. Luckily, we often worked with one of the best, Ken Butters. If the pilot can get close and match the speed of the wolf, darting is like shooting at a stationary target. Usually, though, the combination of terrain, trees, and the wolf's elusive maneuvering makes it more challenging.

## The Realities of Darting Wolves

John Burch darted most of the wolves for us and quickly grew highly competent, darting wolf after wolf almost routinely. A few of his darting attempts, however, did not go quite according to textbook. One such case involved the white breeding female of the McLeod Lake Pack. The aerial spotters found her and her packmates among thick trees in the flats northwest of Kantishna; visibility was poor, with fog, light snow, and ice crystals hanging in the air. Both daylight and fuel were short.

The helicopter dropped Tom Meier off on a river to reduce weight and maximize maneuverability. It then came in slowly toward the wolves, hovering just over the treetops. The Super Cub radioed that the wolf was heading for a small swamp where it could be darted. Suddenly John realized that the dart had been in his rifle barrel for 10 minutes or more, and it was -30°F (-34°C) out. The drug was probably frozen.

At that moment Ken asked, "Ready?" The wolf was at the opening, and Ken was about to dive on her. John lunged out of the window and aimed. The wolf ran in a tight arc. Ken followed. John knew the time was not right, but he had only one chance. He shot just as Ken pulled into a hover.

The whole world turned white from the rotor wash blasting the fluffy snow. The dart missed, and the wolf disappeared. "S——!" Ken regained his horizon on a small clump of grass and flew straight up like an elevator to the treetops. They decided to try again.

The wolf approached another opening, a pond a little bigger than the swamp. Ken hovered over the treetops trying to push her onto the pond. However, his rotor wash blasted the snow again, obscuring their view. Snow blown in by the rotor covered Ken's back and John's lap. John recalled the following finish to his frustrating foray:

> I was breathing hard, my breath fogged my glasses, my left fingers burned with cold, we were tight on daylight and fuel, and we had lost sight of our wolf. All of a sudden the Cub says the wolf is crossing the pond! Life doesn't get any better than this!
>
> Ken and I see her running straight across the pond. He dives while I aim. Ken closes the gap. The wolf is almost across the pond when I fire. The dart hits her in the butt. Ken wrenches the helicopter hard to the left, and I almost lose the rifle out the window. A huge cloud of snow almost envelopes us as Ken pulls into a hover. He utters the longest string of four-letter words I've heard from him.
>
> The Cub loses the wolf in the near whiteout. Ken lands immediately on the pond to conserve fuel and to let the Cub search. I suddenly remember Tom standing out on the river, freezing his ass off, wondering what's going on. Three minutes later the Cub spots the wolf still traveling in the thick trees. Ken and I pick up Tom and wait.

It's now 5 minutes since darting, but the Cub reports no drug effect. I'm sure the dart hit the wolf (aren't I?). Maybe it bounced off. Maybe the internal charge didn't fire, or the drug froze. This always happens when you're shy of daylight and fuel. The Cub tells us there is no place close to the wolf to land anyway. Great!

Seven minutes after dart time, the Cub says the wolf stumbled. Then definitely, yes, at 10 minutes the wolf is down, but her head is up and she is struggling. We take off and look for the closest place to land. The Cub says there's a small opening 200 yards from the wolf, but they doubt we can land in it.

The skilled Vietnam war veteran proves them wrong and wiggles the helicopter down.

"Hurry up, it's getting dark," he warns. Tom and I sink to our crotches in snow as we wade hurriedly toward the wolf. The Super Cub guides us through the thick trees by radio. Finally we grab the wolf, give her more drugs, and process her as fast as possible. The Super Cub immediately heads home.

In the end it worked; the helicopter refueled from a nearby fuel cache, and the crew got home just before dark.

## The Darts and Drugs

The reason the wolf did not drop right away is that the dart did not completely inject all the drug. A charge in the dart fires when the dart hits something, forcing a rubber plunger down the dart barrel, which then expels the drug. All the drug was not injected because the internal charge was a partial dud.

We used two kinds of drug mixtures. Through the first half of the study, we used a mixture of ketamine and xylazine. The ketamine renders the wolf unconscious, and the xylazine is a tranquilizer that mellows the creature and helps the anesthetic work faster. We used 800 milligrams of ketamine and 150 milligrams of xylazine. To reverse the xylazine and promote rapid recovery of the drugged wolves, we injected them with yohimbine at a dosage of 0.15 milligram per kilogram of body weight (Kreeger et al. 1987).

The second mixture we used was a combination of tiletamine (an anesthetic) and zolazapam (the tranquilizer) at a dose of 500 milligrams of mixture per wolf (Ballard et al. 1991). As yet, there is no reversal agent for this combination. However, the drugged wolves usually were mobile within 4 to 6 hours and fully recovered by the next day.

## Handling Wolves

When we captured a wolf, the most important task was to attach a radio collar around its neck (figure 2.4). We also clipped a numbered plastic ear tag in each ear. Then, if the collar came off and the wolf was recaptured, we still knew which wolf it was; this happened seven times. We weighed (plate 8) and measured each wolf; examined it for wounds, scars, or abnormalities; and measured teats or testes to check for breeding status (Mech et al. 1993).

We distinguished between pups and non-pups in autumn based on tooth eruption (Van Ballenberghe and Mech 1975). Unfortunately, for the winter period no published information exists that allows distinguishing definitively between pups and yearlings, or between yearlings and adults, although we recently learned about a boney protuberance on the ankle of pups (ADFG, unpublished).

We used tooth wear and the length of testes to help distinguish among these age classes, based on testes' lengths of known-aged wolves from Minnesota and elsewhere. Testes' lengths (centimeters) of pups in winter were about 2.5; of yearlings, 3.8 to 5.0; and of adults, 4.2 to 5.5 (L. D. Mech, unpublished).

We also drew blood samples from each wolf

*Figure 2.4. Radio collars weighing 1.3 pounds (580 grams) were placed on 147 wolves from 30 packs in and around Denali. (Photo by L. David Mech.)*

for disease antibody screening, for general blood characteristics (Seal et al. 1975; Seal and Mech 1983), and for genetic analyses (Lehman et al. 1992; Smith et al. 1997). When done, we injected each wolf with an antibiotic to help reduce the chance of capture-induced infection (Kreeger 1996). After recovering from the drug, all the captured wolves except loners promptly reunited with their packs.

We usually tried to keep two or three members of each pack radio-collared. We did this because wolves disperse or die at high rates, and because their radio collars sometimes come off or fail. The radios had an estimated life of 3 years, although some lasted as long as 5. Thus, we always tried to re-radio each pack while it still contained at least

one member with a working collar. It was much easier and more economical to capture and radio-collar another wolf that way than to find them again by snow-tracking.

## Following the Signals

We routinely radio-tracked wolves by flying in the Super Cub from pack to pack and homing in on the radio-collared wolves in each. "Homing in" requires two directional antennas, one on each wing strut (figure 2.5). The signal from each antenna feeds through a cable and switch box to the receiver. The switch allows the listener to hear a signal from either antenna or both at once. The pilot and biologist could both hear the signal through the plane's intercom and still talk to each other.

*Figure 2.5. A directional antenna on each wing strut of the aircraft facilitated finding radio-collared wolves. (Photo by L. David Mech.)*

Aerial radio-tracking involves listening to the signal strength and switching between right and left antennas as the plane approaches the wolf (Mech 1983). The higher the aircraft, the farther a signal can be heard. As the plane gets closer, the signal gets louder. If stronger from the right, then that is where the wolf is. The plane is turned until the signal strength is equal from both sides, which indicates the plane is pointed at the wolf. When the signal is loudest, it is time to circle and try to see the wolves, continually switching between antennas and maneuvering the plane until the wolves are spotted or the signal is isolated. We saw wolves during 84% of our attempts.

We located the wolves an average of three times per month with a Super Cub and a Cessna 185 aircraft. Not all packs were located during each flight, and some packs were located more frequently than others. We also located wolves more often in late winter and spring than during summer, late autumn, and early winter; our summer data are especially sparse.

Once we spotted the wolves, we recorded their number, color, behavior, and number of pups, and mapped their location. Dens or rendezvous sites were also of special interest to us. We also searched for any kill remains and tried to note the species, age, and sex. This sometimes required a few low and slow passes to look for small antlers or other clues. We then mapped and photographed the kill locations to aid in revisiting them on the ground.

## Examining Kill Remains

We examined prey carcass sites from the ground as soon as possible after locating them, depending on helicopter availability or other means of access, to determine species, cause of death, sex, age, and condition of prey (plate 9). The position of the carcass, presence of blood, signs of struggle, and manner of feeding provided clues as to whether wolves killed or merely scavenged a particular carcass. We determined the sex of prey by the presence of antlers or antler pedicels (moose), antler size (caribou), horn shape and size (sheep), mandible, metatarsus or metacarpus length (caribou and sheep), or pelvis shape (all species).

For aging wolf-killed prey, we collected teeth, usually incisors, for sectioning and counting cementum annuli (Wolfe 1969), which we had done commercially (Matson's, Milltown, Montana). We determined the ages of younger animals by tooth-eruption pattern. Sheep were aged by annular rings on the horns and by tooth eruption and tooth sectioning.

We collected marrow (usually from the femur bone), dried it, and weighed it to determine per-

*Figure 2.6.* The authors collected jaws and various other bones from all wolf-killed prey to determine the animal's age, sex, and condition. (Photo by Thomas J. Meier.)

cent fat content (Neiland 1970) as a possible indicator of poor condition. The marrow fat percentages we report are probably higher than actual because some specimens were not retrieved until long after the animals had died, and the marrow had probably dehydrated.

We checked all bones from kill sites for abnormalities, and collected certain bones, if available, for cleaning and examination (figure 2.6).

## Wolf-Carcass Examination

A final aspect of the wolf research was the collection and necropsy of dead wolves. We collected wolf carcasses by finding any wolf whose collar was transmitting a mortality signal. The radio pulse rate doubles after 4 hours of no movement. Even when wolves sleep, they move enough to prevent switching to mortality mode. We could still be fooled, however, when the collar malfunctioned or when the collar was chewed off an animal (Thiel and Fritts 1983). Luckily both these problems were rare.

We tried to recover dead wolves as quickly as possible but had to leave many for a month or two

because there was no practical way to recover them until a helicopter was available. During the long winters, when most wolves die, the carcasses stay preserved. Sometimes, however, scavengers such as ravens, foxes, and even other wolves ate enough to make it difficult or impossible to collect the data we wanted.

We were most interested in cause of death and the animal's age, condition, and reproductive history (females). We could often make a good guess at the cause of death from tracks in the snow and the position and appearance of the carcass. We tried to corroborate these clues by our ground examination and necropsy. The most common cause of death was other wolves, which was easy to figure out because of puncture wounds and much internal trauma. We took the few carcasses whose deaths we could not explain to Dr. John Blake, DVM, at the University of Alaska, where he performed a thorough necropsy.

We also collected skinned carcasses of wolves from hunters and trappers in the surrounding area. These provided valuable information about the number of wolves harvested in the area, where

*Figure 2.7. The helicopter was also used to dart caribou cows for radio-collaring. (Photo by L. David Mech.)*

they were taken, and their age, sex, condition, and reproductive history.

## Caribou Research Techniques

Many of the methods we used for caribou research were similar to those used for wolves. This section focuses on the differences.

### Capturing Caribou

We darted caribou much like we darted wolves, and Layne Adams did most of the darting (figure 2.7). Caribou are usually easier to find initially, as there are so many more, and they are generally in the open. When a helicopter approaches a herd of caribou, they tend to stay together, whereas wolves usually scatter. Thus, the darter must quickly assess the age and sex of the caribou based on body and antler size and genitals. Sexing caribou in this way may sound easy, but both males and females possess antlers, and young males are about the same size as adult females. We mainly captured cows, so we had to rely on seeing a vulva on the animal selected. With a practiced eye, we could do this consistently, though in the early

years of the study we darted a few bulls by mistake. One of the authors, who shall remain nameless, was responsible for a young bull we mistakenly radio-collared in our first such capture effort. The bull carried the name "Bruce," in honor of the gunner, for the remainder of his tenure in our study.

We processed caribou much like we did wolves, weighing, measuring, and radio-collaring them. We also blood-sampled them, pulled a small canine tooth for aging, gave them antibiotics, and reversed their drug. That allowed the caribou to be on its feet and running 2 to 3 minutes later.

### Caribou Herd Composition Surveys

Many important questions about caribou could not be answered with radio-tracking alone. How many caribou are in the herd? How many bulls and cows? How many cows were pregnant? How many calves survived through each season? We attempted to answer these questions with caribou herd composition surveys.

We conducted four kinds of caribou herd composition surveys each year (Adams et al. 1989). All were done similarly, and the radio-collared animals greatly facilitated the surveys. We started by locating large herds of caribou by radio-tracking our marked animals. Then, using a helicopter, we flew low closely behind the caribou and determined the age class, sex, and number of caribou in each group.

Classifying caribou required three observers and the pilot. The observer in front, usually Adams, aged each caribou by size (calf or adult) and sexed them as described earlier. This information was read into a tape recorder for later tally. The two observers in back mapped the location of each group classified to avoid classifying them twice, and kept a running tally of the total number of caribou classified so we knew when a large enough sample had been obtained to be meaningful.

We made composition counts four times per year: (1) a natality (or pregnancy) survey in May at the peak of calving, (2) a post-calving survey in June, (3) a fall survey near the peak of the rut, and (4) a recruitment (or calf survival) survey in April before calving.

From these counts, we generated ratios to determine how many cows still had their calves and what the bull:cow ratio was. Bull:cow ratios must be determined during the rut, the only time bulls and cows are consistently together. During pregnancy counts, the observer looks for distended udders, which only pregnant cows develop (Bergerud 1964). The pregnancy counts are conducted in the middle of calving season because late calvers do not develop an udder until a week or so before birth, and the udders of cows that lose a calf soon "dry up."

### Caribou Photocensus

We used a couple of methods to count caribou. In late May each year, we used a helicopter to count and classify all the caribou we could find on the calving ground. Since most were in fairly large groups, we probably missed only a few animals. We could estimate the number of cows in the herd by taking the number of cows we counted and di-

viding it by the proportion of our radio-collared cows that were within the area we surveyed. We could calculate the bulls and calves in the herd using calf:cow and bull:cow ratios that we determined in the fall.

We also conducted photocensuses in 1987, 1990, and 1991. A common technique for counting caribou (Davis et al. 1979; Valkenburg et al. 1985), a photocensus takes advantage of the aggregating behavior of caribou on hot, still days in late June and early July. When the weather is hot, caribou amass on high-elevation snowfields to avoid the swarms of flies and mosquitoes.

By radio-tracking our collared animals and searching the right habitats from two to three Super Cubs and a Cessna 185 with a camera port, we were able to locate and photograph these aggregations and count the smaller groups, all in one day. Most of the photography fell to the Cessna 185 crew, but the "Cub jockeys" also had to do their share. It is a thrilling job to photograph caribou groups in steep mountainous terrain from the open window of a Super Cub circling over them.

Once we had the photos, it was just a matter of counting all the maggotlike images of caribou on the white snow background. In the 3 years that we conducted both types of surveys, herd estimates from each were within about 1% of each other (Adams, Dale, and Mech 1995).

We used additional techniques to study caribou calves, and will describe these techniques in chapter 7.

## Basic Wolf Study Data

Gathering the data on which this study was based required over 10,000 hours of flight time in airplanes and helicopters from March 1986 through May 1994. During that time we made 170 captures of 147 wolves in 30 packs (some individuals were captured more than once), primarily those living in the northern two-thirds of the park. Even though wolves also use the part of Denali south of

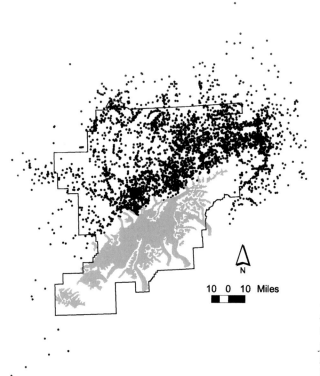

*Figure 2.8.* Composite of all the locations where radio-collared wolves were found during the study. Each dot represents one location where a wolf or pack was found.

the Mountain, we concentrated on the much larger area to the north (figure 2.8).

Of the 30 wolf packs we studied, 23 lived at least partly in Denali National Park and Preserve, and the remaining 7 lived just outside it. In addition, we gathered data from 12 more nearby packs to which our radio-tagged wolves dispersed or that were radio-tagged by the ADFG. Our analyses of wolf mortality and dispersal, however, are based on the 23 park packs (table 2.1).

We were able to radio-track and monitor some wolves for over 6 years, and we followed one pack (East Fork) for over 8 years (see chapter 3); some members were still being monitored as of this writing in 1996 (L. Adams et al., unpublished). We located radio-tagged wolves and their packmates for a total of 7,304 wolf-locations, and examined the remains of 1,294 kills, including 512 moose, 514 caribou, 169 sheep, and 99 miscellaneous.

## Age, Sex, and Weight of Captured Wolves

We usually avoided capturing obvious pups, and often tried to capture known members of breeding pairs; thus, our capture sample did not represent the age structure of the wolf population. Based on the average Denali pack size of nine wolves in fall (table 2.2), and the average litter size of four pups (table 2.3), a "typical" pack would consist of two adult breeders, four pups, two yearlings, and one 2-year-old. Thus, nearly half the wolves in the population should be pups, about 20% yearlings, and 30% adults. Our capture sample consisted of 24% pups, 30% yearlings, and 46% adults (estimated ≥ 2 years old).

Of the 147 wolves we captured between

March 1986 and May 1994, 72 were females and 75 males. The mean weight of female wolves aged as pups or yearlings was 76 (range 58–98) pounds, or 35 (range 26–45) kilograms. The mean weight of male pups and yearlings was 85 (30–115) pounds, or 39 (14–52) kilograms. Two male pups weighing less than 50 pounds (23 kilograms) were not radio-collared. The mean weight of adult females (more than 2 years old) was 88 (70–105) pounds, or 40 (32–48) kilograms; adult males, 103 (78–135) pounds, or 47 (35–61) kilograms.

### Wolf Colors

Of the wolves radio-collared for the first time, 126 (86%) were various shades of gray; 13 (9%), black; 8 (5%), tan, light, or white (see figure 2.2). Some wolves become paler as they age; 3 wolves described as gray at first capture were described as white when recaptured 5 years later. Most of the white wolves we observed were older, with worn teeth. In winter 1990-91, of 196 wolves from 18 packs we observed in and around Denali, 9% were black, the same as in our radio-collared sample.

Black wolves were radio-collared from the Alma Lakes, Bearpaw, Birch Creek, Chilchuk-abena, Chitsia Mountain, and Highpower packs. These packs were clustered in the northwestern part of the study area (figure 2.9), an area low in elevation and heavily forested. Black wolves may be at a disadvantage when hunting or avoiding humans in more open country. In the early 1970s Denali's Savage Pack consisted of black wolves that lived in open, mountainous terrain in the eastern part of Denali, but they did not survive there (Haber 1977).

We also observed black wolves in several packs north and east of Denali: Rex Dome, Tatlanika, Totek Hills, Walker Dome, and Nineteenmile packs. These packs had either been radio-collared by ADFG or were dispersal sites for radio-collared Denali wolves. Most of this area is also forested. A black wolf briefly joined the Headquarters Pack in

**Table 2.1.** Wolf packs included in this study

| Pack | Code | Years studied |
|------|------|---------------|
| Alma Lakes | AL | 1986 |
| Birch Creek | BC | 1987–93 |
| Birch Creek North | BN | 1991–92 |
| Bearpaw | BP | 1987–88 |
| Castle Rocks | CA | 1988 |
| Chilchukabena | CB | 1990–92 |
| Chitsia Mountain | CM | 1989–94 |
| Clearwater | CW | 1986–89 |
| Ewe Creek | EC | 1987–94 |
| East Fork | EF | 1986–94 |
| Foraker River | FO | 1988–94 |
| Highpower | HP | 1988–93 |
| Headquarters | HQ | 1986–94 |
| Jenny Creek | JC | 1993–94 |
| Little Bear | LB | 1988–94 |
| McLeod Lake | ML | 1987–94 |
| McKinley River | MR | 1988–94 |
| McLeod West | MW | 1991–94 |
| Pirate Creek | PC | 1987–88 |
| Swift Fork | SF | 1988–89 |
| Slippery Creek | SC | 1991–92 |
| Stampede | ST | 1988–94 |
| Sushana | SU | 1986–94 |
| Savage | SV | 1992–94 |
| Thorofare | TF | 1992–94 |
| Turtle Hill | TU | 1992–94 |
| Windy Creek | WC | 1987–90 |

*Note: The two-letter codes are used throughout the text.*

1994 but apparently drowned in the Nenana River that spring.

Our hypothesis that black wolves tend to survive better in forested areas tends to be inconsistent with data from Gates of the Arctic National Park, where wolves are legally hunted from snowmobiles. Black wolves there tend to inhabit the open terrain as often as the forested area (L. Adams, unpublished). Nevertheless, the geographic segregation of black wolves in the forested areas of Denali is striking.

A litter of black pups was produced by two

**Table 2.2.** Maximum fall wolf pack sizes in Denali National Park and Preserve

| Pack | 1986 | 1987 | 1988 | 1989 | 1990 | 1991 | 1992 | 1993 | Total | N | Mean | SD | SE |
|------|------|------|------|------|------|------|------|------|-------|---|------|----|----|
| Headquarters | 2 | 2 | 7 | 14 | 11 | 10 | 5 | 9 | 60 | 8 | 7.5 | 4.3 | 1.5 |
| East Fork | 9 | 8 | 19 | 27 | 29 | 16 | 15 | 9 | 132 | 8 | 16.5 | 8.1 | 2.9 |
| Clearwater | 6 | 6 | 4 | 8 | | | | | 24 | 4 | 6.0 | 1.6 | 0.8 |
| Alma Lakes | 3 | | | | | | | | 3 | 1 | 3.0 | 0.0 | 0.0 |
| McLeod Lake | | 7 | 12 | 12 | 20 | 13 | 13 | 15 | 92 | 7 | 13.1 | 3.9 | 1.5 |
| McLeod West | | | | | | 11 | 17 | | 28 | 2 | 14.0 | 4.2 | 3.0 |
| Birch Creek | | 11 | 23 | 15 | 16 | 6 | | | 71 | 5 | 14.2 | 6.3 | 2.8 |
| Birch North | | | | | | 5 | | | 5 | 1 | 5.0 | 0.0 | 0.0 |
| Bearpaw | | 10 | 1 | | | | | | 11 | 2 | 5.5 | 6.4 | 4.5 |
| Windy Creek | | 8 | 5 | 8 | 17 | | | | 38 | 4 | 9.5 | 5.2 | 2.6 |
| Totek Hills | | 15 | 7 | 12 | | | | | 34 | 3 | 11.3 | 4.0 | 2.3 |
| Ewe Creek | 6 | 8 | 5 | 3 | 4 | 3 | 3 | | 32 | 7 | 4.6 | 1.9 | 0.7 |
| Chulitna | 2 | 5 | | | | | | | 7 | 2 | 3.5 | 2.1 | 1.5 |
| Pirate Creek | | | 9 | | | | | | 9 | 1 | 9.0 | 0.0 | 0.0 |
| Castle Rocks | | | 8 | | | | | | 8 | 1 | 8.0 | 0.0 | 0.0 |
| Swift Fork | | | 2 | | | | | | 2 | 1 | 2.0 | 0.0 | 0.0 |
| Highpower | | | 8 | 10 | 12 | 11 | 10 | | 51 | 5 | 10.2 | 1.5 | 0.7 |
| McKinley River | | 10 | 10 | 8 | 10 | 9 | 7 | 3 | 57 | 7 | 8.1 | 2.5 | 1.0 |
| Sushana | 2 | | | | | | | | 2 | 1 | 2.0 | 0.0 | 0.0 |
| Stampede | | | 7 | 10 | 4 | 2 | 2 | 3 | 28 | 6 | 4.7 | 3.2 | 1.3 |
| Little Bear | | | 7 | 12 | | 23 | 12 | 12 | 66 | 5 | 13.2 | 5.9 | 2.6 |
| Foraker | | | | 7 | 9 | 8 | 7 | 6 | 37 | 5 | 7.4 | 1.1 | 0.5 |
| Chitsia | | | | 4 | 8 | 12 | 9 | 8 | 41 | 5 | 8.2 | 2.9 | 1.3 |
| Chilchukabena | | | | | | 6 | 7 | | 13 | 2 | 6.5 | 0.7 | 0.5 |
| Slippery Creek | | | | | | 5 | 1 | | 6 | 2 | 3.0 | 2.8 | 2.0 |
| Tonzona | | | | | | 5 | | | 5 | 1 | 5.0 | 0.0 | 0.0 |
| Ferry | | | | | | 7 | | | 7 | 1 | 7.0 | 0.0 | 0.0 |
| Reindeer | | | | | | | 7 | | 7 | 1 | 7.0 | 0.0 | 0.0 |
| Yanert | | | | | 20 | 5 | 18 | | 43 | 3 | 14.3 | 8.1 | 4.7 |
| Thorofare | | | | | | | 2 | 7 | 9 | 2 | 4.5 | 3.5 | 2.5 |
| Turtle Hill | | | | | | | 8 | 7 | 15 | 2 | 7.5 | 0.7 | 0.5 |
| Savage | | | | | | | 5 | 8 | 13 | 2 | 6.5 | 2.1 | 1.5 |
| Jenny Creek | | | | | | | | 6 | 6 | 1 | 6.0 | 0.0 | 0.0 |
| | | | | | | | | | | | | | |
| Total | 30 | 90 | 134 | 150 | 160 | 157 | 148 | 93 | 966 | | | | |
| Sample Size | 7 | 11 | 16 | 14 | 12 | 18 | 18 | 12 | | 108 | | | |
| Mean | 4.3 | 8.2 | 8.4 | 10.7 | 13.3 | 8.7 | 8.2 | 7.8 | | | 8.9 | 5.6 | 0.5 |
| SD | 2.8 | 3.4 | 5.7 | 5.8 | 7.4 | 5.1 | 5.1 | 3.4 | | | | | |
| SE | 1.0 | 1.0 | 1.4 | 1.6 | 2.1 | 1.2 | 1.2 | 1.0 | | | | | |

**Table 2.3.** Minimum pup production of Denali wolf packs based on pup counts in autumn

| Pack | 1986 | 1987 | 1988 | 1989 | 1990 | 1991 | 1992 | 1993 | Total | N | Mean | SD | SE |
|------|------|------|------|------|------|------|------|------|-------|---|------|----|----|
| Headquarters | 0 | 0 | 5 | 7 | 3 | 3 | 2 | 7 | 27 | 8 | 3.4 | 2.8 | 1.0 |
| East Fork | 2 | 2 | 12[a] | 9 | 9 | 3 | 7 | 4 | 48 | 8 | 6.0 | 3.8 | 1.3 |
| Clearwater | 0 | 2 | 0 | 6 | | | | | 8 | 4 | 2.0 | 2.8 | 1.4 |
| McLeod Lake | | 3 | 5 | 4 | 11[a] | 5 | 4 | 5 | 37 | 7 | 5.3 | 2.6 | 1.0 |
| McLeod West | | | | | | | 4 | 8 | 12 | 2 | 6.0 | 2.8 | 2.0 |
| Birch Creek | | 4 | 12[a] | 2 | 1 | 3 | | | 22 | 5 | 4.4 | 4.4 | 2.0 |
| Bearpaw | | 4 | | | | | | | 4 | 1 | 4.0 | 0.0 | 0.0 |
| Windy Creek | | 3 | 0 | 5 | 9 | | | | 17 | 4 | 4.3 | 3.8 | 1.9 |
| Totek Hills | | 4 | | | | | | | 4 | 1 | 4.0 | 0.0 | 0.0 |
| Ewe Creek | | 1 | 2 | 0 | 2 | | | | 5 | 4 | 1.3 | 1.0 | 0.5 |
| Chulitna | | 5 | | | | | | | 5 | 1 | 5.0 | 0.0 | 0.0 |
| Pirate Creek | | | 7 | | | | | | 7 | 1 | 7.0 | 0.0 | 0.0 |
| Castle Rocks | | | 6 | | | | | | 6 | 1 | 6.0 | 0.0 | 0.0 |
| Highpower | | | 5 | 3 | 5 | 3 | 3 | | 19 | 5 | 3.8 | 1.1 | 0.5 |
| McKinley River | | | 0 | 1 | 5 | 4 | 2 | 1 | 13 | 6 | 2.2 | 1.9 | 0.8 |
| Stampede | | | 5 | 6 | | 0 | 0 | 0 | 11 | 5 | 2.2 | 3.0 | 1.3 |
| Little Bear | | | 5 | 5 | | 11[a] | 6 | 3 | 30 | 5 | 6.0 | 3.0 | 1.3 |
| Foraker | | | | 4 | 3 | 3 | 3 | | 13 | 4 | 3.3 | 0.5 | 0.3 |
| Chitsia | | | | 0 | 5 | 5 | 3 | 1 | 14 | 5 | 2.8 | 2.3 | 1.0 |
| Chilchukabena | | | | | | 3 | 3 | | 6 | 2 | 3.0 | 0.0 | 0.0 |
| Slippery Creek | | | | | | 3 | 0 | | 3 | 2 | 1.5 | 2.1 | 1.5 |
| Reindeer | | | | | | 3 | | | 3 | 1 | 3.0 | 0.0 | 0.0 |
| Yanert | | | | | | 0 | 6 | | 6 | 2 | 3.0 | 4.2 | 3.0 |
| Thorofare | | | | | | | 0 | 5 | 5 | 2 | 2.5 | 3.5 | 2.5 |
| Turtle Hill | | | | | | | 5 | 3 | 8 | 2 | 4.0 | 1.4 | 1.0 |
| Savage | | | | | | | 2 | 4 | 6 | 2 | 3.0 | 1.4 | 1.0 |
| Jenny Creek | | | | | | | | 4 | 4 | 1 | 4.0 | 0.0 | 0.0 |
| | | | | | | | | | | | | | |
| Total | 2 | 28 | 64 | 52 | 53 | 53 | 54 | 37 | 343 | | | | |
| Sample Size | 3 | 10 | 13 | 13 | 10 | 15 | 16 | 11 | | 91 | | | |
| Mean | 0.7 | 2.8 | 4.9 | 4.0 | 5.3 | 3.5 | 3.4 | 3.4 | | | 3.8 | 2.8 | 0.3 |
| SD | 1.2 | 1.5 | 3.9 | 2.7 | 3.3 | 2.5 | 2.5 | 2.1 | | | | | |
| SE | 0.7 | 0.5 | 1.1 | 0.7 | 1.0 | 0.6 | 0.6 | 0.6 | | | | | |

[a] Represents two litters.

gray parents in the Chulitna River Pack. The male, former Headquarters wolf 231, was a typically colored gray wolf, but the female had a striking white stripe down her back. It is unusual for two light-colored wolves to produce black offspring. Male 231 may not have been the father, or his odd-colored mate may have had an unusual genetic makeup.

## Pack Sizes

Annual pack size depends on the number of pups produced, the number surviving, the number of

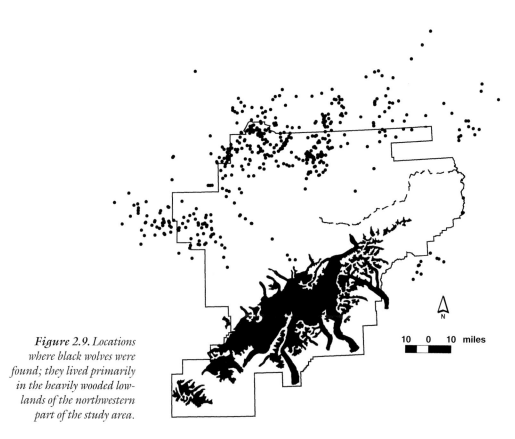

*Figure 2.9. Locations where black wolves were found; they lived primarily in the heavily wooded lowlands of the northwestern part of the study area.*

1- to 3-year-old members dispersing, and the overall survival rate. As will be discussed in chapter 5, dispersal helps buffer variations in food availability, with more wolves dispersing during leaner years.

Denali wolf packs ranged in maximum size from the basic pair to as many as 29 members (table 2.2), averaging 9 in fall and 7 in spring (table 2.4). Annually, mean pack size varied from 4.3 to 13.7, and individual packs during the study contained an average of 2 to 17 members per year (tables 2.2 and 2.4).

### Wolf Pack Territory Sizes

Denali's wolf packs occupied territories that ranged in size from an estimated 200 to 1,000 square miles (500 to 2,500 square kilometers), the size probably depending on prey abundance, the activities of neighboring packs, and each pack's individual habits (see chapter 4).

Determining territory size from radio-tracking data is complex, and any attempt yields only general estimates. The estimate obtained enlarges with the number of radio locations used to estimate it (Fritts and Mech 1981; Bekoff and Mech 1984; Ballard et al. 1987). However, it also depends on the temporal distribution of the locations (50 locations in 1 day would yield a much smaller estimate than 50 spread over 1 year, for example).

Even the specific method of delineating the

**Table 2.4.** Maximum spring wolf pack sizes in Denali National Park and Preserve

| Pack | 1986 | 1987 | 1988 | 1989 | 1990 | 1991 | 1992 | 1993 | 1994 | Total | N | Mean | SD | SE |
|---|---|---|---|---|---|---|---|---|---|---|---|---|---|---|
| Headquarters | 6 | 1 | 2 | 7 | 10 | 9 | 7 | 4 | 2 | 48 | 9 | 5.3 | 3.2 | 1.1 |
| East Fork | 11 | 6 | 7 | 18 | 24 | 18 | 11 | 10 | 6 | 111 | 9 | 12.3 | 6.3 | 2.1 |
| Clearwater | 5 | 3 | 4 | 2 | | | | | | 14 | 4 | 3.5 | 1.3 | 0.7 |
| Alma Lakes | 4 | | | | | | | | | 4 | 1 | 4.0 | 0.0 | 0.0 |
| McLeod Lake | | 4 | 7 | 8 | 10 | 16 | 13 | 11 | 11 | 80 | 8 | 10.0 | 3.7 | 1.3 |
| McLeod West | | | | | | 7 | 11 | | | 18 | 2 | 9.0 | 2.8 | 2.0 |
| Birch Creek | | 7 | 11 | 22 | 16 | 9 | | | | 65 | 5 | 13.0 | 6.0 | 2.7 |
| Birch North | | | | | | 6 | | | | 6 | 1 | 6.0 | 0.0 | 0.0 |
| Bearpaw | | 5 | 4 | | | | | | | 9 | 2 | 4.5 | 0.7 | 0.5 |
| Windy Creek | | 7 | 6 | 5 | 8 | | | | | 26 | 4 | 6.5 | 1.3 | 0.7 |
| Totek Hills | | | 7 | 7 | | | | | | 14 | 2 | 7.0 | 0.0 | 0.0 |
| Ewe Creek | | | 5 | 4 | 2 | 3 | 5 | 2 | | 21 | 6 | 3.5 | 1.4 | 0.6 |
| Chulitna | | 2 | | | | | | | | 2 | 1 | 2.0 | 0.0 | 0.0 |
| Pirate Creek | | | 2 | | | | | | | 2 | 1 | 2.0 | 0.0 | 0.0 |
| Castle Rocks | | | 2 | | | | | | | 2 | 1 | 2.0 | 0.0 | 0.0 |
| Highpower | | | 5 | 7 | 10 | 8 | 8 | | | 38 | 5 | 7.6 | 1.8 | 0.8 |
| McKinley River | | | 10 | 8 | 8 | 5 | 8 | 3 | 3 | 45 | 7 | 6.4 | 2.8 | 1.1 |
| Stampede | | | 2 | 7 | 7 | 3 | 3 | 2 | 3 | 27 | 7 | 3.9 | 2.2 | 0.8 |
| Little Bear | | | 2 | 7 | 7 | 13 | 14 | 12 | 13 | 68 | 7 | 9.7 | 4.5 | 1.7 |
| Foraker | | | | 2 | 7 | 4 | 3 | 6 | 7 | 29 | 6 | 4.8 | 2.1 | 0.9 |
| Chitsia | | | | 4 | 4 | 8 | 7 | 6 | 4 | 33 | 6 | 5.5 | 1.8 | 0.7 |
| Chilchukabena | | | | | | 3 | 3 | | | 6 | 2 | 3.0 | 0.0 | 0.0 |
| Slippery Creek | | | | | | 2 | 3 | | | 5 | 2 | 2.5 | 0.7 | 0.5 |
| Tonzona | | | | | | 5 | | | | 5 | 1 | 5.0 | 0.0 | 0.0 |
| Dillinger | | 10 | | | | | | | | 10 | 1 | 10.0 | 0.0 | 0.0 |
| Last Chance | | | | | | 4 | | | | 4 | 1 | 4.0 | 0.0 | 0.0 |
| Reindeer | | | | | | 9 | | | | 9 | 1 | 9.0 | 0.0 | 0.0 |
| Yanert | | | | | | 7 | 7 | | | 14 | 2 | 7.0 | 0.0 | 0.0 |
| Thorofare | | | | | | | 2 | 2 | | 4 | 2 | 2.0 | 0.0 | 0.0 |
| Turtle Hill | | | | | | | 3 | 7 | 6 | 16 | 3 | 5.3 | 2.1 | 1.2 |
| Savage | | | | | | | | 3 | 6 | 9 | 2 | 4.5 | 2.1 | 1.5 |
| Jenny Creek | | | | | | | | 2 | | 2 | 1 | 2.0 | 0.0 | 0.0 |
| | | | | | | | | | | | | | | |
| Total | 26 | 45 | 76 | 108 | 113 | 139 | 108 | 70 | 61 | 746 | | | | |
| Sample Size | 4 | 9 | 15 | 14 | 12 | 19 | 16 | 13 | 10 | | 112 | | | |
| Mean | 6.5 | 5.0 | 5.1 | 7.7 | 9.4 | 7.3 | 6.8 | 5.4 | 6.1 | | | 6.7 | 4.3 | 0.4 |
| SD | 3.1 | 2.8 | 2.9 | 5.6 | 5.7 | 4.4 | 3.9 | 3.6 | 3.5 | | | | | |
| SE | 1.6 | 0.9 | 0.7 | 1.5 | 1.6 | 1.0 | 1.0 | 1.0 | 1.1 | | | | | |

**Table 2.5.** Average annual terrritory sizes (km$^2$) of Denali wolf packs based on minimum convex polygons of radio locations[a]

| | Number of locations per year | | | | | | | | |
| | For all locations[b] | | | For > 20 locations | | | For > 40 locations | | |
| Pack | Mean | Min | Max | Mean | Min | Max | Mean | Min | Max |
| --- | --- | --- | --- | --- | --- | --- | --- | --- | --- |
| Headquarters | 607 | 174 | 931 | 607 | 174 | 931 | 695 | 557 | 931 |
| East Fork | 1384 | 648 | 2086 | 1384 | 648 | 2086 | 1489 | 850 | 2086 |
| Clearwater | 1793 | 1098 | 2100 | 1793 | 1098 | 2100 | 1793 | 1098 | 2100 |
| Alma Lakes | 2560 | 2560 | 2560 | 2560 | 2560 | 2560 | 2560 | 2560 | 2560 |
| McLeod Lake | 1379 | 717 | 2152 | 1379 | 717 | 2152 | 1379 | 717 | 2152 |
| McLeod West | 338 | 117 | 559 | | | | | | |
| Birch Creek | 1618 | 495 | 2991 | 1618 | 495 | 2991 | 2108 | 1505 | 2991 |
| Birch North | 189 | 189 | 189 | | | | | | |
| Bearpaw | 615 | 586 | 644 | 615 | 586 | 644 | 644 | 644 | 644 |
| Windy Creek | 750 | 565 | 913 | 750 | 565 | 913 | 884 | 854 | 913 |
| Totek Hills | 996 | 535 | 1426 | 1116 | 805 | 1426 | | | |
| Ewe Creek | 501 | 137 | 984 | 771 | 445 | 984 | 934 | 883 | 984 |
| Chulitna | 963 | 963 | 963 | 963 | 963 | 963 | | | |
| Pirate Creek | 403 | 403 | 403 | 403 | 403 | 403 | | | |
| Castle Rocks | 475 | 475 | 475 | 475 | 475 | 475 | 475 | 475 | 475 |
| Swift Fork | 271 | 271 | 271 | | | | | | |
| Highpower | 928 | 233 | 1417 | 990 | 622 | 1358 | 1358 | 1358 | 1358 |
| McKinley River | 1839 | 743 | 4335 | 1839 | 743 | 4335 | 2655 | 974 | 4335 |
| Sushana | 358 | 358 | 358 | | | | | | |
| Stampede | 758 | 368 | 1204 | 944 | 583 | 1204 | 1102 | 1000 | 1204 |
| Little Bear | 833 | 460 | 1303 | 888 | 460 | 1303 | 1303 | 1303 | 1303 |
| Foraker | 805 | 264 | 1186 | 1062 | 868 | 1186 | | | |
| Chitsia Mtn. | 821 | 365 | 1287 | 935 | 510 | 128 | | | |
| Chilchukabena | 530 | 502 | 557 | 557 | 557 | 557 | | | |
| Slippery Creek | 784 | 689 | 878 | 689 | 689 | 689 | | | |
| Tonzona River | 1215 | 1215 | 1215 | | | | | | |
| Last Chance | 127 | 127 | 127 | | | | | | |
| Reindeer | 175 | 130 | 220 | | | | | | |
| Yanert | 478 | 433 | 523 | | | | | | |
| Thorofare | 459 | 453 | 464 | 459 | 453 | 464 | | | |
| Turtle Hill | 512 | 445 | 578 | 512 | 445 | 578 | 578 | 578 | 578 |
| Savage | 286 | 228 | 344 | 344 | 344 | 344 | | | |
| Jenny Creek | 88 | 88 | 88 | | | | | | |

[a] The polygons are the smallest polygons that encompass all the outermost locations.

[b] Because these areas are annual averages, those given for all locations and for > 40 locations are not always the same.

**Table 2.6.** Age at first breeding for Denali wolves, 1986 to 1989

| Wolf | Date captured | Age (mon) | Year born | Breeding history[a] | Age (yr) at first breeding |
|------|---------------|-----------|-----------|---------------------|----------------------------|
| 217 | 03/31/86 | 22 | 1984 | EF 1989 and 1990 | 4 or 5 |
| 343 | 10/21/88 | 17 | 1987[b] | EC 1990–92+ | 3 |
| 347 | 10/22/88 | 5 | 1988[c] | BC 1990, BN 1991 | 2 |
| 359 | 12/06/88 | 19 | 1987[b] | CM 1990–92+ | 3 |
| 361 | 03/18/89 | 22 | 1987 | CW 1989 | 2 |
| 367 | 03/18/89 | 10 | 1988 | MW 1991? | 2 or 3 |
| 387 | 11/20/89 | 18 | 1988[b] | FO 1991 | 3 |

Note: Ages are estimated except where otherwise indicated.

[a] Two-letter abbreviations refer to the pack (see table 2.1) in which the animal bred.

[b] Known minimum age.

[c] Known age.

**Table 2.7.** Rates of wolf dispersal from Denali

| | | | Dispersers | | | | | |
|------|----------------|-------------|-------|-----------|-------|------|-------|------|
| | | | Total[b] | | | | From study area | |
| Year | Radio-collared wolves | Wolf-years[a] | Known | Probable[c] | Total | Rate | Total | Rate |
| 1986 | 14 | 7.6 | 5 | 1 | 6 | 0.79 | 6 | 0.79 |
| 1987 | 23 | 13.7 | 4 | 1 | 5 | 0.36 | 4 | 0.29 |
| 1988 | 35 | 21.5 | 3 | 2 | 5 | 0.23 | 4 | 0.19 |
| 1989 | 32 | 24.8 | 3 | 2 | 5 | 0.20 | 3 | 0.12 |
| 1990 | 34 | 23.7 | 7 | 1 | 8 | 0.34 | 5 | 0.21 |
| 1991 | 42 | 25.8 | 7 | 1 | 8 | 0.31 | 2 | 0.08 |
| 1992 | 50 | 30.3 | 8 | 1 | 9 | 0.30 | 8 | 0.26 |
| 1993 | 44 | 31.4 | 3 | 3 | 6 | 0.19 | 6 | 0.19 |
| 1994 | 31 | 21.8 | 2 | 2 | 4 | 0.18 | 3 | 0.14 |
| Total | 305 | 201 | 42 | 14 | 56 | 0.28 | 41 | 0.21 |

[a] Rates are based on wolf-years of monitoring, 1 wolf-year represents monitoring 1 wolf for 1 year.

[b] Includes dispersers that remained in the study area.

[c] Probable dispersers are wolves whose signals were suddenly lost under circumstances in which radio failure or other causes of signal loss were unlikely.

territory based on the radio locations will influence the estimate. In a crescent-shaped distribution of radio locations, how tightly does one adhere to the actual points in drawing a territory "boundary"? If one includes the bowl of the crescent as part of the territory, that would produce a much larger area than if one did not.

Because such considerations alter the actual territory size estimates by varying amounts, it is useful to present estimates based on different sample sizes (table 2.5).

## Reproduction

Like wolves elsewhere (Mech 1970), Denali wolves first bred at ages 2 to 4 years (table 2.6). Three male and two female wolves appeared to have paired as yearlings, breeding at about 22 months of age. Eleven male and nine female wolves were thought to have paired as 2-year-olds, breeding at 34 months. In at least eight cases, new packs started by younger breeders failed to survive 2 years later. Older wolves may be more successful breeders than younger wolves, both because of greater experience and the possession of better-established territories.

Packs bred annually, and during this study they produced an average of at least 3.8 pups per litter in mid to late May (table 2.3). They denned in holes in hillsides or other sandy areas, below the lower branches of conifers, or in shallow pits (see chapter 5). To our knowledge, only during 14 of 91 pack years did wolf packs fail to produce pups (table 2.3).

Even though in most areas usually only one pair of wolves produces a litter in each pack (Mech 1970), Denali packs produced multiple litters in at least six cases during our study (see chapter 4). Two packs raised as many as 12 pups in a single summer (table 2.3). Multiple litters were produced when annual snowfall began increasing after a few years of being below average (table 1.1) and when female weights and population density began increasing and prey became especially vulnerable (see chapter 8).

## Wolf Dispersal

Most wolves of both sexes disperse from their natal territories by the age of 3 years (Fritts and Mech 1981; Peterson et al. 1984; Messier 1985; Mech 1987; Ballard et al. 1987; Fuller 1989; Gese and Mech 1991), and form new packs when they locate dispersers of the opposite sex and a vacant area to set up a territory (Rothman and Mech 1979).

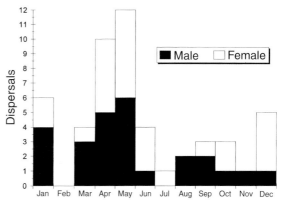

*Figure 2.10.* The commonest time of year for dispersal was April and May.

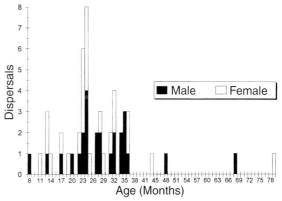

*Figure 2.11.* Denali wolves tended to disperse when 1 to 3 years old.

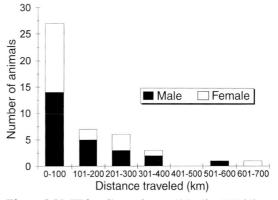

*Figure 2.12.* Wolves dispersed up to 435 miles (700 kilometers) away from Denali. (See also figure 2.13.)

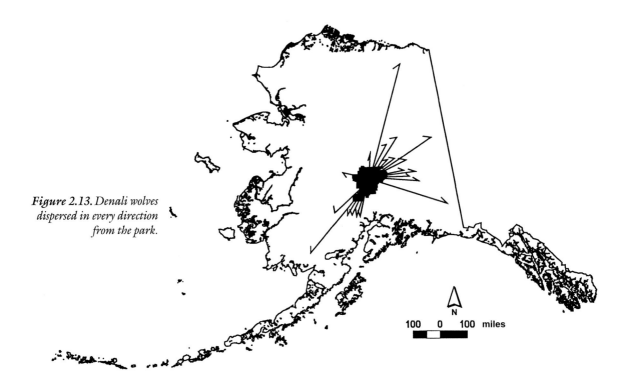

*Figure 2.13. Denali wolves dispersed in every direction from the park.*

N

100    0    100   miles

Denali wolves also fit this pattern (appendix 1). An average of 28% of our radio-collared wolves dispersed annually from their packs, and 21% from the study area (table 2.7). Of 56 that dispersed from park packs, 29 were males and 27 were females. Most dispersed alone, but some left in dyads, and in one case 11 wolves (3 of them radio-collared) dispersed together (see chapter 5).

The most common time of year for dispersal was April and May (figure 2.10), and the average dispersal age was about 30 months for males and 28 months for females. Because dispersal peaked near the time when pups are born, most wolves dispersed when they were about 1, 2, or 3 years old (figure 2.11). Only 8% of dispersers left their packs when they were more than 3 years old.

Average minimum dispersal distance was 83 miles (133 kilometers) for both males and females (figure 2.12). The actual average could have been much higher because our data are biased against

the wolves that dispersed the farthest, which we did not track. About half the dispersers traveled 44 miles (70 kilometers) or less before settling down. Many of them started new packs or joined existing packs in or near the study area.

However, 13 wolves (6 females and 7 males) dispersed more than 100 miles (160 kilometers) from their capture pack. We usually found out where these far travelers had gone only when they were killed and their collars were turned in, sometimes years later. Thus, Denali dispersers that made it to inaccessible areas or locales where wolves are not subject to much human presence would have gone undetected.

The longest movement that we know of by a Denali wolf was by Headquarters Pack female 219, which left the study area in March 1987 and was shot by an Inupiat hunter near the Canning River in April 1991, 40 miles (64 kilometers) from the Arctic Ocean. Her total move (straight-

**Table 2.8.** Mortality causes and rates for radio-collared Denali wolves[a]

| Year | Radio-collared wolves | Wolf-years[b] | Wolf-killed | Pathology | Accidents[c] | Unknown natural[d] | Human[e] | Capture related? | Total deaths | Mortality |
|---|---|---|---|---|---|---|---|---|---|---|
| 1986 | 14 | 8 | 1 | 0 | 0 | 0 | 0 | 0 | 1 | .13 |
| 1987 | 23 | 14 | 2 | 0 | 0 | 0 | 0 | 0 | 2 | .15 |
| 1988 | 35 | 22 | 5 | 2 | 0 | 0 | 1 | 0 | 8 | .37 |
| 1989 | 32 | 25 | 4 | 0 | 0 | 2 | 0 | 0 | 6 | .24 |
| 1990 | 34 | 24 | 1 | 1 | 3 | 1 | 0 | 0 | 6 | .25 |
| 1991 | 42 | 26 | 3 | 1 | 0 | 1 | 0 | 2 | 7 | .27 |
| 1992 | 50 | 30 | 4 | 0 | 0 | 5 | 3 | 0 | 12 | .40 |
| 1993 | 44 | 31 | 2 | 0 | 0 | 1 | 2 | 1 | 6 | .19 |
| 1994 | 31 | 22 | 0 | 0 | 2 | 5 | 2 | 0 | 9 | .41 |
| Total | | 202[b] | 22 (39%) | 4 (7%) | 5 (9%) | 15 (26%) | 8 (14%) | 3 (5%) | 57 (100%) | |
| Average annual mortality | | | .11 | .02 | .02 | .07 | .04 | .01 | | .27 |

[a] Includes wolves from packs living at least partly inside Denali National Park.

[b] Annual mortality rates are based on wolf-years of monitoring; 1 wolf-year represents monitoring of 1 wolf for 1 year.

[c] Four killed by avalanche and 1 drowned.

[d] Probably mostly wolf-killed.

[e] One killed illegally in the park, 2 killed legally in the preserve, and 5 (an annual average of 2% of the population) killed outside the park and preserve.

line) was 435 miles (696 kilometers). Other Denali wolves dispersed to southwestern and eastern Alaska (figure 2.13). In other areas, wolves have dispersed as far as 550 miles (886 kilometers) (Fritts 1983).

Probably many more of our far-dispersers went undetected, for many signals disappeared, and we never found them. Because known radio failures were rare, most probably represented far-dispersers, and in our dispersal analyses we assumed this.

Dispersing Denali wolves headed in every direction (figure 2.13). Because we were unable to follow each disperser when it left the population, we do not have detailed information about dispersal routes.

## Wolf Mortality

The primary mortality cause of 57 wolves aged 9 months or older in Denali Park and Preserve during our study was death from other wolves (see chapter 4), and that cause claimed about five times the rate of wolf deaths as any other known natural cause such as accidents or disease (table 2.8). Accidents included four burials in avalanches (Boyd et al. 1992) (figure 2.14) and one drowning.

Kills of radio-collared wolves by humans included 8 (14%) of 57 deaths over a 9-year period, or less than 4% of our study population per year (table 2.8). They included 1 illegal shooting in the park, 2 legal trappings in the preserve, and 5 legal killings outside the park and preserve. Half the harvest occurred in packs in the northeastern cor-

*Figure 2.14. Dave Mech digs a radio-collared wolf out of an avalanche; both members of the breeding pair were buried in 1990. (Photo by L. David Mech.)*

ner of our study area that lived primarily outside the park and preserve. Thus, in the park and preserve itself, human kills included only 3 (5%) of the 57 deaths over a 9-year period and 3 of 202 wolf-years of monitoring, or an estimated 1% of the Denali wolf population per year.

Disease and other pathologies such as physical ailments (1 ruptured disk!) claimed only 4 animals. However, we were unable to investigate mortality causes of wolves younger than 9 months old. On the other hand, only about 9% of the 1- to 2-month-old pups we observed died before autumn (see chapter 8).

3

# Denali
# Wolf Packs

One of the best-known wolf packs the world over is Denali's "East Fork Pack," made famous by Adolph Murie's description in *The Wolves of Mount McKinley* (1944). Now, half a century later, does this pack still exist? Certainly wolves still use much of the same area as Murie's East Fork Pack, including its den. In fact, many people believe that the East Fork Pack is the only pack in Denali National Park and Preserve or that it is the main pack out of only a few. The claim has even been made that the East Fork Pack has maintained the same genetic lineage for 56 years (Haber 1996). However, the claim was undocumented, and in fact until the advent of molecular genetics techniques (Lehman et al. 1992) could not have been documented.

Given the high rate of turnover and genetic interchange in the Denali wolf population (see chapter 4), it is highly unlikely that the wolves currently occupying the East Fork Pack territory are any closer related to the wolves Murie (1944) or even Haber (1977) studied than are any other Denali wolves. Few if any wild wolves survive beyond 13 years (Mech 1988b), and because wolves tend to avoid inbreeding (see chapter 4), most wolves replacing old breeders are likely to be unre-lated, contrary to Haber's (1996) claim. Within a few generations, the genotypes of any pair would either be entirely replaced or extremely diluted.

But Denali supports far more wolf packs than the one occupying the East Fork area. There usually are at least 15 wolf packs in Denali at any time. Earlier workers studied packs near the East Fork River along the park road because of their accessibility. However, aircraft and radio-tracking allowed us to study nearly all of the park's packs.

## Wolf Pack Composition

Wolf packs consist of a breeding pair of wolves and their offspring from one or more years (Murie 1944), although infrequently they include other related individuals (Mech and Nelson 1990b) and even single adoptees (see chapter 4). The breeding male and female are usually unrelated (see chapter 4). When a breeder is lost, it may be replaced by an unrelated disperser from another pack, or if the remaining breeder is a recent unrelated immigrant (step-parent), then a young pack member may assume the breeding role and breed with it (Rothman and Mech 1979; Fritts and Mech 1981;

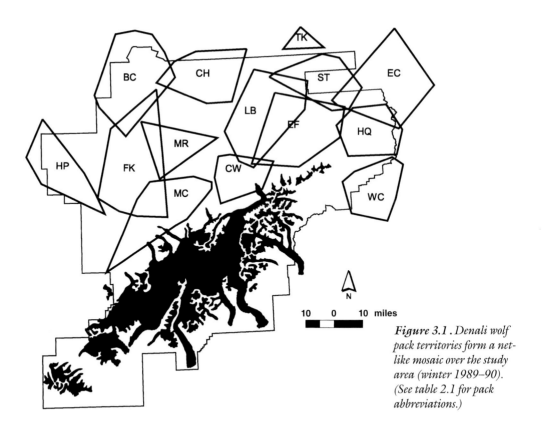

*Figure 3.1. Denali wolf pack territories form a net-like mosaic over the study area (winter 1989–90). (See table 2.1 for pack abbreviations.)*

Mech and Hertel 1983; Peterson et al. 1984; Fuller 1989; Mech 1995a).

Each wolf pack occupies a certain piece of the Denali terrain, and although the specifics vary over time, as we will show in chapter 4, the Denali wolf population functions in a mosaic of interlocking wolf pack territories that lies like a net over the area (figure 3.1).

We will now examine some of the wolf packs we have studied the longest that form the cells of this network. Histories of the packs for which we had less data are given in appendix 2. The packs are named for prominent features inside their territories.

## Birch Creek Pack

The Birch Creek Pack occupied the lake country east of Lake Minchumina in the northwest region

of the preserve and outside the boundary, but it made forays for 35 to 40 miles (60–70 kilometers) in several directions from there (figure 3.2).

It was difficult to study wolves in this area. The heavily wooded terrain made it hard to find and capture wolves. Also, several radio collars in the Birch Creek Pack were chewed off by pack-mates (Thiel and Fritts 1983), making this one of only two packs in the study area in which this happened.

The core territory of the Birch Creek Pack included a minimum of 500 square miles (1,270 square kilometers) of lowland forest, lakes, and rivers containing a moderate density of moose, very few caribou, and many beavers. Several beaver skulls were found at a commonly used den complex both times we visited it.

We started studying the Birch Creek Pack in

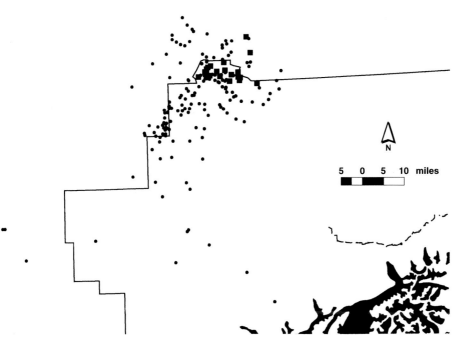

**Figure 3.2.** *Birch Creek Pack territory including long forays (distant dots) and splitting off of Birch Creek North Pack (squares). Dashed line represents the end of the park road.*

April 1987, when we radio-collared yearling male 257 near the junction of Hult Creek and Birch Creek, and yearling female 263 near Doghouse Lake. The pack contained at least 2 black and 4 gray wolves at that time. Track surveys in winter 1984–85 had indicated at least 8 wolves in this area (Dalle-Molle and Van Horn 1985). The radio collar from male 257 was picked up in August 1987, having been chewed off.

In early winter 1987–88, the pack consisted of 5 black and 6 gray wolves including at least 1 pup. We radio-collared young male wolf 301 near Beaverlog Lakes in February 1988. Female 263 disappeared from the pack in summer 1988.

We discovered a large, heavily used den complex in the pack's territory during summer 1988. Two litters of pups may have been raised there, as

fall observations showed 23 wolves in the pack, about half of which were black and half, gray. In October 1988, we radio-collared 2 female pups from this pack and recollared male 301. Female 345's chewed-off collar was found in February 1988.

In late winter 1988–89, 22 wolves remained in the pack, and we radio-collared 2 more members when we found them in upper Slippery Creek. They were on an extraterritorial foray more than 70 miles (120 kilometers) from where we captured wolves from the same pack the previous winter, but they again raised at least 2 pups in the 1988 den in summer 1989.

Sixteen wolves comprised the Birch Creek Pack in winter 1989–90. The production of pups in 1990 was inferred from sightings of wolves in

**Table 3.1.** Ungulate prey found with selected Denali wolf packs, 1988–93[a]

| Pack | Moose | Caribou | Sheep |
|---|---|---|---|
| Headquarters | 41 | 10 | 13 |
| Clearwater | 17 | 26 | 6 |
| Pirate Creek | 4 | 3 | |
| East Fork | 43 | 28 | 26 |
| Totek Hills | 6 | 1 | |
| Windy Creek | 9 | 8 | |
| McLeod Lake | 29 | 75 | 3 |
| Ewe Creek | 7 | 6 | 11 |
| McKinley River | | 16 | |
| Chitsia Mountain | 6 | 5 | |
| Foraker River | 13 | 5 | |
| Highpower | 13 | 11 | |
| Castle Rock | 7 | | |
| Stampede | 11 | 16 | |
| Little Bear | 14 | 20 | |
| Yanert | 1 | 8 | |
| Turtle Hill | 3 | 10 | 2 |
| Birch Creek[b] | 16 | 7 | |

[a] *Because of uneven tracking effort and other biases, these data only grossly represent the variation among packs in their use of various prey.*

[b] *Data combined for Birch Creek pack before and after splitting.*

known den areas, and the presence of 20 wolves in the pack in winter 1990–91. This count did not include male 301, which dispersed to the east. After spending more than a year in the Bearpaw River/ Nineteenmile area, he dispersed farther north and east and was snared in March 1993 near Old Minto, 100 miles (160 kilometers) from his natal territory.

This pack probably fed primarily on moose and caribou (table 3.1), and on October 18, 1990, John Burch spotted 10 members of the Birch Creek Pack feeding on a cow moose while her calf stood in shallow water less than 5 yards (meters) away, watching the whole episode.

The Birch Creek Pack split in winter 1990–91, dividing the original territory into a north half and a south half (figure 3.2). Wolf 371 and 10 others occupied the south half of the territory, and were found at a new den in summer 1991. Yearling male 449 was captured from this "south pack" in March 1991, but died of unknown natural causes near the Birch Creek North territory in summer 1991. At least 6 wolves, including 3 pups, remained in the south pack in fall 1991. Female 371 died of unknown causes in the south territory northeast of Carlson Lake in winter 1991–92, ending our contact with the Birch Creek Pack.

## Birch Creek North

After splitting from the Birch Creek South Pack, the Birch Creek North Pack contained 9 wolves including adult female 369 and adult female 347, which we recaptured in March 1991. She was identified by her ear tags, after losing her collar in 1989. Pup female 431 was also radio-collared but was killed at the capture site by a hunter who had flown in. Female 369 was killed by wolves northwest of Jeannes Lake in early April 1991.

We do not know if the Birch Creek North Pack produced any pups in spring 1991. Female 347 localized (remained in a small area) in spring, but this does not necessarily indicate that she had pups (Mech et al. 1996). At least 5 wolves remained in this pack in fall 1991. Female 347 died in a trapper's snare in March 1992 east of Lake Minchumina.

## Chitsia Mountain Pack

We studied the Chitsia Mountain Pack from winter 1988–89 through 1994. It occupied an area of about 390 square miles (1,000 square kilometers), formerly occupied by the Alma Lakes, Bearpaw, and McKinley River packs in the north-central part of the park and to the north (figure 3.3). The degree to which these various packs were related is not known, except that they ranged from all-gray to nearly all-black packs, and appear to have replaced one another with varying degrees of interpack strife. The various packs (excluding the

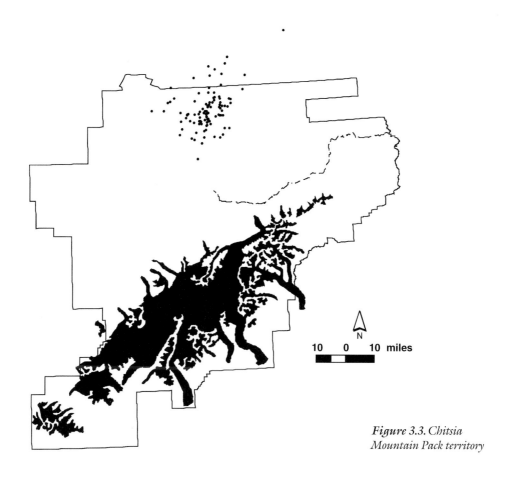

*Figure 3.3. Chitsia Mountain Pack territory*

McKinley River Pack) may represent unsuccessful attempts by new pairs and small groups to occupy an area surrounded by larger existing packs.

The Chitsia Mountain Pack territory contains a low density of moose and caribou, and Tom Meier and John Burch several times saw the Chitsia wolves feeding on salmon along Moose Creek.

In December 1988, we found tracks of 8 or more wolves on the Clearwater Fork of the Toklat River, from near Stampede Airstrip to the mouth of the East Fork River. We saw 2 wolves near the mouth of the East Fork and radio-collared gray female 359. She was accompanied by a black companion, which appeared larger but subordinate.

The 2 traveled widely and were found as far away as Wien Lake and Lake Minchumina before settling down in the Bearpaw area. There they were joined by 2 gray McKinley River wolves, males 315 and 379, in spring 1989. The latter wolf soon dispersed, but male 315 remained with female 359. They apparently did not den in 1989 but did collect another member. Thus, in fall 1989, the Chitsia Mountain Pack consisted of 3 gray members and 1 black. To our knowledge, this type of assemblage of 4 wolves from at least two packs has not been reported, although it might be similar to known packs containing 2 related wolves and an unrelated member of the opposite sex (Mech and Nelson 1990b).

The pack denned for the first time in 1990. It used the same den as the defunct Bearpaw Pack (appendix 2), bolstering our suspicion that female

359 and the black member were a remnant of that pack of black wolves. Five pups, of mixed colors, were seen with the Chitsia Mountain Pack in September 1990, and 8 wolves were seen throughout winter 1990–91.

In May 1991, breeding female 359 produced at least 5 pups at a new den, and the pack included 10 grays, 1 black, and 1 silver-gray in fall 1991. We found both radio-collared male 461 from this pack and male 407 from the Chilchukabena Pack some 200 yards (meters) apart killed by wolves near the Kantishna River in March 1992. This may have indicated a fight between the two packs. By spring, the Chitsia Mountain Pack had shrunk to 7.

The pack probably denned at the Bearpaw den in summer 1992, and 3 pups were seen in fall. The pack included 7 wolves in spring 1993, and 8 that fall, so pups were probably again produced. Female 359 (whose gray coat was now white) died of unknown causes in summer 1994, and female 463 dispersed to the northeast and died of unknown causes in winter 1994–95.

## Clearwater Pack

The Clearwater Pack was a living example of the kind of turmoil that sometimes characterizes a pack trying to maintain a territory. Track surveys in winter 1984–85 suggested that a pack of 6 wolves occupied an area from the Kantishna Hills to the Toklat River, and south to the Alaska Range (Dalle-Molle and Van Horn 1985). During the early years of our study, the Clearwater Pack occupied about 790 square miles (2,000 square kilometers) in this region (figure 3.4). The Denali Caribou Herd spent much of its time there, including calving and wintering. The territory also contained relatively high moose densities (Meier 1987) but few sheep.

We began monitoring the Clearwater Pack on March 31, 1986, by radio-collaring 10-month-old female wolf 213, adult male 223, and yearling female 151 from a pack of 5. The pack frequented an area from Wigand Creek into the Kantishna Hills

and south to Moose Creek. The Clearwater Pack frequented two den sites near Wigand Creek in summer 1986 but left them after July, and we found no further evidence of pups.

Lone female wolf 227, radio-collared near the Muldrow glacier in April, joined the Clearwater Pack in July 1986. She had been alone during 29 observations before that. However, whether she had dispersed earlier from this pack and was now rejoining it (Mech and Seal 1987), or whether she was actually joining it anew is unknown.

Yearling female 213 drifted away from the Clearwater Pack in winter 1986–87 and moved northeast beyond our study area. She was recollared by ADFG personnel when she joined with other radio-collared wolves in the Lignite Creek area, some 40 miles (65 kilometers) away; eventually she was trapped and killed in February 1988, near Dot Lake, 175 miles (290 kilometers) east of the Clearwater Pack territory.

Two-year-old female 151 spent much of her winter alone in the Clearwater Pack territory and dispersed southwest beyond the study area in early April 1987. She was shot by a land-and-shoot hunter in February 1988 on the Styx River, 145 miles (240 kilometers) southwest of the pack territory.

The Clearwater Pack consisted of 3 wolves for much of winter 1986–87: male 223, female 227, and younger male 250, which was captured near the Toklat River in March. Female 227 denned on Canyon Creek in the Kantishna Hills in May and June and was seen with 4 pups on June 16.

It appeared that between May 15 and July 26, 1987, breeding male 223 and young male 250 rarely, if ever, visited the Clearwater Pack den. During the 11 times when we located 223 between these dates, he was 14 to 27 miles (22–43 kilometers) from the den. He and 250 spent much time with a new small wolf at the south end of the territory (south of McKinley Bar), where caribou were calving. We found female 227 at or near the den on 4 of 10 occasions during the same period, and never saw her with any other wolf except her

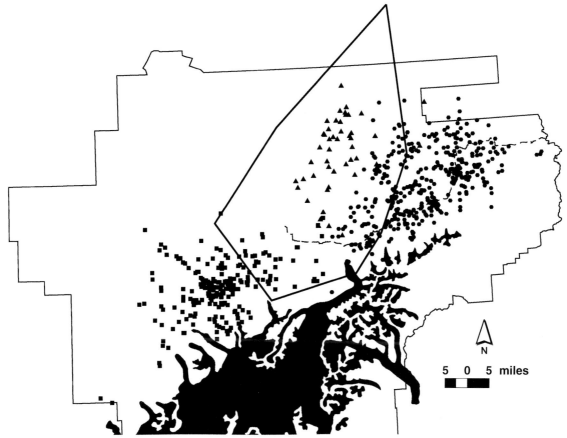

**Figure 3.4.** Clearwater Pack territory during 1986 to 1989 (polygon), and packs that occupied it after the demise of the Clearwater Pack; dots represent the East Fork Pack during 1986 to 1990; squares, the McLeod Lake Pack during 1987 to 1990; triangles, the Little Bear Pack during 1989 to 1990.

pups. In July, female 227 and the pups traveled southward and rejoined 223. Two of the pups survived into fall.

Separation of the male and the rest of the pack from the breeding female and pups for much of summer is extremely unusual and has been reported only once before (Mech 1995b). In all the other Denali packs we followed during summer, we would find the various pack members at or near the den at least some of the time. One possible explanation is that wolf 223 may not have been the original mate of 227 and thus may not have been so bonded to 227 as to feed her and her pups.

Young male 250 paired with the unknown smaller wolf and occupied the southern part of the Clearwater territory until early November, when his collar failed. What is known about his subsequent history is related as part of the Pirate Creek Pack history (appendix 2).

Through winter 1987–88, the Clearwater Pack consisted of male 223, female 227, and presumably their 2 pups, 1 of which we radio-collared (311). Female 227 did not appear to localize at a den in spring 1988. On one occasion in June she was seen entering a den hole near the Thorofare River, but wolves will check out dens even if not pregnant (Mech et al. 1996). By fall 1988, the pack still consisted of wolves 223, 227, and 311, and 1 noncollared individual.

In early 1989, Clearwater Pack cohesion was greatly disrupted. Two-year-old male 311 dispersed and joined the Headquarters Pack, as described later. Breeding male 223 was killed by wolves on Alder Creek in January 1989. In March, 227 was found with 2 noncollared companions, both of which we radio-collared (female 361 and male 363). However, in April, 227 was killed by several other wolves along Clearwater Creek.

Female 361 remained in the Clearwater territory and produced 6 pups in 1989; thus, she must have bred while the previous breeding female, 227, was still alive. It is likely that 361 was the sibling to 311 born in 1987, and as such was the only remaining member of the Clearwater Pack.

After joining the Clearwater females, male 363 was found briefly with the McLeod Lake Pack, which made us believe that McLeod was his natal pack (Mech 1987). He then rejoined 361 to raise a litter of 6 pups in summer 1989.

Male wolf 363 died of unknown causes on Moose Creek in December 1989. When his remains were investigated later in the winter, the remains of 2 dead pups were found with him. All had been consumed by other wolves, which had spent much time at the site. It appeared that the pups had been orphaned and starved to death. Another pup was found killed by wolves near upper Moose Creek in March. The fate of female 361, which disappeared about the same time that 363 died, is unknown.

By 1989, the Clearwater Pack territory was more restricted, occupying only about 390 square miles (1,000 square kilometers), as the territory was squeezed more and more by neighboring packs. By winter 1989–90, the Clearwater Pack appeared to be extinct.

These events marked the end of the Clearwater Pack, and in late winter both the Little Bear and East Fork packs were using the Moose Creek area where the Clearwater Pack had lived. Although there were sightings of wolves on the caribou calving grounds in May, no active dens were found in the area, and as of fall 1990 it did not appear that any new wolves had recolonized the McKinley Bar and Moose Creek areas. Parts of the Clearwater Pack territory were eventually occupied by the Little Bear, Turtle Hill, and Stampede packs.

## East Fork Pack

In deference to Adolph Murie's (1944) work, we continued to call the pack inhabiting the area around the East Fork of the Toklat River the East Fork Pack. However, as indicated earlier, today's East Fork wolves would have no closer relatedness to those in the area in the 1940s than would any other Denali packs (see chapter 4).

The East Fork Pack is of great interest to park staff and visitors, being the most readily observable pack in the park and carrying the legacy of Murie's study and writing, although few, if any, of the genes of his pack. The wolves regularly travel, make kills, and occupy rendezvous areas within sight of the park road. The low shrubs, tussock tundra, and alpine tundra abundant in the area provide wide-open views that facilitate the observation of wolves.

During our study, this pack occupied a territory of 585 to 780 square miles (1,500 to 2,000 square kilometers), centered around Sable Pass and almost entirely within the park (figure 3.5). The pack occasionally made forays north to the mouth of the East Fork of the Toklat River, east to Riley Creek, and west to Boundary Creek and the Muldrow Glacier. The East Fork territory contains excellent moose and sheep habitat and is used by the Denali Caribou Herd.

Our contact with the East Fork Pack began on March 31 and April 1, 1986, when we radio-tagged 3 members in the Teklanika-Sanctuary area. The pack included 10 gray wolves. A pack of 13 wolves had been seen there in November 1984, of

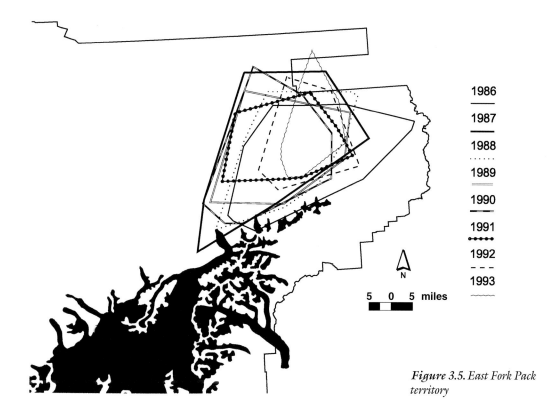

1986
1987
1988
1989
1990
1991
1992
1993

5 0 5 miles

N

*Figure 3.5.* East Fork Pack territory

10 in April 1985, and of 13 in September 1985 (Dalle-Molle and Van Horn 1985).

Our radio-collared male 221 and a light-colored wolf assumed to be the breeding female were first found at a den on the East Fork of the Toklat River on May 7. Two pups were seen there on June 14, and they remained there until July 28, when they moved to a rendezvous site less than 1 mile (1.6 kilometers) away. They remained there until mid-September, when they began moving with the pack, which then included 9 members.

Yearling male 215 had dispersed from the pack in June and was trapped 210 miles (350 kilometers) east-southeast at Tanada Lake in Wrangell–St. Elias National Park in February 1989. He reportedly was a member of a pack of 6 when killed.

During an unusual foray by the East Fork Pack east to Riley Creek in January 1987, yearling male 239 was captured in a live-snare we had set for the Headquarters Pack wolves. This wolf remained with the East Fork Pack until late February, then dispersed southeastward for more than 50 miles (80 kilometers), but returned to the territory in May 1987 and stayed with the pack until September. He then dispersed to the northeast and was shot near the Wood River 75 miles (125 kilometers) away in April 1989.

The East Fork Pack contained 6 wolves in spring 1987. Observers reported spotting 5 pups at the East Fork den in early summer 1987, but only 2 were seen after mid-June. These 2 began traveling with the pack in late September.

Breeding male 221 began spending less time with the pack in midsummer 1987. Although he had been limping for many years, he still appeared in reasonable health and was seen killing a yearling moose by himself near the park road in July. His radio signal was last heard in August 1987.

Male 221's breeding position was usurped by a large gray male, 5051, which we radio-collared in November 1987 along the Toklat River. The pack at that time consisted of 8 wolves including 5051, subordinate female 217, a white-shouldered breeding female, the 2 pups, and 3 other wolves of unknown sex and age. Seven wolves remained in the pack in spring 1988.

The dominant breeding female denned on the East Fork in 1988, but a second East Fork Pack female whelped at a den on the Teklanika River. In June, this female carried her pups one by one up the park road to the main den, merging the two litters. Murie (1944) also reported wolves merging two litters in this area.

This made a total of 12 pups in the pack, all of which survived at least until mid-September, when the pack numbered 19 wolves, including radio-collared female 217 and breeding male 5051. Eighteen wolves remained in the pack in spring 1989.

The pack also produced two litters of pups in 1989; the white-shouldered female again occupied the East Fork den, and 217 used an old den a mile away. Wolf 217 had not been the second breeding female the previous year and had probably never bred until 1989. She merged her litter with the other pups early in summer. In late summer, a total of 10 pups from the combined litters were seen near the main den.

The highest pack count observed in early winter 1989–1990 was 27 wolves, of which 26 remained at least until March. In March 1990, we radio-collared male yearling 395 in the Stony Creek drainage, newly occupied by the East Fork Pack after the demise of the Clearwater Pack. He remained with the East Fork Pack only until summer 1990 and then dispersed. He was shot in February 1991 near the mouth of the Mulchatna River 335 miles (560 kilometers) southwest of the East Fork Pack territory.

In 1990, 3 East Fork females produced litters of pups. The white female produced 2 pups, denning once more along the East Fork River, and a noncollared gray female had 5 near the main fork of the Toklat River. The latter group attracted much attention when they appeared on the park road in July. Later in the summer, the wolves combined these two litters and moved farther from the road.

Female 217 split away from the main East Fork Pack and produced 2 or 3 pups in an open-pit den near Gorge Creek (Mech 1993). She later moved the pups to Stony Creek, closer to where the rest of the pack's pups were located, but apparently she never combined them with the pack's other litters during the summer. She was found within 2 miles (3 kilometers) of the primary rendezvous site of the main pack, however, and East Fork male 5051 was found with her at her rendezvous site.

In fall 1990, we saw 29 wolves in the main East Fork Pack. In addition, female 217 and 3 other wolves, presumably her mate and 2 pups, had "budded" off the main pack to form a new pack and were still using the west edge of the East Fork territory. In February 1991, female 217 was killed by wolves in upper Little Moose Creek in the Kantishna Hills—probably by the Little Bear Pack since they were in the area; we do not know what happened to her 3 companions.

By March 1991, the East Fork Pack appeared to have shrunk to 18 or 19 wolves. They again produced at least two litters of pups in 1991, both north of the Toklat bridge. Two pups were seen with white breeding female 1080, and at least 1 other pup was seen at a nearby den at the same time. Later in summer, these two litters were combined in the same vicinity. At least 3 pups were seen in fall 1991. The pack at that time numbered 16 wolves. Breeding female 1080 died of unknown natural causes in October 1991 near the upper Sushana River; she was estimated to be about 11 years old.

Although this large pack preyed regularly on moose, caribou, and sheep, it did not disdain smaller prey. On September 27, 1991, Tom Meier recorded the almost absurd chase by 13 East Fork wolves of snowshoe hares in the Wyoming Hills area northwest of Toklat and saw them catch one and miss one; the remains of two hare kill sites were also visible in the immediate area.

In November 1991, we radio-collared adult female 467 and young adult male 469 from the pack near the Teklanika River. The latter dispersed to the northeast in April 1992 and seemed to have joined a small pack on the Totatlanika River 58 miles (96 kilometers) away later that year. His collar was heard in mortality mode near the Tatlanika River in August 1993, but the site was well outside the study area, so we could not investigate it further.

Eleven wolves were seen in the East Fork Pack in spring 1992. Female 467 produced pups at a den on the Teklanika River, and the pack numbered 15 in fall, including female 467 and male 5051. Male 5051 and 3 other East Fork wolves (2 young adult females and a female pup) were trapped just outside the park boundary near the mouth of the Sanctuary River in November 1992. Ten wolves were seen in the pack in late winter.

Adult male 513, which behaved like the new dominant male, was captured in March 1993 on the upper Sushana River. Female 467 frequented both the Teklanika and East Fork dens in May and June 1993, and 4 pups were seen in early winter, when the pack numbered 10 wolves. By spring 1994, it had dropped again to 6 wolves.

## Foraker River Pack

The Foraker River Pack territory, mostly in the western part of the 1980 addition to the park, contains a low density of moose and is occupied year-round by a few members of the Denali and Tonzona caribou herds (figure 3.6). The pack lived primarily on moose, but also killed caribou. John Burch once watched a member of this pack cache a caribou fetus.

The pack was formed when female wolf 321 dispersed from the McKinley River Pack in fall 1988 and paired with a male on the west edge of the McKinley River Pack territory. After producing their first pups in 1989, this pack consisted of 7 wolves during winter 1989–90. We radio-collared yearling female wolf 387 in November 1989, an apparent adoptee. Breeding female 321 denned in 1990, but in June she died of unknown causes within 1 mile (1.6 km) of the den. Later in summer, 2-year-old female 387 was seen with 3 pups, and in winter 1990–91 the pack included 9 members.

In March 1991, we radio-collared yearling male 441, but he soon left the Foraker River Pack and paired off to found the Slippery Creek Pack to the northeast. In May 1991, wolf 385, a young male from the Highpower Pack, joined the Foraker River Pack. Three pups were seen with female 387 at a den along the Foraker River in May 1991. In early December 1991, wolf 387 was found dead 4 miles (6 kilometers) from the Highpower Pack, probably having been killed by them.

Only 4 wolves were seen in the Foraker River Pack in spring 1992, and we radio-collared adult female 493. The pack included 4 adults and 3 pups in fall 1992. Adult male 385 was caught by a local trapper in the northwestern preserve area outside the pack's normal territory in March 1993 and was attacked by other wolves while in the trap. We radio-collared adult male 517, his probable replacement, later in March. We only monitored the pack lightly in 1993 and continued tracking it through spring 1994. It contained 7 members then, indicating probable reproduction in 1993.

## Headquarters Pack

We monitored 1 to 15 wolves per year in the park headquarters area throughout the entire study, from March 1986 through December 1994. During this time, there was a complete turnover of wolf packs there, as described later. The Headquarters Pack territory averaged about 235 square miles (600 square kilometers), centered in the

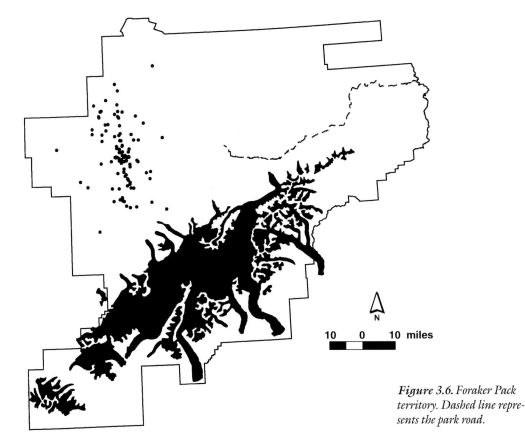

*Figure 3.6. Foraker Pack territory. Dashed line represents the park road.*

Riley Creek and Savage River drainages west of park headquarters (figure 3.7).

The Headquarters wolves made occasional forays west to the Sanctuary River, east into the Yanert River drainage, and south to the Cantwell area. Their territory contains some of the largest concentrations of moose found in Denali, as well as sheep and occasional members of the Denali and Delta caribou herds.

These wolves fed on all three species and seemed to have scavenged many moose that had been hit by trains along a highway and a railroad running up the Nenana valley through their territory. This pack also seemed to compete often with bears, for we saw them interacting with bears at 10 kills.

The first wolf we radio-collared in the study

was Headquarters adult female 205, which we live-snared near the George Parks Highway on March 18, 1986. She was the apparent breeding female in a pack of 6 wolves. Surveys in 1985 had also suggested the presence of a pack of 6 wolves in the Headquarters area at that time (Dalle-Molle and Van Horn 1985). We also radio-collared female 219, probably a 1985 pup, at Triple Lakes in April.

In mid-April, the Headquarters Pack had a series of serious altercations with the East Fork Pack on the Savage River near their mutual boundary (figures 3.5 and 3.7). Based on tracks, it appeared that first the Headquarters Pack killed an East Fork male pup there, and then the East Fork Pack killed Headquarters female 205 there two days later.

We radio-collared Headquarters male pup

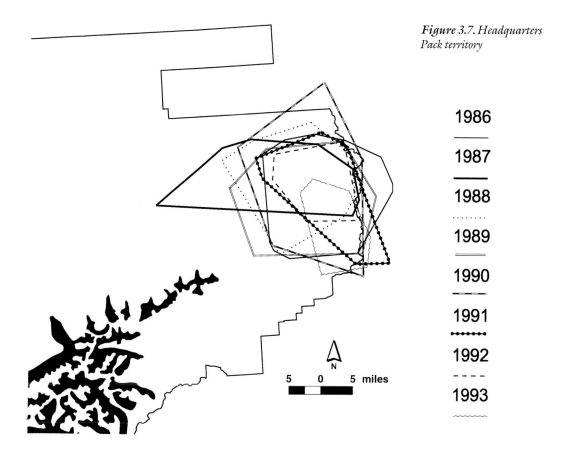

*Figure 3.7. Headquarters Pack territory*

1986
——
1987
——
1988
⋯⋯⋯
1989
═══
1990
——
1991
•••••••
1992
- - - -
1993
〰〰〰

231 on Mount Fellows later in April. We saw no evidence of denning or pup production in 1986, providing evidence that 205 had probably been the breeding female. Four wolves, including female 219 and male 231, were seen in the territory in September. Male 231 dispersed 50 miles (80 kilometers) to the southwest in October and was seen with a distinctively marked new companion. The new pair subsequently founded the Chulitna River Pack, described in appendix 2.

Female 219 moved about widely in the eastern part of the Headquarters Pack territory, sometimes with 1 companion, and was last found in the study area in late March 1987; she then dispersed. In April 1991, she was shot near the Canning River, 40 miles (64 kilometers) from the Arctic Ocean and 420 miles (700 kilometers) north of her natal pack territory. She was with 3 other wolves at the time.

We radio-collared adult female 241 on Riley Creek in early February 1987. She traveled in the Headquarters Pack territory with 1 companion but was killed by wolves in early March near Revine Creek. We then live-snared male 251, thought to be her former companion, near the park dump later in March. (Wolf 251 was gray when estimated to be 22 months old. By 66 months, he was turning whitish, and by 102 months he was white.)

Wolf 251 occupied the Headquarters territory alone until June, and thus, no reproduction took place in this territory in 1987. We then radio-collared his new companion, female 307, between the Savage and Sanctuary Rivers in February 1988.

This new Headquarters pair (251 and 307) raised a litter of 5 pups in 1988 at a den on a tributary of Riley Creek. The newly reestablished pack occupied an area south of the park road, west of the George Parks Highway, and east of the Teklanika River. Radio-collared 2-year-old male wolf 311, originally from the Clearwater Pack some 30 miles (50 kilometers) to the west, then joined the Headquarters Pack in March 1989 and remained with them for a year. Six pups were born to female 307 in 1989 at a den on Jenny Creek. Fourteen pack members were seen in fall 1989, indicating the probable survival of all pups born in 1988 and 1989, along with the breeding pair and adopted wolf 311. The pack had grown from 1 member to 14 in only 2 years.

The Headquarters Pack numbered 10 in late winter 1989–90, indicating that some members had dispersed and/or died. One pup was probably shot along the George Parks Highway, and adopted wolf 311 began ranging separately from the pack, but still within the territory, in February. He was usually accompanied by 1 other wolf, which we speculate was a female he had lured from the Headquarters Pack.

Wolf 311 and his mate then budded off from the Headquarters Pack and raised at least 2 pups in the Nenana Canyon area in summer 1990. In early winter 1990, a female wolf and a pup were legally trapped in the Nenana Canyon–Healy area by a local trapper. Male 311 moved east and appeared to join the Last Chance Pack of wolves in the upper Tatlanika Creek drainage (see appendix 2).

The main Headquarters Pack again denned on Jenny Creek in 1990, producing at least 3 pups. Male 251's radio collar failed in May, but we recollared him in November. Eleven wolves were seen in the pack in fall 1990, and 9 in spring 1991. We recollared female 307 in March 1991.

In 1991, the pack produced at least 3 pups in the Riley Creek den. Ten wolves were seen in the pack in fall 1991, but this number shrank to 7 by March 1992. Male 251 appeared to have been in-

jured on a foray into the upper Nenana River area (south of the Alaska Range) in March 1992, but he survived.

The pack again denned in the Riley Creek area in 1992 and numbered 4 adults and 2 pups in fall 1992, but no more than 4 total in spring 1993. They denned in the same area in 1993, and 2 radio-collared adults and 7 pups were observed in fall 1993. Female 307's radio collar failed in July 1993. Male 251 died from a capture-dart wound in November 1993.

Wasting no time, female 307 (located by snow-tracking) paired with black male 9401 in December 1993. We radio-collared both adults in March 1994. Male 9401's signal came from the Nenana River in May, indicating death from an unknown cause. Nevertheless, female 307 denned near Carlo Pass in spring and summer 1994. The pack numbered 6 animals in fall 1994.

One can see from this pack that regardless of the loss and turnover of pack members, some wolves usually remain in the territory and that the pack ends up breeding during most years despite the high mortality. Was the Headquarters Pack the same pack in 1994 as in 1986?

## Little Bear Pack

The Little Bear Pack was probably formed about 1988 when the Clearwater Pack stopped using the Kantishna Hills part of their territory. The Little Bear territory lay almost entirely in the Kantishna Hills, although the pack occasionally traveled east to Stony Creek (figure 3.8). The territory covered 310 to 510 square miles (800 to 1,300 square kilometers). It contained moderate numbers of moose and varying numbers of the Denali Caribou Herd, but no sheep. In March 1989, we radio-collared 2 young male wolves, 373 and 375, on Little Bear Creek, and we monitored this pack through spring 1994.

The pack numbered 12 wolves in fall 1989. Yearling male 373 strayed east to the Sushana River in February 1990 and was killed by the Stam-

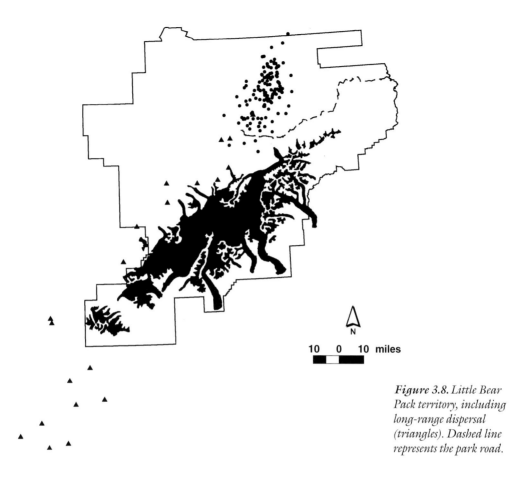

*Figure 3.8.* Little Bear
Pack territory, including
long-range dispersal
(triangles). Dashed line
represents the park road.

pede Pack. We radio-collared female pup 391 in March 1990. Yearling male 375 probably dispersed in March, and female 391 drowned in the Clearwater Fork of the Toklat River in May 1990. This left no radio-collared wolves in the pack until March 1991, when we radio-collared adult male 437 and yearling females 433 and 435 in the Myrtle Creek area. There were 13 wolves in the pack.

Male 437 dispersed from the Little Bear Pack in late summer 1991 and spent from about September 12 to November 11 with the Stampede Pack. He then joined the Ferry Pack about November 14, but we did not keep track of him after that. By February 18, 1992, however, he had been killed by humans 40 miles (65 kilometers) away from his natal pack.

Females 433 and 435 remained with the pack, and in spring 1991 the pack denned in the Kantishna Hills, probably having two litters and producing at least 11 pups. There were 23 wolves in the Little Bear Pack in fall 1991. In November 1991 we radio-collared 2 yearlings, female 457 and male 459.

The Little Bear Pack was split in winter 1991–92 during at least 16 of the 21 times we located it, and in May 1992 all of the radio-collared animals dispersed. Wolves 433, 435, 459, and 8 others headed southwest together, eventually settling on the South Fork of the Kuskokwim River, some 150 miles (250 kilometers) from their home territory. Female 457 also dispersed southwest, apparently alone. (See also chapter 5.)

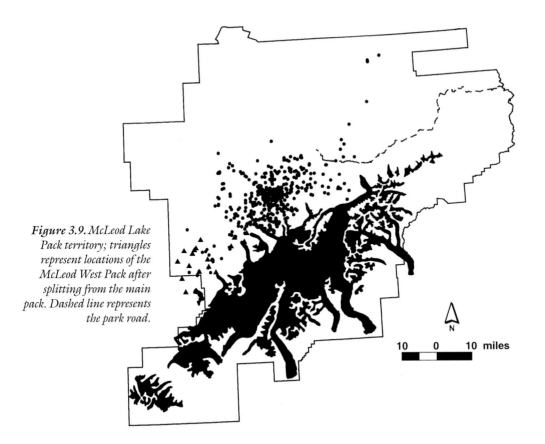

*Figure 3.9.* McLeod Lake
Pack territory; triangles
represent locations of the
McLeod West Pack after
splitting from the main
pack. Dashed line represents
the park road.

In September 1992, we radio-collared year-ling female 503 and breeding female 507 along Stony Creek. There were still 12 wolves in the pack at that time, including 6 pups. Wolf 503 disappeared in March 1993, but 507 remained with the pack through the end of the study. She produced at least 3 pups in summer 1993. We radio-collared yearling female 541 in September 1993 and last located her in the territory in April 1994. The pack included 13 members at that time. Female 507 was killed by wolves in April 1995.

## McLeod Lake Pack

The McLeod Lake Pack ranged over an area of up to 780 square miles (2,000 square kilometers) to-ward the southwestern end of the park between the Muddy River on the east and White Creek on

the west and just northwest of the Alaska Range (figure 3.9). This area contains a large moose pop-ulation (Meier 1987) and about half of the Denali Caribou Herd's calving range, and this pack some-times made extensive use of caribou calves (see chapter 7).

We radio-collared the first 2 McLeod Lake wolves near the terminus of the Peters Glacier in March 1987. Adult male 253 and pup or yearling male 255 traveled with 2 other wolves in the area south and west of Wonder Lake. Track surveys in winter 1984–85 had indicated that a pack of at least 8 wolves had been in this area, but that 5 of these had been killed by aerial poachers in Febru-ary 1985 (Dalle-Molle and Van Horn 1985).

We last heard 255 in July 1987. Four pups were seen with a noncollared white wolf near Slippery Creek in July. That fall the pack consisted of male 253 (probably the breeder), the white breeding female, yearling male 792 (radio-collared in November near McLeod Lake), one other adult, and 3 pups. Pack size remained at 7 through the winter. We radio-collared the white female (309) in February 1988 near Birch Creek.

### Use of Ground Nests

The McLeod Lake Pack produced 5 pups in May 1988. Because the denning habits of the McLeod Lake Pack, especially its choice of dens, were so different from those of the other Denali packs and those reported elsewhere (Mech 1970), we describe them here.

Each year that McLeod female 309 was known to have bred (1988, 1989, and 1990) she bore her pups in an open nest under spruce trees and later moved them to the Stomach Lake den. In 1988 she localized under spruces on May 8 and moved her pups 700 yards (meters) to the den about May 20. In 1989, she began using different spruces on May 9, and was seen carrying her pups 5,700 yards (meters) to the Stomach Lake den on May 30. In 1990 she localized under still different spruces on May 7 and moved her pups to the Stomach Lake den on May 10, a distance of 700 yards (meters).

We do not understand why this female denned in the open rather than in a hole in the ground, unless the available holes still had frost or too much moisture. In any case, wolf pups are at risk to predation by other carnivores, especially bears (Hayes and Baer 1992), and wolves must be highly aggressive to ward off such animals from around dens (Murie 1944). Thus, ground nests would seem to be risky.

In fact, we twice watched McLeod wolves defending the pack's pups against bears. Intermittently over the period of an hour on June 25, 1988, Tom Meier and a pilot saw a single wolf defending the pups after the pack had moved its pups to a series of ground holes. Meier described what happened:

> When we first arrived, male wolf 253 and a small grizzly bear were lying 10 feet apart, some 50 feet from the den. Periodically, they would approach one another. The wolf would dodge and bite at the bear's nose or rump. Twice the wolf moved off around 100 yards but returned to the bear and den and would lie down, usually with a spruce between it and the bear, but would sometimes lie within 5 feet of the bear with its back to the bear. We saw the wolf actually bite the bear twice on the rump, two to three times on the nose. The bear got to within a few feet of the den. The bear was never seen to use its paws. The situation was the same when we left as when we arrived. Female 309 was 10 miles away feeding on a moose kill. We later found that the pups had survived.

On May 18, 1992, John Burch watched 5 McLeod wolves chase a grizzly away from one of their open-nest dens. The bear was in the area for 5 to 10 minutes, and the wolves actually bit the bear at least twice before it left.

In fall 1990, female 309 died (described in the following section), and the new breeding female was not radio-collared. Pups were observed at the Stomach Lake Den on May 31. In 1992 either female 465 or 473 (or both) bore pups at an open-nest site, localizing under spruces May 7–21. They then moved the pups 860 yards (meters) to another spruce patch, and on May 28 another 900 yards (meters) to the Stomach Lake Den. In 1993, the McLeod Lake wolves used a different den, a hole in the ground 7,800 yards (meters) southeast of the Stomach Lake Den, which did not appear to have been used before.

### Pack History

Regardless of the types of dens the McLeod Pack used, the animals were consistently successful raising pups, and the pack thrived. In early winter 1988, the pack contained 12 animals, including breeding male 253, alpha female 309, and 2-year-old male 792. Wolf 792 died in December 1988, apparently of a heart-valve infection, and wolf 253's collar failed in November 1988.

We radio-collared 2 10-month-old females, 365 and 367, in March 1989. The pack produced at least 4 pups in 1989, and thus the pack consisted of 12 members that fall, including wolves 309 and 367. Female 365 probably dispersed in October. Ten wolves were seen in the pack in spring 1990. We radio-collared female yearling 409 in May on the caribou calving grounds.

In June 1990, a large, light-colored, radio-collared male wolf was seen with wolf 409, and we realized that male 253, last heard from in 1988, was still in the pack with a nonfunctioning radio collar. We changed his radio collar in September. Female 309 bore 5 pups in early summer 1990, but a total of 11 pups were seen with the pack in September. Thus, the pack must have produced two litters.

In October, female 309 died from a prolapsed intervertebral disc that paralyzed her hindquarters, causing eventual starvation. She showed several signs of advanced age. After the loss of 309, the pack consisted of 19 wolves in fall 1990.

### The Splitting of the Pack

The McLeod Lake Pack remained at 15 or 16 wolves throughout winter 1990–91. In May 1991, the pack split, with 3-year-old wolves 367 and 409 and 5 others taking the western half of the territory (creating the McLeod West Pack), and 253 and 8 others retaining the eastern half. The main McLeod Lake Pack produced 5 pups in upper Birch Creek, and the McLeod West Pack produced 4 in the Barren Creek area.

In November, we radio-collared yearling female 453 and adult female 465 near upper Iron Creek. The main McLeod Lake Pack at that time numbered 13 wolves, all of which remained through the winter.

In March 1992, in order to study predation on the caribou calving grounds, we tried to radio-collar the entire McLeod Lake Pack and did get 9 additional wolves, most of them yearlings and pups (471, 473, 481, 483, 485, 487, 489, 491, and 497). One small wolf remained uncollared.

Female 481 dispersed northeastward in April 1992 and was seen with a very young pup of unknown origin near the Savage River in May. She did not remain in that area, however, and was last heard somewhere northeast of the study area.

The McLeod Lake Pack produced 4 pups in May 1992, with 465 being the suspected breeding female. Female 491 was killed by the 11 dispersing members of the Little Bear Pack in May 1992. Female 453 joined the McLeod West Pack in late May 1992. Male 489 dispersed eastward in June and was last found in December 1992 with 1 other wolf near the Valdez Creek Mine on the Denali Highway, 100 miles (160 kilometers) east of the McLeod Lake territory.

Radio collars on male 485 and female 483 failed in June 1992. In fall 1992, the main McLeod Lake Pack numbered 13 wolves, including 4 pups and radio-collared wolves 253, 465, 471, 473, 487, and 497. Female 471 disappeared in December and probably dispersed.

There were 10 wolves in the pack in March 1993, when we radio-collared 5 more McLeod Lake wolves, including female 483 (recaptured, having recently lost her collar) and 4 pups (519, 521, 523, and 525). Five new pups were born in May.

### Chewed-Off Collars

Male 253 died of unknown causes near Hauke Creek in August 1993. About the same time, female 483 had her radio collar chewed off. We then realized that the McLeod Lake Pack members were learning to chew each other's collars off, just like a

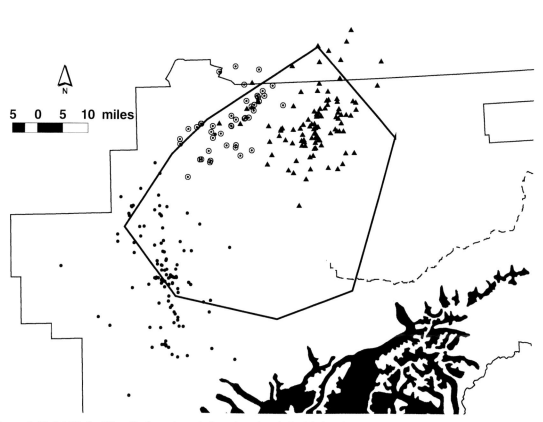

*Figure 3.10.* McKinley River Pack territory (polygon) and packs budded off from it; triangles represent the Chitsia Mountain Pack during 1989 to 1993; circles, the Chilchukabena Pack during 1991 to 1992; and dots, the Foraker Pack, from 1988 to 1993. Dashed line represents the park road.

pack had learned in Wisconsin years before (Thiel and Fritts 1983).

Fifteen wolves (including 5 pups) were seen in the pack in early winter 1993–94. Three radio-collared McLeod Lake East wolves died during winter of unknown natural causes: female 465, female 473, and male 525.

Male 519 and 4 more McLeod Lake wolves lost their radio collars over fall and winter 1993–94. We recaptured 3 of them and fitted them with more-chew-resistant collars, which continued to transmit into 1995.

## McLeod West Pack

When the McLeod Lake Pack split in May 1991, 7 wolves including 3-year-olds 367 and 409 moved west to the Barren Creek area and produced 4 pups. The McLeod West Pack numbered 11 wolves in fall 1991 in a territory of 220 square miles (560 square kilometers), ranging from the Herron River southwest to just west of the Swift Fork of the Kuskokwim River, and from the Alaska Range northwest to the Cottonwood Hills (figure 3.9). This area contains a high number of moose, some sheep, and the eastern range of the Tonzona Caribou Herd.

Female 409 died of unknown natural causes in March or April 1992. Female 367 disappeared after April 1992, probably having dispersed. The only other record we obtained for the pack was when female 453 joined it, at least temporarily in fall 1992, when 17 wolves were seen, including 8 pups. Wolf 453's signal was heard in mortality mode in the Heart Mountain area in January 1994, but we were unable to investigate from the ground to determine whether the wolf died or her collar had been chewed off.

## McKinley River Pack

Tracks in winter 1984–85 suggested a pack of 4 to 6 wolves in the area west of the Kantishna Hills and east of the new park boundary. In December 1987, we followed tracks of 10 wolves including pups for 25 miles (40 kilometers) down the McKinley River from north of Eagle Gorge to near Chilchukabena Lake. The wolves had eaten salmon carcasses along the river.

Tom Meier related the interesting circumstances surrounding the radio-collaring of members of the McKinley River Pack:

> On March 1, 1988, while tracking the Bearpaw Pack (see appendix 2), we found that collared female 261 had been killed by other wolves. Tracks led to the breeding male, which we knew by his size and color. We found him wounded 2.5 miles to the northeast, and followed tracks from him to the remaining 5 Bearpaw wolves 3 miles north. Tracks from the attack site led us to the 10-member McKinley River Pack at a moose kill 4 miles to the south, partway into the Kantishna Hills. We collared male 315 and female 321, both young adults from that pack.

Over the next several days, the McKinley River Pack stayed in the Bearpaw territory, while the Bearpaw Pack visited several of their old kills. By March 5 the Bearpaw Pack had reunited with its wounded male. Two weeks later, we found Bearpaw yearling female 313 killed by other wolves, and the McKinley River Pack was 4 miles (6 kilometers) away.

The McKinley River Pack remained in the less than 200 square miles (500 square kilometers) of the Bearpaw territory for 6 weeks before moving back west to what was presumably their original territory (figure 3.10). The 10 wolves traveled widely over a 1,560-square-mile (4,000-square-kilometer) area in summer 1988, trespassing into neighboring territories. They did not localize at a den, apparently producing no pups that year.

Radio-collared female 321 left the main pack in July 1988 and paired with another wolf along the Foraker River and Birch Creek, founding the Foraker Pack. Male 315 and newly radio-collared male 379, also a young adult, left the McKinley River Pack in March 1989 and joined 2 other wolves to found the Chitsia Mountain Pack.

Thus, the McKinley River Pack appeared to have budded and colonized two adjacent areas in 1 year. The structure of both the Foraker River and Chitsia Mountain packs suggested that more than 1 wolf may have left the McKinley River Pack to form each of them. In fact, we suspected for a time that these two groups were all that was left of the original pack. However, track searches in November 1989 indicated that a pack of at least 7 wolves still occupied the lower McKinley River–Bear Creek area, separate from the other two groups.

We reestablished contact with the McKinley River Pack in March 1990, when we radio-collared breeding female 401 and yearling male 407 along the McKinley River. The pack then consisted of 8 animals, indicating that pups probably had been produced in 1989.

Female 401 denned west of Slippery Creek in summer 1990 and produced 5 pups. The pack was also augmented in fall 1990 by the adoption of 2-year-old male 397, originally a Stampede Pack

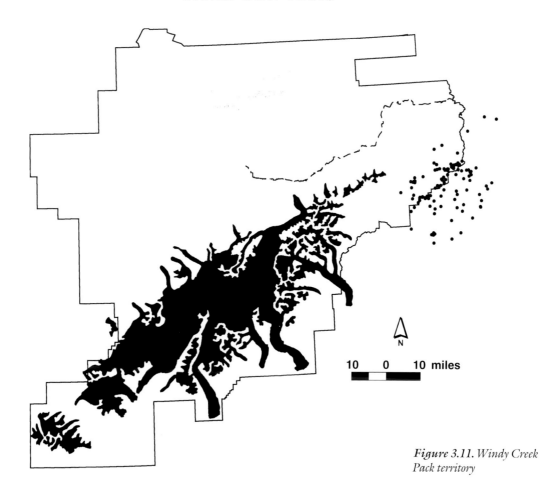

*Figure 3.11. Windy Creek Pack territory*

wolf. About the same time, 2-year-old male 407 began frequenting the north edge of the pack's territory, near Chilchukabena Lake, with at least 2 companions, to found the Chilchukabena Pack.

Eight wolves were seen in the McKinley River Pack in fall 1990, but only 5 were seen the following spring. In March 1991, we found these wolves around the carcasses of 17 caribou, spread over a 1-square-mile (3-square-kilometer) area east of the McKinley River. There they later denned and raised 4 pups in spring.

When we radio-collared adult female 451 from this pack near Moose Creek in November 1991, the pack numbered 9 wolves. Eight were seen with this pack later in winter.

In summer 1992, females 401 and 451 both occupied dens a few miles apart, but only 2 pups and 5 adults were seen in fall 1992. Male 397 lost his collar in September 1992. Female 451 was found dead along Moose Creek in late winter 1992–93, having apparently been shot and wounded from an airplane. Only 3 wolves remained in the pack, female 401, male 397 (no longer radio-collared), and male 533, radio-collared in March 1993.

Female 401 again denned east of the McKinley River in 1993, but her radio collar failed in July. We saw 2 adults and 1 pup in fall 1993 and radio-collared both male 397 and male 533 in March 1994. The third wolf seen with them was thought to have been a pup, and if so, the fate of female 401, a relatively large wolf not likely to be mistaken for a pup, remains unknown. Wolves 397 and 533 were legally trapped outside the park in February 1997.

## Windy Creek Pack

The Windy Creek Pack occupied an area of not more than 350 square miles (900 square kilometers) in the Windy Creek, Jack River, and Chulitna River drainages along the southeast corner of the park (figure 3.11). This area contains high moose densities, intermittent high caribou densities, and some sheep. Windy Creek wolves fed primarily on moose and caribou (table 3.1).

In February 1987, a cow moose was seen on upper Windy Creek defending the carcasses of her two calves against wolves. She kept predators and scavengers away from the two carcasses for 11 days, after which they were finally eaten by the Windy Creek Pack (see chapter 5).

We radio-collared 2 members of this pack, males 243 and 245, near the carcasses. Seven wolves were present in the pack in February, decreasing to 6 by March. During the previous winter, track surveys had indicated at least 11 wolves in this area, but 3 of them were poached inside the park in March 1985 (Dalle-Molle and Van Horn 1985).

Three pups were seen in summer 1987 at a den near Little Windy Creek, and apparently all survived to fall. Five adults remained with the pack into the fall, including both radio-collared animals. The Windy Creek Pack occupied a relatively small area during the first 10 months we monitored it, mostly in the Windy Creek and Cantwell Creek drainages south of the Alaska Range.

The pack made two known forays north into the Alaska Range, and in December 1987 the wolves were found 15 miles (25 kilometers) southeast at Caribou Pass, south of the Denali Highway, where many caribou of the Nelchina herd were wintering.

Although wolf 245 was found near the den in summer 1988, no pups were seen in the fall. The pack appeared to be spending more time outside Denali, in the Jack River and Chulitna River drainages, than it had in 1987. The signal from male 243 was last heard in April 1988, and he presumably dispersed or was killed. The pack contained 5 wolves in winter 1988–89.

In March 1989, we radio-collared breeding female 377 in the Yanert River valley. That was the only time we found the pack north of the Alaska Range.

The Windy Creek Pack produced 5 pups in summer 1989 at the den near Little Windy Creek, and the pack contained 8 wolves in fall 1989 and spring 1990. They denned some 20 miles (32 kilometers) farther south in 1990 than in previous years, using a den occupied by the Chulitna Pack in 1987 and by other packs in previous years (W. Ballard, pers. comm.). Six pups were seen at that den.

The Windy Creek Pack then began spending little time as far north as Windy Creek. We found no evidence that other wolves were occupying that area except for two visits by the Headquarters Pack, which in itself may have suggested a vacancy there.

We last heard breeding female 377 in August 1990, her collar having apparently failed. A total of 17 wolves were seen in the Windy Creek Pack in November 1990, suggesting that two litters of pups may have been produced. We radio-collared female pup 413 at that time. Attempts to locate the pack later in winter failed, and we heard no radio signal from wolves 245 or 377 after that time.

In early June 1991 a wolf that looked like it was radio-collared and that fit female 377's description was seen suckling at least 3 pups at the Chulitna River Den. This was the last record we have for the Windy Creek Pack.

From these pack histories and those in appendix 2, it should be clear that Denali's wolf packs are dynamic and that the Denali wolf population is a vibrant entity pulsing over time and space. Individual wolves come and go and live and die, and so do packs. Throughout this constant churning, however, the population persists. There is an East Fork Pack, for example, but probably any genetic relationship it has with the one Murie studied in the early 1940s is slight at best. The next chapter will examine the processes through which the packs like the East Fork Pack interact within the population.

# Denali Wolf Social Ecology

The wolf packs discussed in chapter 3, as well as those in appendix 2, can be considered the cast of characters in an ongoing play, and for the rest of this book we will examine the play itself.

The plot is simple but profound: each breeding pair of wolves and its pack compete with each of the others to maximize their genetic representation in the next generation (Dawkins 1976). Although evolution ultimately acts on individuals, family groups like wolf packs also benefit from cooperation and from competition with other groups because of their genetic relatedness, the process known as kin selection (Darwin 1859; Wilson 1975).

Put another way, each pack strives to survive and provide as much food and security as possible for as many of its own offspring as possible in the face of other packs attempting to do the same. This imperative fosters a great deal of competition. A major subplot in the grand drama, then, involves the interplay of the packs in the population, and we shall examine that in this chapter.

Wolves are highly competitive. Pups only weeks old compete fiercely with littermates, and with their own parents, for food (L. D. Mech, un-

published). Even mates compete with each other in some ways, although each must also cooperate to nurture the pair's shared genetic investment in their offspring. This fierce individual competition carries right on up the wolf's social organization to express itself among packs as well.

## Wolf Pack Territoriality

Resident wolf pairs and their offspring inhabit extensive territories that they attempt to keep exclusive by various methods, discussed here. Because wolf packs are so closely tied to geography, it is handy to give them geographic names, for example, after some prominent stream, lake, or hill in their territory. It seems like a simple task, but there are pitfalls caused by the complexities of the packs' dynamic behavior.

The Birch Creek Pack exemplifies the complications. Early in the study, we were eager to radio-collar wolves from the "Flats" area of the park, west of Kantishna Hills. When we found 10 wolves on Birch Creek in February 1987, we radio-collared 1 and promptly named this the Birch Creek Pack. However, this pack must have been a long way from home when we found it, for it was soon

100 miles (160 kilometers) from our study area. We renamed it the Dillinger River Pack (see appendix 2).

We eventually transferred the Birch Creek name to another pack we captured 2 months later, again on Birch Creek. This pack stayed around for several years, but it seldom frequented Birch Creek. These wolves, too, had been on a foray outside their territory when we found them. Both the McLeod Lake and Foraker packs spent more time than that pack had around Birch Creek, but the name stuck. And occasionally, on one of its long winter treks, the Birch Creek Pack did visit Birch Creek. In winter 1990–91, the pack split into two, each occupying part of the territory, and we dubbed one of them the Birch Creek North Pack.

Superimposed on such problems is the very real possibility that a wolf pack territory is dynamic or ever changing, presumably around some central area. Seasonal and annual data plotted for individual packs give this impression (Mech 1977a; Fuller 1989). However, with simulated wolf pack territories of 10,000 stationary points, comparisons of several random selections of 50 to 100 points yield the same impression (L. D. Mech, unpublished; J. Burch, unpublished); thus, the deduction from actual wolf data could merely result from sampling error.

Or it could be real. Wolf packs sometimes do make major shifts of territories. Even snow-tracking of actual wolf routes, which yields far more data about wolf locations than does radio-tracking, also indicates much boundary shifting (Peterson 1977; Peterson and Page 1988).

Wolves could also be territorial in a spatiotemporal sense. Conceivably the territories could overlap only spatially such that over any short period neighboring wolf packs would remain separate, but over time their locations could overlap (Mech 1970). The usual territory advertisements such as scent-marking and howling (discussed later) thus might generally suffice to keep neighboring packs apart. With this model, any meeting

of packs and resulting aggression would be aberrations, accidents, or failures.

Whatever the case, wolf pack territories do at times overlap along the edges (Peters and Mech 1975; Peterson 1977), and it could be that the larger the territories, the larger the percentage of overlap (Lehman et al. 1992).

## Effect of Prey on Wolf Pack Spacing

A main factor that influences the dynamics of wolf pack spacing is prey density and the dynamics of prey movements, that is, migration and/or nomadism. In this respect, an interesting comparison can be made between wolf social ecology in Minnesota and Denali. In Minnesota, where the wolf's main prey is white-tailed deer, with a comparatively high density of biomass (weight of prey per area), pack territories are relatively small (see discussion later).

Although the annual boundaries of Minnesota wolf packs appear to shift, each tends to shift around a central point, as described earlier, and disruption of pack territorial structure is low (Mech 1973, 1977a, 1986, unpublished; Fritts and Mech 1981; Fuller 1989), except when prey density is low or it decreases suddenly (Mech 1977b, unpublished).

In Denali, on the other hand, pack territories are larger and no doubt harder to defend. Prey, caribou in particular, move unpredictably, and wolves may use one part of their territory for weeks while the caribou are there, and may not even visit the other parts.

For example, the McKinley River Pack (see chapter 3), which at times covered some 1,560 square miles (4,000 square kilometers), remained in an area of only about 100 square miles (250 square kilometers) from about February 7 to April 14, 1991 (10 of 10 observations). Deep snow during this period allowed them to make a multitude of caribou kills there.

Thus, pack territory boundaries in Denali may at times be poorly defined and irregularly

**Figure 4.1.** *Ewe Creek Pack territory; note major shift between 1986–89 (dots) and after 1989 (triangles). Solid line represents the Denali National Park and Preserve boundary; dashed line, the park road.*

patrolled. In any case, we will show that at least during our study, wolf pack territorial spacing in Denali appeared to be more dynamic than in Minnesota.

### Stability of Territory Boundaries

Some packs permanently shifted their boundaries during our study. The Ewe Creek Pack lived on the northeast edge of the park in 1986–89 but later moved east of the Nenana River and George Parks Highway (figure 4.1). The McLeod Lake and Birch Creek packs each split in two, dividing their territory (discussed later). Several dispersers from the McKinley River Pack budded off, settled on the edge of that pack's territory, and formed new packs that occupied parts of that territory.

When the Clearwater Pack died out in late 1989, parts of its territory were occupied by its neighbor packs, East Fork, McLeod Lake, and Little Bear, for the rest of that winter; later the Little Bear Pack, and eventually the Turtle Hill Pack, actually settled there (figure 3.4).

To assess the stability of Denali wolf pack territories over long periods, the East Fork Pack is a good case to examine (figure 4.2). From 1939 to 1941, Murie (1944) defined this pack's territory as extending perhaps as far east as the Sanctuary River and west to Wonder Lake, based on ground tracking and observations. From 1966 to 1974, the territory of this pack, which Haber (1977) called the Toklat Pack, was defined as extending east only to the Teklanika River and west to Wonder Lake, based on ground and aerial snow-tracking and observations (Haber 1977).

Our radio-tracking data based on 715 locations at which 10 known radio-collared wolves

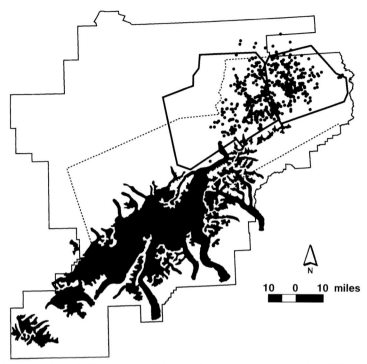

**Figure 4.2.** *Shift of pack territory boundaries over several decades. Dots represent East Fork Pack locations during 1986 to 1994; eastern polygon represents territory boundary of the Savage Pack; and western polygon, the Toklat Pack during 1966 to 1974 (Haber 1977). Dashed boundary represents the "Old Park."*

were located from 1986 to 1993 indicate that the East Fork Pack territory stretched eastward to the Savage River and westward to about the toe of the Muldrow Glacier some 15 miles (24 kilometers) east of Wonder Lake. During this period, the boundary Haber (1977) defined between his Savage Pack and his Toklat Pack separated our East Fork Pack territory neatly in half (figure 4.2). Thus, in 20 years, if not sooner, there was 100% spatial displacement in whether a given location was on the edge or center of the territory of the pack that inhabited that area.

This land-tenure history of the East Fork Pack is not necessarily typical. Generally, we believe, pack territory boundaries are held roughly in place by each neighboring territory (Mech 1973, 1986; Peterson 1977; Fritts and Mech 1981; Fuller 1989; Hayes 1995). Even when a given territory is

disrupted, for example, by its owners being killed by neighbors as will be discussed later, the borders of the other neighboring packs will continue to delineate at least parts of the original territory.

Wolf packs probably do not maintain precise permanent territory boundaries, except for those restricted by topographic features such as lakes, barren mountains, or human constructs such as villages and highways. Thus, in any given location, territory boundary shifting may be occurring somewhere at any time (table 4.1, figure 4.3). We view wolf pack territories as elastic discs (Huxley 1934) pushing one way and then another against neighboring elastic discs (Packard and Mech 1980).

In terms of degree of territory-spacing dynamics, areas like Minnesota and Denali may be on opposite ends of a continuum. Both show the same

**Table 4.1.** General history of turnover in wolf packs in various territories in Denali National Park and Preserve

| | Territory number[a] | | | | | | | | | | | | | | | | | | | | | | |
|---|---|---|---|---|---|---|---|---|---|---|---|---|---|---|---|---|---|---|---|---|---|---|---|
| Year | 1 | 2 | 3 | 4 | 5 | 6 | 7 | 8 | 9 | 10 | 11 | 12 | 13 | 14 | 15 | 16 | 17 | 18 | 19 | 20 | 21 | 22 | 23 |
| 1986 | HQ[b] | EF | | CW | SU | EF | | | CW | CW | | | | | | AL | | | | | | | |
| 1987 | 251 | EF | | CW | EC | EF | WC | CU | CW | CW | MR | MR | | MR | MR | BP | BC | BC | ML | ML | | TH | |
| 1988 | HQ | EF | | ST | EC | EF | WC | WC | CW | PC | MR | MR | | MR | CA | MR | BC | BC | ML | SF | HP | TH | |
| 1989 | HQ | EF | | ST | EC | EF | WC | WC | CW | CW | MR | MR | | FO | FO | CM | BC | BC | ML | ML | HP | TH | |
| 1990 | HQ | EF | | ST | ST | EF | WC | WC | LB | ML | MR | CB | EC | FO | FO | CM | BC | BC | ML | ML | HP | TH | |
| 1991 | HQ | EF | YT | ST | ST | EF | | | LB | ML | MR | CB | EC | SC | FO | CM | BC | BN | ML | TZ | HP | TH | RH |
| 1992 | HQ | EF | YT | ST | SV | TF | | | LB | TU | MR | CB | EC | SC | FO | CM | BC | | ML | MW | HP | TH | RH |
| 1993 | JC | EF | YT | ST | SV | TF | | | LB | TU | MR | | | EC | MR | FO | CM | | | ML | MW | | TH | RH |
| 1994 | HQ | EF | YT | ST | SV | EF | | | LB | TU | MR | | | MR | FO | CM | | | ML | | | TH | |

[a] Territory numbers represent general areas of Denali (figure 4.3) where packs held territories. However, because packs regularly expanded and contracted territories, there was more overlapping and dynamism than implied in these more arbitrary designations.

[b] Different pack designations for a given territory indicate new packs with no known genetic ties to previous packs in that territory.

basic structure but differing degrees of disruption. No type of pack interaction that we saw in Denali has not been observed in northeastern Minnesota (Mech 1977a,b, 1986, unpublished). However, the frequency of disruptive dynamics appears higher in Denali, probably because of the lower prey density there and the greater movement of prey.

## Territory Sizes

In chapter 2 we cautioned that even with radio-tracking data it is difficult to estimate the full extent and actual location of wolf pack territories, and that various methods can be used to make the estimates. Whatever estimates are used, however, two conclusions about Denali pack territory sizes are clear.

First, there is considerable variation (table 2.5). For example, the Headquarters Pack of 7 to 14 wolves in 1989 used a territory estimated at 230 square miles (590 square kilometers), whereas the McKinley River Pack of 10 wolves in 1988, some 50 miles (80 kilometers) away, used a territory of about 1,700 square miles (4,300 square kilometers).

Second, Denali wolf pack territories are among the largest reported. Denali's largest territory, that of the McKinley River Pack, was about the largest on record, including those in northeast Alaska (Stephenson and James 1982), those just east of the park (Ballard et al. 1987), those in Wood Buffalo National Park, Alberta (Carbyn et al. 1993), and those on Ellesmere Island, Northwest Territories (Mech 1988a, 1995a). In all five other areas, the largest territory estimate was about 1,000 square miles (2,600 square kilometers), although the Ellesmere territory, being based on incidental observations rather than radio-tracking, was probably considerably larger than estimated. It is noteworthy that the McKinley River Pack's territory was so large that the pack was able to bud off "daughter packs" with which to share the space (see below).

One larger wolf pack territory has been reported. The Talkeetna Mountain Pack, discussed in chapter 5 (Burkholder 1959), covered some 2,450 square miles (6,272 square kilometers), but it appeared that this pack was nomadic during the 6 weeks it was studied.

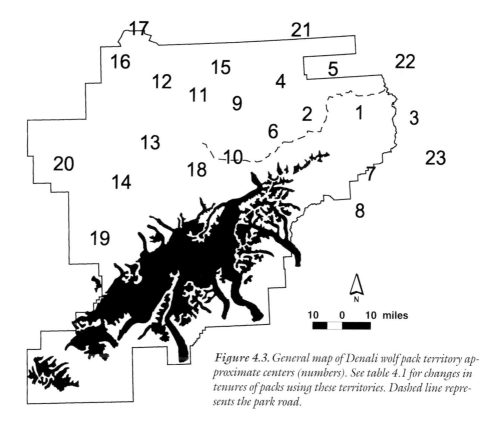

*Figure 4.3.* General map of Denali wolf pack territory approximate centers (numbers). See table 4.1 for changes in tenures of packs using these territories. Dashed line represents the park road.

Wolf pack territories in Denali (figure 4.4) are approximately 10 times as large as those in similarly saturated populations in lower latitudes such as in Minnesota (Mech 1973; Van Ballenberghe et al. 1975; Fritts and Mech 1981; Fuller 1989), Wisconsin (Wydeven et al. 1995), and Isle Royale (Jordan et al. 1967; Peterson 1977). This relationship probably reflects the higher density of prey at lower latitudes, as indicated earlier.

Wolf pack territory sizes tend to be smaller where prey biomass is greater (Messier 1985; Fuller 1989), and migratory prey such as caribou tend to increase annual territory size. In Denali we did not have data on prey density good enough to determine if there was such a relationship among our packs and their prey. However, since food supply is such a basic factor in the life of any animal, and since the main reason that wolves use space is

to obtain food (see chapter 5), this relationship no doubt applies to Denali wolves as well.

Comparing two Denali packs illustrates this relationship. Earlier we described how the Headquarters Pack occupied a territory only one-seventh as large as the McKinley River Pack territory, 50 miles (80 kilometers) away. The Headquarters Pack territory contains some of the highest concentrations of Dall sheep and moose in the park, as well as some caribou. The McKinley River territory contains no sheep, usually few caribou, and an estimated moose density only one-eighth that of the Headquarters territory (Meier 1987).

Contrary to intuition, wolf pack size seems to influence territory size only slightly (Potvin 1988; Fuller 1989) except where human harvesting of wolves is high (Peterson et al. 1984; Ballard et al. 1987). Denali wolves tend to follow earlier find-

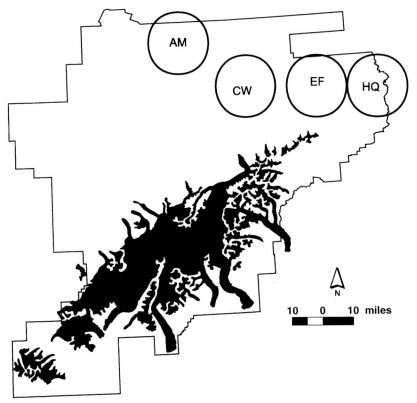

***Figure 4.4A.*** *Estimates of extents of Denali wolf pack territories, winter 1985–86; circles represent packs with insufficient locations to portray entire territory. (See table 2.1 for pack abbreviations.)*

ings with unharvested wolves elsewhere in showing only a slight relationship between pack size and territory size.

The larger the territory, the less likely it is that wolves will be in any single spot at a given time. This presumably makes it harder to effectively patrol and defend a large territory. It is not surprising, then, that the wolves living farthest north, with the largest territories, such as Denali's (figure 4.4), showed the most overlap among territories (Lehman et al. 1992). Although some of the overlap is real, an unknown degree is also due to our sampling method. The northern wolf populations also have the most migratory prey.

It is possible that under conditions of highly migratory or rare prey, the system of defended ter-

ritories may break down altogether (Stephenson and James 1982). Conceivably our Dillinger River Pack and the dispersing Little Bear Pack (see chapter 3) may be examples of packs using this modified lifestyle.

## Territorial Maintenance

Wolf packs maintain their territories in at least three ways: (1) scent-marking with urine and feces (figure 4.5), (2) howling, and (3) direct aggression.

Scent-marking appears to be the most elaborate and probably the least understood method of territorial advertisement and maintenance (Peters and Mech 1975). As wolves travel around their territories, they scent-mark frequently on various conspicuous objects such as snowbanks, bushes,

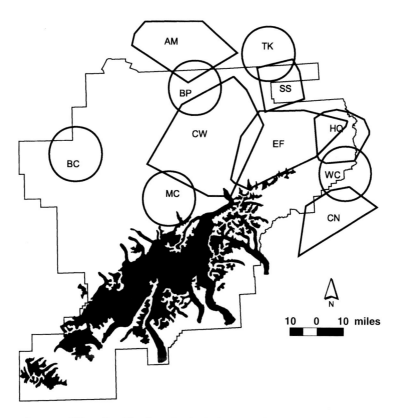

**Figure 4.4B.** *Estimates of extents of Denali wolf pack territories (polygons), winter 1986–87; circles represent packs with insufficient locations to portray entire territory. (See table 2.1 for pack abbreviations.)*

logs, and so on. In Minnesota during winter, packs sometimes marked with raised-leg urinations as often as 20 times per 0.6 mile (1.0 kilometer), and they marked twice as much around the edges of their territories as in the centers (Peters and Mech 1975). That these marks have an aversive effect on neighbors was observed on Isle Royale (Peterson 1977).

Howling is another method of advertising a pack's presence and helping to maintain the pack territory (Harrington and Mech 1979). Howling can sometimes be heard as far as 6 miles (9.6 kilometers) away, and in the more open areas of Denali perhaps farther, based on observations on the Arctic tundra (L. D. Mech, unpublished). Howling and scent-marking complement each

other in that one provides current but temporary information about a pack's location while the other gives a longer record of areas a pack has used and probably an indication of when they used it (Peters and Mech 1975).

## Strife among Wolves

Although we did not collect enough information in Denali to add to what is known about wolf scent-marking or howling, we did record considerable data about the third method of territorial maintenance, direct aggression (figure 4.6). Of 57 radio-collared wolves that died while in the study area, 39% (from 17–20 packs) were known to have been killed by neighboring wolf packs (table 2.8). Another 26% died of unknown natural causes,

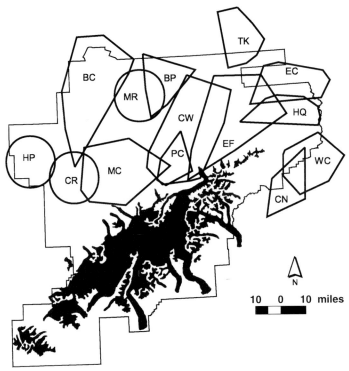

**Figure 4.4C.** *Estimates of extents of Denali wolf pack territories (polygons), winter 1987–88; circles represent packs with insufficient locations to portray entire territory. (See table 2.1 for pack abbreviations.)*

most of which were also probably wolf kills. Thus, as much as 65% of the wolf mortality was probably due to other wolves. This is the highest rate reported by any study. Many of our intraspecific deaths took place around prey carcasses, and most of the wolves killed were not eaten.

Biologists have long known that wolves will attack and sometimes kill wolves from other packs (Murie 1944; Mech 1966a, 1977b, 1994a; Van Ballenberghe and Erickson 1973). Only recently, however, have enough data become available to begin to shed light on some of the correlates of this behavior.

In northeastern Minnesota, 9 (56%) of 16 wolves killed in their territories by other wolves were killed in a narrow band within 0.6 mile (1 kilometer) inside the estimated boundary (Mech 1994a). The zone in which they were killed comprised only 29% of the area of the average territory

(50 square miles, or 129 square kilometers); thus, a significant disproportion were killed in this border area. These findings suggest that wolf aggressiveness in these cases was related to territorial competition.

Our Denali data tend to confirm the Minnesota findings. Since wolf pack territories are larger in Denali, we used a 2-mile (3.2-kilometer) band just inside their territory borders, constituting the outer 29% of their territory, as in the Minnesota analysis. Eight of the 12 (75%) Denali wolves killed by other wolves within their own territories died in this narrow strip (table 4.2).

There is evidence that the areas of actual territorial overlap discussed earlier include buffer zones or regions claimed by each neighboring pack but owned by neither (Mech 1977c). This theory holds that neither pack spends much time in buffer zones because of fear of meeting their

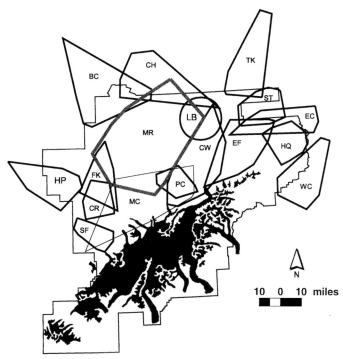

**Figure 4.4D.** *Estimates of extents of Denali wolf pack territories (polygons), winter 1988–89; circles represent packs with insufficient locations to portray entire territory. (See table 2.1 for pack abbreviations.)*

neighbors, although both packs scent-mark the zones.

Most wolf-killing by neighbors occurs either outside the territories or in these narrow zones. Because neither pack spends much time in buffer zones, prey inhabiting them are safer from attack and thus survive longer (Hoskinson and Mech 1976; Peters and Mech 1975; Nelson and Mech 1981; Fritts and Mech 1981; Rogers et al. 1980).

We did not collect enough wolf location data in Denali to further test the buffer-zone theory except to note the large apparent overlap among our wolf pack territories (figure 4.4). The shifting and temporary nature of Denali territory boundaries calls into question the universality of long-term buffer zones, but it does not rule out the possibility of temporary or shifting buffer zones in areas like Denali.

In Denali and Minnesota, both breeders and nonbreeders of both sexes were killed by other wolves. Without knowing how well our radio-collared wolf sample represented the proportion of breeders in the populations, it is impossible to determine whether breeders or nonbreeders were killed disproportionately. Mech (1977b) reported that intraspecific strife in his northeastern Minnesota wolf population resulted in the deaths of breeders more often than subordinate wolves. After many more years, however, he found that a substantial proportion of wolves killed by other wolves were immature (L. D. Mech, unpublished). This seems to suggest that more than just breeding competition is involved in such aggression. As already indicated, the level of intraspecific strife seen in our study (table 2.8) is the highest reported in any wolf population. In most other sizable wolf populations that have been studied, humans were the major cause of mortality. We suggest that widespread intraspecific strife and the resulting disruption of pack and population struc-

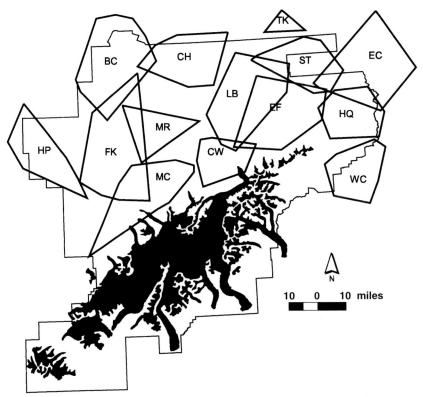

*Figure 4.4E. Estimates of extents of Denali wolf pack territories (polygons), winter 1989–90; circles represent packs with insufficient locations to portray entire territory. (See table 2.1 for pack abbreviations.)*

ture are a normal consequence of wolf territoriality in the absence of extensive human interference.

The annual mortality rate from all causes, averaging 27% (see chapter 8), had little apparent effect, however, on wolf numbers or reproduction in Denali, for other wolves were always ready to breed. In fact, the disintegration of six packs following the death of breeders killed by other wolves provided most of the opportunities for successful formation of new packs during our study (see below).

## Spatial Organization of Pack Territories

Wolves probably visit all parts of interior Alaska, except for the highest mountains, from time to time. They frequent some areas far more often than others, however, depending on availability of prey. Each pack has its favorite hunting areas

and its characteristic dens and travel routes. If a pack dies out, it is likely to be replaced by another pack with different habits and different territory boundaries.

In Denali, for example, the Bearpaw Pack supplanted the Alma Lakes Pack in 1987, and it was supplanted by the McKinley River Pack and its offshoot, the Chitsia Mountain Pack, in 1988 (table 4.1; figure 4.2). Way off to the southeast of them, the Turtle Hill Pack sprang up in 1992 where the Pirate Creek Pack had died out during winter 1988–89. Meanwhile, in the northeast end of the park, the Sushana, Ewe Creek, Stampede, and Savage packs successively used the same area.

In two of these cases of pack replacement, the new pack used the same den as the former pack had. The prey base in these areas remained essentially the same for the earlier and later residents,

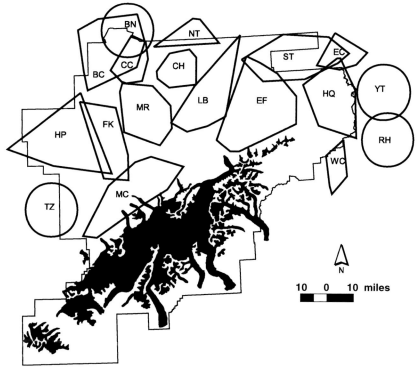

**Figure 4.4F.** *Estimates of extents of Denali wolf pack territories (polygons), winter 1990–91; circles represent packs with insufficient locations to portray entire territory. (See table 2.1 for pack abbreviations.)*

except for differences in caribou and moose migration due to different weather. Changes in wolf and prey density in neighboring territories may have put different pressures on the territorial ambitions of succeeding packs in a given area, however.

Furthermore, a replacement pack may have hunting preferences and travel habits different from their predecessors. Thus, the Alma Lakes Pack used areas farther to the north, and the Chitsia Mountain Pack used areas farther to the west, than the Bearpaw Pack, although all three successively occupied the area along the lower Bearpaw River. The Turtle Hill Pack traveled far north into the Kantishna Hills in winter when food became scarce in the area southeast of Wonder Lake. But several years earlier, the Pirate Creek Pack, faced with the same prey scarcity in this area, had starved.

(An alternative explanation for this behavior

that we cannot rule out, however, is that because of possible changes in annual conditions, the original packs using these areas might also have shifted territory use similarly if they had not been replaced.)

The pattern formed by the territories of these peripatetic and interacting wolf packs has been described as a mosaic similar to that of a jigsaw puzzle. However, the pieces of this jigsaw puzzle are constantly changing and overlapping (figure 4.4).

Use of an area by a population of wolf packs, then, is highly dynamic in several ways: (1) packs may make extraterritorial forays into other pack territories, (2) new packs may form, (3) one pack may usurp another's territory (Carbyn 1981), (4) packs may shift their territory boundaries either seasonally or permanently, (5) packs may use overlapping territories, (6) members may bud off a pack to form new neighboring packs, (7) packs

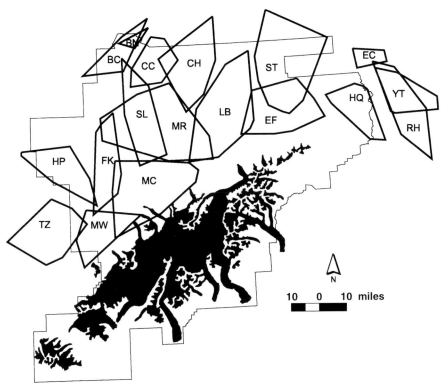

*Figure 4.4G. Estimates of extents of Denali wolf pack territories (polygons), winter 1991–92; circles represent packs with insufficient locations to portray entire territory. (See table 2.1 for pack abbreviations.)*

may sometimes split permanently, and (8) packs may forsake certain areas of low prey density, leaving gaps among territories; although some gaps may reflect our lack of data, most are no doubt real (figure 4.4).

## Dynamics of Wolf Pack Spacing

Wolf-pack spacing dynamics are partly a reflection of the turnover in individual wolves, and that turnover was great. An average of 27% of our radio-collared wolves died each year, while an annual average of 28% dispersed from the packs in which they were first captured (see chapter 2). As discussed earlier, 39% to 65% (from 17–20 packs) of our radio-collared wolves were killed by neighboring wolf packs. Harvest outside the Denali park and preserve boundary accounted for 9% of our mortality (table 2.8).

Thus, for example, of 85 wolves we studied that were younger than 3 years of age, 36 (42%) dispersed from the study area and 15 (18%) died before turning 3 years of age; only 13 (15%) remained in the Denali population more than 5 years (table 4.3). Radio-collared wolves older than 3 years of age at capture lived an average of 7 years; thus, their average tenure as adults in the Denali population was 4 years (see chapter 8). Therefore, even if a wolf population is stable in overall numbers, the individuals that comprise it are constantly changing through mortality and dispersal.

Six study packs disintegrated after the death of one or more members from natural causes (table 4.4). All were replaced by newly formed packs. Many other new pairs and larger social groups formed but did not persist (see below).

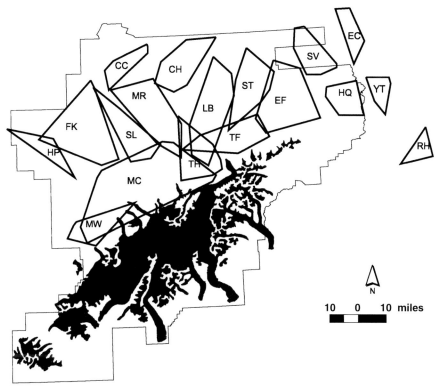

**Figure 4.4H.** *Estimates of extents of Denali wolf pack territories (polygons), winter 1992–93; circles represent packs with insufficient locations to portray entire territory. (See table 2.1 for pack abbreviations.)*

## Extraterritorial Forays

Even within a mosaic of pack territories, some wolves may live "outside the grid," moving from territory to territory. This is certainly true of lone, dispersing wolves, which can travel tremendous distances across many pack boundaries before settling down (Mech and Frenzel 1971; Fritts and Mech 1981; Messier 1985; Fuller 1989). Such a wolf in Denali was male 411, which traveled alone from his capture in November 1990 through December 1991. He drifted back and forth over our study area and beyond, a distance of about 100 miles (160 kilometers) across, until he was snared miles east of the park. Such wolves are searching for a mate and a vacancy in which to start their own pack (Rothman and Mech 1979).

Packs sometimes also drift around. Because caribou, sheep, and moose migrate during autumn

and spring, some Denali packs may find themselves without prey in winter. They respond, however, by traveling long distances, usually along frozen waterways and windblown ridges.

The Dillinger River Pack that we found on Birch Creek must have crossed the territories of many wolf packs in their 100-mile (160-kilometer) travel away from Denali. While we were monitoring the Little Bear Pack, a group of 11 of them (about half the pack) dispersed together and traveled about 150 miles (250 kilometers) before settling down or splitting up (see chapter 3).

We also witnessed movements by the Birch Creek Pack of 50 miles (80 kilometers) in several directions, by the Turtle Hill Pack of 30 miles (48 kilometers) to the north, and by the East Fork Pack of 20 miles (32 kilometers) to the east. These winter moves may last a few days or weeks, and

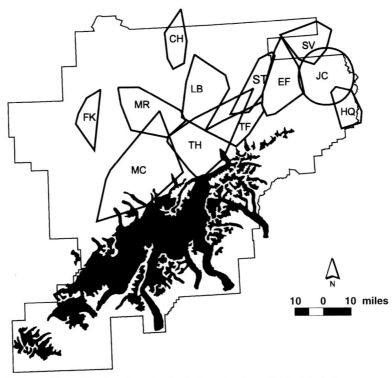

*Figure 4.4I.* Estimates of extents of Denali wolf pack territories (polygons), winter 1993–94; circles represent packs with insufficient locations to portray entire territory. (See table 2.1 for pack abbreviations.)

probably happen when neighboring packs are away from the area intruded upon. The high rate of killing of wolves by other wolf packs shows that these travels can be risky, however. Of 22 wolves we found killed by other wolves, 9 (41%) were 3 to 14 miles (5–22 kilometers) outside their estimated territory borders (table 4.2). In Minnesota, 6 (27%) of 22 wolf-killed wolves were killed outside their estimated territories (Mech 1994a).

### New Pack Formation

At least 16 new wolf pairs or packs formed in Denali during our study (table 4.5). These were detected when one or more of the wolves was already radio-collared (*n* = 9), or when a new pack was discovered by snow-tracking in a formerly vacant area (*n* = 7). Two new pairs died out without producing pups, 5 produced pups but did not successfully establish a territory for at least a year, and 9

succeeded in producing pups and founding packs that persisted for at least a year. The only similar information of which we are aware is for a Minnesota wolf population, where 67% of 15 adult dispersers, 31% of 26 yearling dispersers, and 25% of 8 dispersing pups succeeded in settling, pairing, and denning (Gese and Mech 1991). No data on pup production were presented in the latter study.

### Pack Budding

Seven of the 9 successful new packs in Denali were formed adjacent to or partly inside the natal territory of a founding member, a process we refer to as pack "budding" (Meier et al. 1995). One pack, the McKinley River Pack, budded off three new packs (the Chitsia Mountain, Foraker River, and Chilchukabena packs) on the edge of its territory over a 3-year period, relinquishing some territory to each

*Figure 4.5. The East Fork Pack breeding male scent-marks part of his territory. (Photo by L. David Mech.)*

(figure 3.10). The Foraker River Pack in turn produced a daughter pack, the Slippery Creek Pack, 3 years after its own formation.

In one case and possibly more, the colonization of an adjacent area immediately followed the demise of the formerly resident pack. The Bearpaw Pack was first radio-collared in April 1987 and consisted of 7 black and 3 gray wolves. Between January and March 1988, all three radio-collared Bearpaw wolves were killed by the all-grey McKinley River Pack, which entered the Bearpaw territory and remained there for much of the winter. At least one noncollared Bearpaw wolf was wounded,

and other pack members probably dispersed or were killed.

Two radio-collared McKinley River wolves, joined by 2 other wolves of unknown origin remained in the Bearpaw territory to found the Chitsia Mountain Pack. The Chitsia Mountain wolves occupied virtually the same territory, and later used the same den, as the defunct Bearpaw Pack.

Contrary to the usual tendency for packs to arise from breeding pairs, two of the new packs that arose from the McKinley River Pack were founded by 3 or more wolves (table 4.5). Both the Chitsia Mountain and Chilchukabena packs began with at least 1 radio-collared McKinley River wolf, 1 black wolf not of McKinley River origin, and 1 gray wolf of unknown origin. Conceivably these new packs were formed by a pair of unrelated breeders and the relative of 1 of them (Mech and Nelson 1990b).

The budding of a new pack on the perimeter of an established pack's range has obvious reproductive value for breeding wolves, and might even reduce interpack strife by replacing hostile, unrelated neighbors with relatives and former associates. However, observations of wolves being killed by close relatives on Isle Royale (Jordan et al. 1967; Peterson 1977) suggest that former associations or close genetic relatedness (Wayne et al. 1991) does not necessarily prevent strife when wolves meet again. We saw no cases of reassociation between packs that had separated, and the incidence of reintegration of a dispersed wolf back into its natal pack appeared no more common than the acceptance of total strangers.

### Pack Splitting

In other cases, all of the founding members of a new pack appeared to come from the same parent pack. Two large wolf packs split into approximately equal halves, subdividing their original territories. The McLeod Lake Pack of 15 wolves split, in early May 1991, into an eastern group of 8 wolves including the breeding male, and a western

*Figure 4.6. Tom Meier (right) and John Burch examine a wolf-killed wolf. (Photo by L. David Mech.)*

group of 7 wolves including 2 young radio-collared females (figure 3.9). The main breeding female in the original McLeod Lake Pack had died in October 1990, prior to the split. Both packs produced pups in summer 1991 and included 13 and 11 members, respectively, in fall. Although we once observed them within a mile (1.6 kilometer) of each other, the two packs occupied separate territories and apparently did not associate.

The Birch Creek Pack also split, in January 1991. This pack of more than 20 wolves split into a northern group of 11, including 2 radio-collared adult females, and a southern of 9, including a radio-collared adult female and a radio-collared yearling male (see chapter 3). We thought both packs denned in summer 1991, although we verified pup production only in the southern pack. As had the McLeod Lake Pack, the two new packs split the territory of the original pack, and no further contact between them was observed.

The splitting of a pack, with subdivision of the territory, may ease social and nutritional stress in a large group and may allow more efficient use of available prey (Murie 1944; Mech 1966a; Haber 1977). The McLeod Lake territory had become elongated as the pack expanded its travels farther southwestward along the Alaska Range. The new McLeod West territory included the western part of this territory, as well as additional area outside the original McLeod Pack territory. That arrangement allowed the exploitation of different moose populations and the calving grounds of two different caribou herds.

Both the McLeod Lake Pack and Birch Creek Pack splits occurred in packs with a history of multiple litters. The McLeod Lake split was preceded 7 months earlier by the death of the breeding female. Splitting in an Isle Royale wolf pack was also linked circumstantially to the death of a dominant member (Jordan et al. 1967; Wolfe and Allen 1973).

We believe that such pack splitting as this may occur when a new breeder from outside the pack is adopted into the pack and pairs with an unpaired maturing member. This new pair along with the original breeders yields two unrelated breeding pairs. At times both pairs may breed while part of the same social group, and then when the parent pack grows too large, the two families may split.

90

**Table 4.2.** Information about radio-tagged wolves killed by other wolves in Denali National Park and Preserve, 1986 through November 1992

| No. | Sex | Age (yr)[a] | Breeder? | Date died | Kilometers from territory edge | Remarks |
|-----|-----|-----|-----|-----|-----|-----|
| 205 | F | 7+ | Y | Apr 1986 | -2.8 | |
| 217 | F | 6+ | Y | Feb 1991 | 10.5 | Pack splitting |
| 223 | M | 8+ | Y | Jan 1989 | 8.2 | |
| 227 | F | 9+ | Y | Apr 1989 | -10.0 | |
| 235 | F | 2+ | Y | Mar 1987 | 0.0 | Member of new pair |
| 241 | F | 2+ | Y | Mar 1987 | 0.0 | |
| 259 | M | 2+ | N | Jan 1988 | -2.5 | Pack exterminated |
| 261 | F | 1+ | N | Mar 1988 | -5.2 | Pack exterminated |
| 313 | F | < 1 | N | Mar 1988 | -3.0 | |
| 333 | F | 6+ | Y | Dec 1988 | 0.0 | Member of new pair |
| 335 | M | 4+ | Y | Nov 1988 | -0.5 | Member of new pair |
| 355 | F | 6+ | Y | Feb 1989 | -4.5 | |
| 357 | M | <1 | N | Jan 1989 | 4.8 | |
| 369 | F | 4+ | Y | Mar 1991 | 8.2 | |
| 373 | M | 1+ | N | Feb 1990 | 22.2 | |
| 383 | F | 1+ | N | Dec 1989–Feb 1990 | 7.8 | |
| 407 | M | 3+ | N | Mar 1992 | -7.8 | |
| 425 | F | 6+ | N | Win. 1991–92 | 7.8 | Few locations |
| 449 | M | 2+ | N | Jul–Sep 1991 | 8.2 | |
| 461 | M | 2+ | N | Mar 1992 | 8.2 | |
| 491 | F | 2 | N | May 1992 | -6.8 | |
| 505 | M | 2+ | N | Nov 1992 | -3.2 | |

[a] Age estimated.

### Production of Multiple Litters

Multiple litters are probably more common than thought (Harrington et al. 1982), and appear to be a long-term pattern for wolves in at least one part of Denali (Murie 1944; Haber 1977; table 4.6). We observed or inferred the existence of multiple litters in nine packs in all habitat types used by wolves in Denali. The East Fork Pack produced as many as three litters one summer (see chapter 3), and two packs raised as many as 12 pups.

Wolves produced multiple litters when food appeared adequate and the wolf population was growing; several multiple litters followed severe winters when we found multiple prey killed in a single bout (see chapter 8). A plentiful food supply around the time of breeding might make breeding among subordinate wolves more likely (Hillis 1990; Boertje and Stephenson 1992), whether inhibition of breeding is mediated by behavior or physiology (Packard and Mech 1980).

### Adoption of Unrelated Wolves

Perhaps the most unusual social interactions we have observed involved strange wolves joining established packs. We noted eight such cases, seven of which involved male wolves 1 to 4 years old (table 4.7). Three cases could have represented a wolf returning to his natal pack after an unsuccessful pairing attempt (Mech and Seal 1987), al-

**Table 4.3.** Fates of 85 wolves caught and radio-collared at 5–35 months old in Denali, 1986–94

| | Died | | | |
| Age | Natural | Human-caused | Left Denali | Remained in Denali |
|---|---|---|---|---|
| By 3 years old | 13 | 1[a] | 36 | 35[b] |
| When 3–5 years old | 13 | 3 | 6 | 13 |
| More than 5 years old | | | | 13 |

Note: Six wolves whose radios failed soon after radio-collaring were omitted from this group. Wolves whose signal disappeared under conditions suggesting dispersal (n = 17) were considered probable dispersers.

[a] Killed outside Denali.

[b] Collar on 1 wolf failed when animal was 39 months old.

though we have no information to support either possibility.

Four other instances of adoption involved wolves of known origin and age, with no known history of contact with the packs they eventually settled in. In at least two of the four cases, the newcomer entered as a subordinate, rather than replacing a lost breeder. This distinguishes this type of adoption from those reported by Rothman and Mech (1979), Mech and Hertel (1983), and Fritts and Mech (1981).

The only female known to have been adopted into another pack was captured as an adult in the Foraker Pack at a time when that pack was thought to consist only of the radio-collared breeding female, an adult male, and their 6-month-old pups. On two occasions, adopted wolves entered packs near the time when similar-aged wolves born into the pack dispersed (table 4.7).

Most reports of the acceptance of strange wolves into packs have been from populations with extensive harvests, where disrupted pack structures would seem more likely to favor new social arrangements (Van Ballenberghe 1983a; Ballard et al. 1987). In Denali, however, wolves were

accepted into intact, long-established packs, new packs with a single generation of pups, and remnants of once larger packs (table 4.7). One wolf remained in the adopting pack for 1 year, and then paired off and denned on the edge of that pack's territory.

The breeding success of other adopted wolves is not yet known, but at least two are thought to have become breeding pack members. Five of six wolves accepted into existing packs prior to 1992 lived for at least 1 year afterward.

It is difficult to understand the benefits of accepting an unrelated, relatively inexperienced wolf into a pack. "New blood" may allow some desirable social realignment of the pack, and certainly introduces genetic novelty if the newcomer remains to become a breeder, or pairs off with one of the pack members. As long as the dominant breeder can prevent the newcomer from breeding his mate, there would be no genetic competition. Furthermore, during periods of plentiful food, there would be a genetic advantage for the dominant breeder if his daughter bred then.

Alternatively, such adoptions may also be merely misplaced sociality of little adaptive significance, although its relatively high rate suggests otherwise. The occurrence of such social tolerance in a population also demonstrating widespread intraspecific strife and intolerance of strange wolves is especially puzzling.

## Genetic Aspects of Wolf Social Organization

If wolf pack-territory boundaries and social spacing are so dynamic, can wolf interrelationships be defined by genetics? Are packs discrete family groups that hold their genetic structure separate from their neighbors for long periods? Could the genetic lineage of a Denali wolf pack (or a wolf pack in any other large population) be maintained intact for many decades, as has been claimed (Haber 1996)?

Considering wolf social ecology, it does not

**Table 4.4.** Summary of information on Denali wolf pack dissolution, 1986–92

| Pack | Longevity | Fates of members[a] |
|------|-----------|---------------------|
| Headquarters | ≥ 1 year, probably an old pack | 6 members in spring 1986 |
| | | F 205 killed by wolves Apr 1986 |
| | | M 231 dispersed Oct 1986 |
| | | F 219 dispersed Feb 1987 |
| | | F 241 killed by wolves Mar 1987 |
| | | 1 other died/dispersed by Mar 1987 |
| | | M 251 remained, paired in June 87 and refounded pack (table 4.5) |
| Bearpaw | ≥ 2 years | 10 members in fall 1987 |
| | | M 259 killed by wolves Jan 1988 |
| | | F 261 killed by wolves Mar 1988 |
| | | F 313 killed by wolves Mar 1988 |
| | | 6 others died or dispersed, 1 survivor may have remained in area |
| | | Replaced by Chitsia Mountain pack, spring 1989 |
| Castle Rocks | 9 months | 8 members in fall 1988 |
| | | F 333 killed by wolves Nov 1988 |
| | | M 335 killed by wolves Nov 1988 |
| | | 6 pups starved |
| | | Replaced by Foraker Pack, fall 1988 |
| Pirate Creek | 14 months | 9 members in fall 1988 |
| | | F 339 died of disease/malnutrition, November 1988 |
| | | Fate of others unknown |
| | | Area occupied by 2 neighboring packs, winter 1988–89 |
| Clearwater | ≥ 3.5 years | 6 members in fall 1986 |
| | | M 223 killed by wolves Jan 1989 |
| | | F 227 killed by wolves Apr 1989 |
| | | M 363 died ? cause Dec 1989 |
| | | F 361 disappeared Dec 1989 |
| | | Pups starved, winter 1988–89 |
| | | Replaced by Little Bear Pack, 1989 |
| Stampede | 2 years | 9 members in February 1990 |
| | | M 349 killed in avalanche Feb 1990 |
| | | F 351 killed in avalanche Feb 1990 |
| | | F 399 pup shot Sep 1990 |
| | | M 397 dispersed to McKinley R. Pack, May 1990 |
| | | 3–4 others died/dispersed; 1 or 2 may have remained in area |

*Source: Reprinted from Meier et al. 1995.*

[a] *Wolves identified by number were radio-collared.*

**Table 4.5.** Summary of information on wolf pair and new pack formation (figure 4.4), 1986–91

| Pack Name | Founded | Founders'[a] Identity/Origin | Type | Location[a] | Longevity/Fate[a] |
|---|---|---|---|---|---|
| Sushana | < Dec 86 | F 235/unknown<br>M 237 / unknown | New pair | Vacant area | 235 killed by wolves;<br>237 to TH Pack |
| Headquarters | Mar 87 | M 251/HQ Pack<br>F 307 / unknown | Pack reformed | HQ Pack territory | Pack survived at least 5 years |
| Pirate Creek | Sep 87 | M 250/CW Pack<br>F 339/unknown | New pair/budded | Edge of CW territory | 339 died, disease; others' fates unknown |
| Castle Rocks | < Mar 88 | F 339/unknown<br>M 335/unknown | New pair | Between ML and HP packs | 333 and 335 killed by wolves; pups starved |
| Stampede | < Mar 88 | F 349/unknown<br>M 351 / unknown | New pair | Vacant area | 349, 351 killed in avalanche; others died or dispersed |
| Little Bear | 1988 | gray M/unknown<br>gray F/unknown | New pair? | Replaced CW Pack | Pack survived at least 3 years |
| Foraker | Aug 88 | F 321/MR Pack<br>gray M/unknown | New pair/budded | Edge of MR territory | 301 died, natural causes; pack survived at least 4 years |
| Swift Fork | < Oct 88 | M 353/unknown<br>F 355/unknown | New pair | Vacant area? | 355 killed by wolves; 353, unknown natural death |
| Chitsia Mountain | Dec 88 | F 359/unknown<br>M 315/MR Pack<br>M 379/MR Pack<br>black M/unknown<br>gray?/unknown | Budded | Edge of MR territory | 379 dispersed; pack survived at least 3 years |

seem possible for a pack's genetic line to remain undiluted for more than a generation. Because wolf packs generally consist of a breeding pair and their offspring, and most offspring disperse and form new packs when they locate dispersers of the opposite sex, genes recombine during each new generation. When a breeding pack member is lost, it may be replaced by a disperser from another pack, or by a pack member if the opposite-sex breeder is a step-parent.

If dispersal distances were consistently long, so that few dispersers settled near their natal packs, this social system could lead to a mosaic of packs in which genetic relatedness among most wolves in a pack is high but relatedness between wolves in adjacent packs is low (Woolpy and Eckstrand 1979). In fact, a pattern of genetic isolation among neighboring wolf packs has been suggested as an adaptive mechanism in the evolution of wolves (Haber 1977, 1996; Shields 1983).

However, by using mitochondrial DNA analysis and nuclear DNA "genetic fingerprinting," we found that wolves in Denali from different packs often showed high levels of genetic similarity, confirming that they were related at the sibling or parent/offspring level (figure 4.7). Furthermore, the degree of relatedness among members of neighboring packs varies among wolf populations

**Table 4.5.** continued

| Pack Name | Founded | Founders'[a] Identity/Origin | Type | Location[a] | Longevity/Fate[a] |
|---|---|---|---|---|---|
| Nenana Canyon | Apr 90 | M 311/HQ Pack gray F/unknown | New pair | Between HQ & EC territories | 311 dispersed; others' fates unknown |
| Chilchukabena | Sep 90 | M 407/MR Pack F 439/unknown gray ?/unknown gray ?/unknown | Budded | Edge of MR territory | 407 killed by wolves; pack survived at least 1.5 years |
| Myrtle Hill | Nov 90 | F 217/EF Pack gray M/unknown | Budded | Edge of EF territory | 217 killed by wolves; others' fates unknown |
| Stampede 2 | Mar 91 | F 427/unknown M 429/unknown M 437/LB Pack M 455/unknown gray?/unknown | Pack reformed | Vacant area? | 427 snared; 437 dispersed; 3 wolves still present Apr 92 |
| Birch Creek North | Jan 91 | F 347/BC Pack F 369/BC Pack 7 other wolves | Pack split | Half of BC territory | 347 snared; 369 killed by wolves |
| Slippery Creek | Apr 91 | M 441/FR Pack F 495/unknown | New pair/budded | Between MR & FR territories | Pack survived at least 1 year |
| McLeod Lake West | May 91 | F 367/ML Pack F 409/ML Pack 5 other wolves | Pack split | Half of ML territory | Pack survived at least 1 year |

*Source: Reprinted from Meier et al. 1995.*

[a] *Wolves identified by number were radio-collared individuals; see Table 2.1 for pack abbreviations.*

(Lehman et al. 1992). The frequency of such similarities between wolves in different packs was higher in a Minnesota wolf population and lower in a Northwest Territories population than in Denali. In all three populations, some packs contained additional wolves that were not the offspring of a single breeding pair.

Sibling or parent/offspring relatedness among wolves in neighboring packs could result from (1) new packs being formed by wolves dispersing from a nearby pack (Rothman and Mech 1979; Fritts and Mech 1981; Peterson et al. 1984; Mech 1987; Fuller 1989; Hayes et al. 1991; Ream et al. 1991; Meier et al. 1995); (2) splitting of existing packs (Jordan et al. 1967; Haber 1977; Mech 1986; Meier et al. 1995); (3) packs adopting wolves from neighboring packs (Rothman and Mech 1979; Fritts and Mech 1981; Van Ballenberghe 1983a; Peterson et al. 1984; Messier 1985; Ballard et al. 1987; Fuller 1989; Hayes et al. 1991; Meier et al. 1995), or (4) breeding between wolves in neighboring packs.

The presence of wolves not related to breeding animals in a pack could result from the adoption of unrelated wolves, the founding of a pack by a group of three or more wolves (Peterson et al. 1984; Messier 1985; Fuller 1989; Mech and Nelson 1990b; Ream et al. 1991), or the presence of more than one breeding female in a pack (Murie 1944; Rausch 1967; Peterson 1977; Haber 1977;

**Table 4.6.** Multiple litters in Denali wolf packs

| Pack | Year | Litters | Females[a] | Pups | Evidence |
|---|---|---|---|---|---|
| East Fork | 1988 | 2 | 1080, ? | 12 | 2 active dens observed |
| Birch Creek | 1988 | 2 | ?, ? | 12 | Large number of pups |
| East Fork | 1989 | 2 | 1080, 217 | 10 | 2 active dens observed |
| East Fork | 1990 | 3 | 1080, 217, ? | 9 | 3 active dens observed |
| Headquarters | 1990 | 2 | 307, ? | 5 | 2 active dens observed |
| McLeod Lake | 1990 | 2 | 309, 367? | 11 | 5 pups seen earlier |
| Windy Creek | 1990 | 2 | 377, ? | 9 | Large number of pups |
| East Fork | 1991 | 2 | 1080, ? | 3 | 2 active dens observed |
| Little Bear | 1991 | 2 | ?, ? | 11 | 2 den areas, large number of pups |

*Source: Reprinted from Meier et al. 1995.*

[a] *Wolves identified by number were radio-collared individuals.*

Harrington et al. 1982; Van Ballenberghe 1983b; Peterson et al. 1984; Ballard et al. 1987; Clarkson and Liepins 1991) if the two females are unrelated or are bred by unrelated males.

Changes in pack composition and territories resulting from intraspecific strife (Jordan et al. 1967; Wolfe and Allen 1973; Van Ballenberghe and Erickson 1973; Mech 1977b, 1994a; Fuller and Keith 1980; Carbyn 1981; Fritts and Mech 1981; Ballard et al. 1987; Fuller 1989) may tend to increase new pack formation and favor other social changes that increase relatedness between packs and decrease relatedness within packs.

### Genetic Relationships among Denali Wolves

Some 53% (10 of 19) of Denali wolves that we tested genetically showed sibling- or parent/offspring-level genetic similarity to wolves in other packs in the population (Lehman et al. 1992). An additional 5 (26%) showed cousin-level relatedness. Nine of 10 packs sampled had at least one such genetic tie to another pack, although the 19 wolves tested represented less than 13% of the 176 wolves in study packs during that period. Thus, many more genetic links probably existed undetected. Our observations of new pack formation, pack splitting, and acceptance of strange wolves into packs demonstrated a minimum of 28 close

genetic connections among wolf packs in this population. Not all of these connections existed at once, because of the turnover of both individual wolves and whole packs in the population. Of 31 radio-collared wolves in the study area as of January 1992, 11 (35%) were living in a pack other than the one from which they were first captured. Most of the genetic similarities we found are congruent with our behavioral observations (figure 4.7). Clearwater wolf number 363, which was thought to have come from the McLeod Lake Pack, showed high genetic similarity to a McLeod Lake wolf. Both the Foraker and Chitsia Mountain packs budded off from the McKinley River Pack, and the wolves tested in these packs resembled McKinley River wolves genetically, although those particular individuals were of unknown origin.

The Little Bear and Stampede packs originated during this study, and their genetic links to more established packs (Birch Creek and East Fork, respectively) are probably indicative of the source of their founding members.

Relatedness among longer-established packs (Clearwater and Birch Creek, McLeod Lake and McKinley River) were at the lower, "cousin" level (Lehman et al. 1992), probably dating to older colonization events.

One genetic link we found seems unrealistic:

**Table 4.7.** Acceptance of Denali wolves into established packs, 1987–92

| | Adoptee | | | Adopting pack | | | | | |
|---|---|---|---|---|---|---|---|---|---|
| No. | Sex | Age[a] | Origin | Date | Name | Size | Age[b] | Composition[c] | Duration/Outcome |
| 237 | M | 2 | Sushana | 03/87 | Totek Hills | 15 | ? | Unknown | Returning to natal pack? Remained at least 3 years |
| 363 | M | 2 | McLeod Lake | 03/89 | Clearwater | 2 | 3+ | Adult F 237 Yearling F 361 | Became only male in pack |
| 311 | M | 2 | Clearwater | 03/89 | Headquarters | 7 | 1 | Adult M 251 Adult F 307 5 pups | 2 pups disappeared about the same time; remained 1 year; paired/dispersed |
| 387 | F | 2 | unknown | F 89 | Foraker | 6 | 1 | Adult F 321 adult M 4 pups | With pack 2+ years; bred in 1991 |
| 397 | M | 1 | Stampede | 09/90 | McKinley R. | 8 | 3+ | Adult F 401 others unknown | Remained at least 1.5 years; 2-year-old male 407 left the pack the same month 397 joined it |
| 385 | M | 2 | Highpower | 05/91 | Foraker River | 4 | 2 | Adult F 387 others unknown | Remained at least 1 year |
| 429 | M | 3 | Stampede? | 02/92 | Totek Hills | 10+ | 4+ | Adult M 455 others unknown | Returning to natal pack? |
| 455 | M | 4 | Stampede? | 02/92 | Totek Hills | 10+ | 4+ | Adult M 429 others unknown? | Returning to natal pack? |

Source: Reprinted from Meier et al. 1995.

[a] Wolf ages based on estimated age at capture.

[b] Pack age: minimum duration of pack (in years) prior to this event.

[c] Wolves identified by number were radio-collared individuals.

male pups 395 and 397 appeared to be related at the sibling level. However, our observations suggested that they were born into the East Fork and Stampede packs, respectively. The nature of the tests and of inheritance itself dictates that various dyads of individuals will show genetic similarity higher or lower than their pedigrees would predict on average (Lehman et al. 1992). Numerical values produced by this method cannot be interpreted unequivocally for every individual.

Among the within-pack genetic relationships we found were two dyads of young female wolves from the same pack showing low relatedness (Lehman et al. 1992). Both packs had contained more than one breeding female in previous years; thus, the members of each dyad we tested could have had different mothers and/or fathers.

Pack budding, pack splitting, and adoption of strange wolves all produce closer genetic links among members of different packs in a wolf population than would be expected if most packs originated from pairs of unrelated, distant dispersers. If adopted wolves were to become breeders, they could greatly decrease genetic isolation in long-

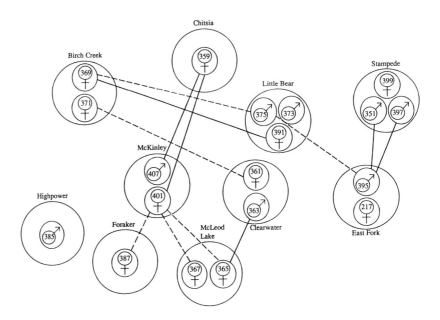

*Figure 4.7. Relatedness suggested by high genetic fingerprint similarities among Denali wolf packs. Solid lines denote similarities more than 2.29 standard errors above the average for unrelated Denali wolves. Dashed lines indicate relatedness 1.52 to 2.29 standard errors above that average. Packs are in relative geographic positions, but distances are not to scale. (Modified from Lehman et al. 1992 and Meier et al. 1995.)*

established packs. However, natural mortality, the changing nutritional needs of growing or shrinking packs, and the dispersal and colonizing strategies described here seem to ensure that the characteristics of the pack-territory mosaic and the genetic makeup of packs in a thriving wolf population will not remain stable for long, contrary to undocumented claims for this same population. Genetic evidence from other wolf populations also supports our interpretation (Kennedy et al. 1991; Lehman et al. 1992).

## Do Wolves Inbreed?

Since the genetic work on Denali wolves we reported earlier (Lehman et al. 1992; Meier et al. 1995), we have sampled many more Denali wolves. These data are still being analyzed, but some trends are obvious. There are many genetic links between wolves in all parts of the Denali population, especially between neighboring packs. Not surprisingly, large packs and packs that have survived a long time show more links with other packs than do smaller and more recent packs. But

dispersal from large, successful packs is not just a one-way movement.

In an attempt to detect what level of inbreeding might occur in our population, we looked at the genetic relatedness of known breeding pairs of wolves both in Denali (table 4.8) and in the Superior National Forest of Minnesota (Smith et al. 1997). If long-lived packs remained genetically isolated from the rest of the population, as has been claimed, then replacement of lost breeders would have to be from within the pack, leading to incest if the nonbreeding members were all the offspring of the breeding pair.

However, we found no evidence of breeding between close relatives in the wolf pairs from either Denali or Minnesota, indicating that wolves tend to avoid incest, in spite of the fact that they have far more opportunities to breed with a sibling or parent than with an unrelated individual. Because the average breeding tenure of individual wolves (tables 4.3, 4.9, and chapter 8) is much shorter than the life span of wolf packs (Mech 1966a; Jordan et al. 1967; Peterson 1977; Peterson and Page 1988; Mech and Hertel 1983; Mech

**Table 4.8.** Histories and relatedness of bonded wolf pairs in Denali National Park and Preserve

| Pack | Male | Female | Relatedness[a] | Duration[b] | Together[c] | | Fate |
|------|------|--------|------------|----------|----------|------|------|
| SV | 511 | 501 | 0.12 | Mar 1993–Oct 1994 | 12/15 | (80%) | 511 shot |
| CW | 223 | 227 | 0.03 | Jul 1986–Jan 1989 | 137/187 | (73%) | 223 killed by wolf |
| CW | 363 | 361 | 0.19 | Mar 1989–Dec 1989 | 21/42 | (50%) | 363 died, cause unknown |
| TU | 4520 | 529[d] | 0.00 | Mar 1993–Oct 1993 | 15/27 | (56%) | 529 killed by wolf |
| EF | 513 | 467 | 0.12 | Mar 1993–Jan 1995 | 14/20 | (70%) | 513 died, cause unknown |
| FO | 441 | 495 | 0.19 | Mar 1992–Sep 1992 | 4/6 | (67%) | 441 died, cause unknown |
| HQ | 251 | 307 | -0.01 | Feb 1988–Nov 1993 | 182/206 | (88%) | 251 capture mortality |
| ST | 351 | 349 | -0.01 | Oct 1988–Feb 1990 | 59/64 | (92%) | Both killed by avalanche |
| TF | 515 | 499 | -0.24 | Mar 1993–Jan 1994 | 16/17 | (94%) | 515 killed by avalanche |
| ST | 455 | 475 | 0.12 | Mar 1992–present | 13/13 | (100%) | Active |

*Source: Adapted from Smith et al. 1997.*

[a] *Average relatedness of siblings or parent-offspring = + 0.5; cousins = + 0.2; Queller and Goodnight 1989.*

[b] *Period when wolves were together and radio-collared.*

[c] *Number (%) of radio locations when pair was together.*

[d] *This is the only pack that did not produce pups.*

1995a), breeders must be replaced often. The genetic evidence indicates that this replacement is usually by wolves from outside the pack or from among pack members that are not related to the remaining breeders.

## Dispersal and Genetic Diversity

Wolf populations are linked genetically by the dispersal of wolves from one area to another. In North America, the wolves from Alaska to eastern Canada, extending north to Ellesmere Island and Greenland and south into Minnesota and other border states could all be considered part of one population. DNA evidence suggests genetic continuity among wolves across vast areas of North America (Roy et al. 1994).

Our observations of wolves dispersing from Denali show how the park's wolves are linked to a much larger area (see chapter 2). Like wolves in other populations, both male and female Denali wolves dispersed long distances (figures 2.12 and 2.13), and our longest known dispersal was 435 miles (695 kilometers).

Because we had only about 20% of the Denali wolf population radio-collared at any time, the movements we observed were only a sample of what was happening. Most dispersed wolves were accompanied by other wolves when they were eventually discovered or killed. If even a fraction of dispersers eventually become breeders, this suggests a great deal of genetic interchange between Denali and the rest of Alaska.

At times, there is probably as much movement of wolves into Denali as out, for densities of wolves outside the park are about the same as or higher than inside (Boertje et al. 1996). We had little chance of detecting immigrants, however, unless we happened to dart one tagged elsewhere, or unless other researchers tracked one from their study area into ours. The likelihood of either depends on the amount of wolf radio-tracking in the vicinity. During most of our study, no wolves were radio-collared in nearby populations. However, in 1995, ADFG began an intensive study east of Denali, and in 1996 we got our first known immigrant.

The extent of wolf harvesting within 500 miles (800 kilometers) of Denali would somewhat limit

**Table 4.9.** Turnover of breeders in the East Fork Pack

| Year | Breeders Male | Female(s) | | | Cause of death |
|---|---|---|---|---|---|
| 1986 | 221 | 1080 | | | |
| 1987 | 221 | 1080 | | | Male 221, old and crippled, disappeared |
| 1988 | 5051[a] | 1080 | GF[b] | | |
| 1989 | 5051[a] | 1080 | 217 | | |
| 1990 | 5051[a] | 1080 | GF[b] | 217 | Female 217 killed by wolves in Kantishna Hills |
| 1991 | 5051[a] | 1080 | GF[b] | | Female 1080, very old, died of natural causes |
| 1992 | 5051 | 467 | | | Male 5051 trapped just outside park boundary |
| 1993 | 513 | 467 | | | |
| 1994 | 513 | 467 | | | Male 513 died of unknown natural causes, Teklanika River |

[a] Other males could also have been breeders.

[b] Noncollared gray female.

the amount of wolf immigration into the park. However, enough remote wolf populations live in this surrounding area and average harvest levels are low enough that harvesting should not prevent wolf immigration into Denali. Even moderately harvested wolf populations in Alaska show high rates of dispersal (Ballard et al. 1987).

The spatial changes we observed in the Denali wolf population and the gene flow that occurs there suggest a spatial organization that is not a static jigsaw puzzle of packs but rather a shifting mosaic. Packs, like individual wolves, have finite life spans. They originate where there is room for them and may flourish for years, producing large numbers of dispersers to ensure their evolutionary success. Eventually, when food is scarce or neighbors are especially successful, they fade out through death and/or emigration.

Even while they thrive, Denali wolf packs are not isolated but are part of a larger continuum,

sending out dispersers to and accepting new members from areas over hundreds of miles away. Thus, Denali's wolf population is affected by the dynamics of surrounding wolf packs and, on a scale of centuries, is at least partly dependent on those populations for genetic diversity. Fortunately, wolf populations in the remainder of Alaska and in most of Canada appear secure enough for the foreseeable future to provide the constant flow of immigrants that will allow Denali's wolves to continue to thrive (Stephenson et al. 1995; Hayes and Gunson 1995).

The chaos and turmoil of the Denali wolf population is typical of other unharvested wolf populations (Mech 1966a, 1986, 1994a, 1995a; Fritts and Mech 1981; Fuller 1989; Peterson 1977, 1995). Nevertheless, through the processes described here, wolves are well adapted to compensate for such disruptions, including those caused by human harvest (Ballard et al. 1987; Hayes 1995; Boertje et al. 1996)

# "The Wolf Is Kept Fed by His Feet"

The old Russian saying that links the wolf's feeding with its feet is quite apt. The animal's large, blocky feet combined with its lanky legs suggest that the wolf is a practiced traveler. It is. At a tireless rate of about 5 miles (8 kilometers) per hour (Mech 1994b), the wolf could travel some 115 miles (190 kilometers) in a day if it did not rest, and it may sometimes do so. Such a feat is not well documented, however, and the wolf must rest after a certain amount of travel. Nevertheless, 50 miles (80 kilometers) in half a day does not seem to be unusual (Mech 1988a).

Denali wolves are no exception. On February 4, 1987, for example, seven to eight wolves of the East Fork Pack traveled at least 21 miles (35 kilometers) from Stony Creek to Igloo Mountain. It was not unusual for us to aerially snow-track wolf packs for such long distances when trying to locate them to capture and radio-collar.

## The Wolf's Prey

The main reason wolves travel so widely is to find prey they can kill (figure 5.1). Denali supports thousands of moose, Dall sheep, and caribou as well as multitudes of smaller prey such as ground squirrels, marmots, beavers, snowshoe hares, and many other smaller creatures (see chapter 1). Nevertheless, the park is huge, and prey are not uniformly distributed over it. Denali's caribou herd may be in only one place, or broken into a few subherds that are only in a few places, in the entire park, and they move frequently. The Dall sheep live scattered in small bands that frequent steep rocky hills and pinnacles to which they can quickly escape from wolves.

Moose are different. Their pure size and brute strength allow them to live here and there among the willows in relatively small home ranges instead of wandering constantly to evade the wolves. Some moose do migrate in fall and spring, to and from lowland areas, but once in their seasonal range, they remain in a fairly small area.

As will be seen in chapter 6, as long as moose remain healthy and in good condition, they merely stand and fight for a few minutes with any wolves that find them, and then go back to their browsing. Thus, wolves must find many moose for each one they can kill. In Isle Royale National Park, Michigan, where moose are the sole winter wolf

101

**Figure 5.1.** *Denali wolves travel far and wide to find prey vulnerable enough for them to catch and kill, usually moose, caribou, or Dall sheep. (Photo by Thomas J. Meier.)*

prey, a pack of 15 wolves had to test about 12 to 13 moose for each one they killed, and that was during late winter and spring, when moose are most vulnerable (Mech 1966a).

Thus, whether to find the caribou herds or the sheep bands or to locate enough moose in order to find a vulnerable one, Denali wolves are constantly faced with the need to travel widely. This need also requires them to maintain a large territory over which they can move and be assured of securing a regular supply of prey.

To maintain their large territories, wolves scent-mark as they travel, leaving urine and feces in conspicuous places to advertise their presence and remind neighbors that they are still present (see chapter 4). In addition, their howling, which often precedes their resumption of travel, also warns neighboring packs. Complementing these territorial warnings is outright aggression against any neighboring packs that are met (see chapter 4).

Because of the great variation in topography, soil, and vegetation across the wide expanse of Denali National Park, each of the wolf packs there occupies a territory that encompasses different combinations of prey (table 3.1). Thus, the Ewe Creek Pack, for example, whose territory included many rugged mountains, fed heavily on Dall sheep, while the Birch Creek Pack inhabiting the flats in the northwest corner of the park may never have encountered a sheep. The East Fork Pack territory included a fair sampling of all three major prey.

***Plates 1-3.*** *(top) Polychrome Pass in the east-central part of Denali. (middle) Mount McKinley, elevation 20,320 feet, is the highest mountain in North America and overshadows the Denali study area. (bottom) In dry years, thousands of acres of northwestern Denali burn from lightning strikes. (Photos by Thomas J. Meier.)*

***Plate 4.*** *Dall sheep are one of the most distinctive and conspicuous mammals of Denali and form one of the wolf's main prey. (Photo by L. David Mech.)*

***Plate 5.*** *Bull caribou sport much larger antlers than do cows; during their autumn rut, these large animals are especially vulnerable to wolf predation. (Photo by John W. Burch.)*

***Plate 6.*** *Moose form the mainstay of the Denali wolf's diet. (Photo by Rick McIntyre.)*

**Plate 7.** *Grizzly bears compete with Denali wolves for prey, especially newborn caribou calves. (Photo by Bruce W. Dale.)*

**Plate 8.** *John Burch and others weigh a radio-collared wolf they are about to release. (Photo by Thomas J. Meier.)*

**Plate 9-11** *(top left) The authors attempted to thoroughly examine the remains of all wolf kills they found, such as this bull caribou. (Photo by John W. Burch.) (top right) The East Fork Pack lounging around a freshly killed caribou. (Photo by L. David Mech.) (bottom) Dall sheep often escape wolves by taking refuge on precipices that wolves cannot reach. Note wolves above sheep. (Photo by Thomas J. Meier.)*

**Plate 12.** *Old prey animals like this 10-year-old Dall ram form a high percentage of individuals that wolves kill. (Photo by L. David Mech.)*

**Plate 13.** *The Denali Caribou Herd numbered from 2,300 to 3,100 during our study. (Photo by L. David Mech.)*

*Plate 14. The Denali Caribou Herd calving ground at the northeastern base of Mount McKinley. (Photo by Layne G. Adams.)*

*Plate 15. A wolf carries a newborn caribou calf back to the den. (Photo by Bruce W. Dale.)*

***Plate 16.*** *Denali wolf pups had a summer survival rate of about 90%. (Photo by Leo Keeler.)*

*Figure 5.2.* Wolves in Denali denned primarily in holes but also used old beaver houses, pits in the ground, and nests under overhanging spruces. (Photo by Thomas J. Meier.)

## Seasonal Wolf Movements

A wolf pack's life history includes two seasonal phases of movement, den-based summer movements and nomadic winter movements. Although the total amount of travel during each season may be similar, the patterns by which wolves use their territories during the two seasons are drastically different because of the great divergences in their lifestyles during these times. To understand wolf movements during these two times of year, it is important to understand these lifestyle differences.

### Summer Headquartering around Dens

During summer, which in Denali lasts from May through September, the manner of movement is dictated by the presence of pups, which are highly sedentary. The pups are born in mid-May and spend their first 8 weeks in and around a den (Mech 1970). Denali wolves produced an average of about four pups per litter (table 2.3), and sometimes they raised two litters in the same den, or at least in the same den complex (see chapter 4).

### Characteristics of Denali Wolf Dens

Denali wolves used dens varying from open nests to old, well-established sites that appeared to have been used for many years, and in some cases are known to have been used intermittently for decades (Murie 1944; Haber 1977). Several den complexes included upward of a dozen holes (figure 5.2), and wolf activity had altered the vegetation surrounding these sites, causing the area to be more grassy or open than it would be otherwise. Most dens were in areas near water, although a few were at least 500 yards (meters) from any obvious pond or stream. There may be intermittent water sources in May that would allow females at these sites to obtain water.

Several sites known to have been used by wolves in the past were occupied by foxes during our study, and wolves also enlarge fox dens for their own use (Murie 1944). One Denali wolf den appeared to have been made from old beaver tunnels along a lakeshore. Most dens were dug-out holes in raised, sandy areas with good drainage. A few took advantage of natural cavelike spaces

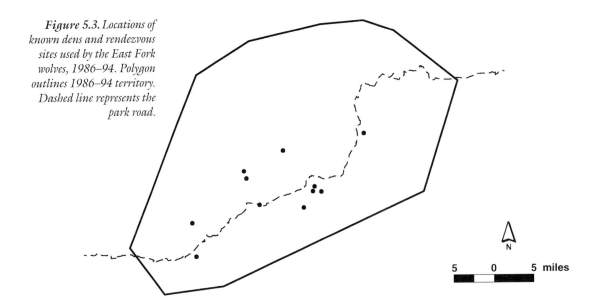

*Figure 5.3. Locations of known dens and rendezvous sites used by the East Fork wolves, 1986–94. Polygon outlines 1986–94 territory. Dashed line represents the park road.*

5   0   5 miles

around rock outcrops. Four litters of McLeod Lake Pack pups were born in open nests under spruces (see chapter 3), and one East Fork litter was born in an open nest in a snow-covered area with little natural shelter at all except for the mother's body (Mech 1993).

Many wolf dens were in spots that commanded extensive views of the surrounding area, probably useful both for hunting and for awareness of intruders. Other dens were hidden away in low-lying or densely wooded areas that were impossible to see from the air. Some dens in wooded areas were easily visible from the air in early May before aspens greened up, and probably benefited from the effects of the sun at that time to thaw and warm the ground. Later in the season they became deeply shaded and impossible to see.

Defining a den as either a site where pups were born or a site with den holes where pups were kept later in the summer, we observed 54 dens, roughly categorized as follows: partly open knoll or ridge in a wooded area, 15; open bluff overlooking a river or stream, 12; wooded hillside, 9; low-lying area near the bank of a river or lake, 9; rock out-crop, fairly far from water, 4; open nest under spruces, 4; open nest in snow-covered tundra, 1.

Individual packs sometimes denned in the same den or same area in consecutive years, but they also sometimes switched dens and areas from year to year, or even in the same summer, similar to wolves in most other locations.

### Summer Movements

The breeding female may move her pups from one den to another during their first 2 months of life, but she keeps them around some kind of shelter. From then through September, they are kept as a group above ground in areas known as rendezvous sites. These are merely resting places where the pups can huddle together when they sleep and wait for the adults to return with food. The adults may move the pups to a few different rendezvous sites over the summer or keep them at one or two. Thus, in a given territory, dens and rendezvous sites are scattered across the territory (figure 5.3). In any case, pups usually do not travel far with the adults until about October.

During this sedentary phase of the pup's life,

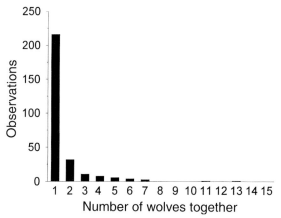

*Figure 5.4. Relative numbers of Denali wolves traveling alone or with others during summer*

the movements of the pack necessarily center around the pups' location. The mother of the pups remains with them during most of the first 3 to 4 weeks of their life. During this time, her mate and any other pack members—usually the pair's offspring of the previous year or 2—also headquarter around the den. All these pack members radiate from the den to hunt and bring food back to the female and the pups (Murie 1944; Haber 1977; Mech 1988a.)

Thus, depending on where the den is in relation to the entire territory, the pack's travel routes will look like a set of spokes out from a hub. After the pups reach 5 to 6 weeks of age, the female often joins the rest of the pack when they go off for the hunt, although it is not unusual for a yearling or 2-year-old animal to remain with the pups (Murie 1944; Haber 1977; Mech 1988a).

The pack members may leave for a hunt independently or together. When they leave together, they may also split up while on the hunt or after a kill and return to the den separately. Thus, wolves most often travel singly in summer (figure 5.4). A tendency to travel singly would increase the pack's efficiency in hunting the smaller prey available during summer, including calves, lambs, beavers, hares, marmots, and ground squirrels.

No doubt the pattern of routes used by the wolves as they radiate from the den varies considerably according to the major type of prey they may be hunting at any given time. In another study area where Mech (unpublished) examined this aspect of wolf movements in more detail, the wolves tended to use different routes away from the den during consecutive days or nights.

The only data available on this subject from the Denali wolf population come from a short period in May 1996. That year, we fitted a couple of wolves from a pack on the caribou calving ground with experimental radio-collars that used the Global Positioning System (GPS) to determine the wolves' locations each hour. During and after the peak of calving, those wolves fanned out from the den each day to habitats used by calving caribou and returned using several different routes (figure 5.5). The value of varying hunting routes might be to increase the chances of surprising more prey. Presumably as prey are hunted they become more wary. Thus, it would be advantageous to vary hunting areas frequently.

*Exceptions: Summer Nomadism*

During the unusual situation when a wolf pack produces no pups or loses its pups early, the wolves no longer headquarter at the den but rather become nomadic over their territory as in winter (Mech 1995b). For example, the McKinley River Pack comprised of eight to nine wolves, which failed to den in 1988, covered a minimum of some 39 miles (65 kilometers), zigzagging around their territory during 6 days in May (figure 5.6).

We also had evidence for an even rarer type of summer lifestyle in the Clearwater Pack during one year. It appeared that between May 15 and July 26, 1987, the Clearwater Pack breeding male and a yearling male we had radio-collared rarely, if ever, visited the Clearwater Pack den (see chapter 3). We found the female at or near the den on 4 of 10 occasions during the same period, and never saw her

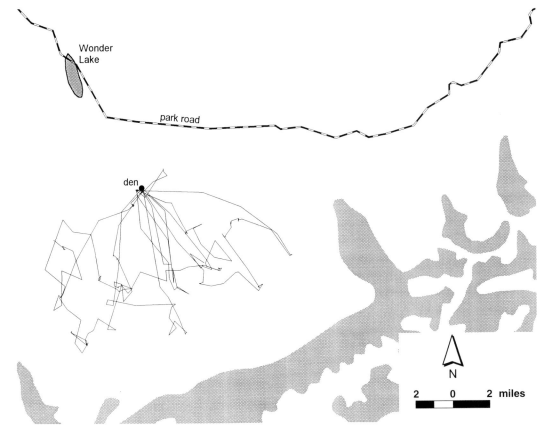

**Figure 5.5.** *Routes of a Turtle Hill wolf to and from its den over a 2-week period in May 1996, based on an experimental GPS collar. Dashed line represents the park road.*

with any other wolf except her pups, contrary to our data from the other packs.

These data suggested that during summer 1987 the Clearwater Pack may have lived like a pack on Ellesmere Island during 1989. In that pack, it appeared that the breeding male, a 2-year-old male, and four yearlings traveled nomadically around the territory independently of the breeding female and a 2-year-old female, which radiated from the den and brought food back to the pups (Mech 1991, 1995a). Conceivably, in both cases the breeding female may have traveled to where the breeding male was hunting and transferred

food that he obtained back to the pups rather than waiting for him to bring it to the den, as is the usual case.

## Winter Movements

The winter phase of wolf movements begins when the pups have grown and developed enough to leave the rendezvous site and join the pack full-time on their hunts, usually about late September or early October. Now no longer restricted by having to return to a certain location, the pack roams about its territory nomadically as a group (figure 5.7). At its 5-mile-per-hour (8-kilometer-per-hour)

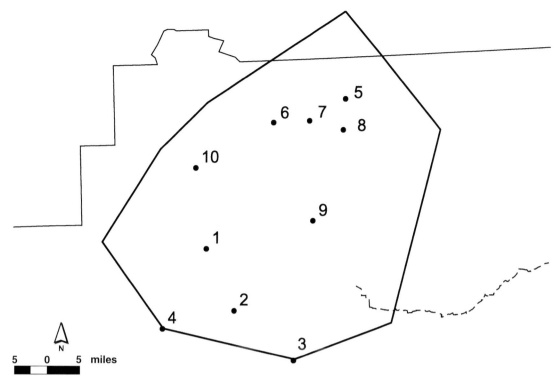

*Figure 5.6. Radio locations of the McKinley River Pack in May 1988; because the pack did not produce pups that year, they did not concentrate near a den but continued traveling nomadically within their territory; numbers indicate sequence of their locations. Dashed line represents the park road.*

gait (Mech 1994b), the pack travels in search of prey, the breeding pair scent-marking every few minutes (Peters and Mech 1975).

Over the weeks and months, the wolves head back and forth around their territory in no apparent spatial pattern. Moving from one caribou herd to another, one moose to the next, or to a band of sheep here or there, they cover as many as 45 miles (72 kilometers) per day (Burkholder 1959; Mech 1966a, 1988a). Alternately feeding on kills, sleeping, eating, resting, and traveling some more, they repeat some variation on this pattern throughout the winter.

A good case in point involved the nine McKinley River wolves from February 11–23, 1989. Starting at the Muddy River, located some

23 miles (37 kilometers) due north of the Mount McKinley summit, the pack traveled at least 39 miles (62 kilometers) north to within 7 miles (11 kilometers) of Bearpaw Mountain. They covered a minimum of 58 miles (93 kilometers) during that trip, and from February 17–18 alone traveled at least 14 miles (24 kilometers). They finally killed a moose on February 20.

## Hunting

To an uninitiated observer watching wolves traveling over the landscape in winter or summer, it may not look like they are hunting. Generally they tend to follow various natural routes like river bars, ridge tops, and game trails. Roads will do too, especially at night, when vehicles are less frequent, and in winter in Denali, when vehicles do not use the park road for more than 6 months. The pack tends to travel single file, more so in winter, when this way of travel promotes efficient wading through snow, but also in summer.

Generally, the breeding pair remains in the front of the line, with their offspring following. The adults call the shots by setting the direction and pace, deciding when to rest, and when to attack prey. Often they go miles without encountering prey. Thus, it looks like they are merely off on an outing (figure 5.1).

However, let the wolves catch the scent of prey, and the true nature of their jaunt becomes evident. Sometimes they see their quarry. Or with smaller creatures, an animal may suddenly spring away from them, causing the whole pack to bolt off in a grand rush. Tom Meier's observation of the 13 East Fork Pack wolves chasing snowshoe hares (see chapter 3) comes vividly to mind.

With their usual large prey, the wolves approach much more deliberately. Although no one knows exactly what information they are gathering as they peer intently at their prey, conceivably they are looking for a strategic advantage, "pondering" their next move, or searching for some weakness on the part of the prey.

### Scanning Prey

There is growing evidence that wolves may scan herds and pick out an individual that might be easier to catch. Although this behavior would seem entirely logical, it would be difficult to gather enough evidence to document it. Most hunting by wolves has been observed from aircraft, usually fixed-wing types spinning around in circles (Mech 1966a,b; Peterson 1977; Haber 1977). It usually is all a biologist can do to observe and record the basic aspects of the hunt. Even from the ground it is difficult to detect the subtleties of the complex interactions going on between predator and prey (Murie 1944; Crisler 1956; Mech 1966a,b, 1970, 1988a; Haber 1977).

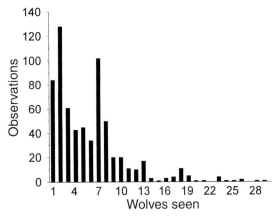

*Figure 5.7. Relative numbers of wolves traveling together in winter*

Nevertheless, an ingenious study in Russia using Borzoi dogs as surrogates for wolves strongly suggested that wolves might actually spot individuals with weaknesses in a prey herd and concentrate on chasing them. Because it is easier to repeatedly observe dog behavior in hunting prey, the researchers turned dogs loose on a herd of saiga antelope (Sokolov et al. 1990).

During each test, the researchers watched the dogs scan the herd and saw that they actually picked out an individual, pursued it, and killed it. Examination of the dog-killed carcasses showed significantly more pathological conditions than in members of the same herd that the scientists collected at random. The dogs were picking out more vulnerable members.

Bolstering the findings of that study was a revealing film taken of wolves in Yellowstone National Park that clearly shows the wolves selecting a limping elk out of a herd, chasing, and killing it (Landis 1995). The wolves at first ran at a speed pacing the herd for a few minutes. Then, suddenly two of them surged forward dramatically after an elk that was slightly but visibly favoring its right hind leg. They continued pursuing that elk through the herd exclusively until after several minutes they caught and killed it.

*Following the Tundra Wolf,* (Peace River Films 1974) showed similar behavior of wolves hunting caribou. However, this film included considerable intercutting of scenes, so the complete sequence was not necessarily as depicted and not in real time, whereas the Landis film was complete with no stopping or intercutting.

## Hunting Caribou

John Burch made an aerial observation in Denali near the confluence of the Savage River and the Teklanika River on March 15, 1990, that shows a possible example of the selection process just described. Although we have no way of knowing whether the target animal was defective, this observation does show how wolves home in on a single, deviant individual:

> A large herd of caribou cows and 10-month-old calves came up over a rise and ran into the resting group of seven Stampede Pack wolves. The caribou scattered into four or five groups with one or two wolves chasing each. The caribou easily outdistanced the wolves.
>
> For some unknown reason a calf split off by itself and ran down a small ridge. A wolf broke off its chase of a group and began pursuing the lone calf. The calf easily outdistanced the wolf until it tried to cross a gully and floundered in the deep snow. While the calf was in the snow, the wolf quickly closed the gap (now distantly followed by another wolf). The calf got through the snow and onto the next small ridge.
>
> Because of the trail the calf had made, the snow in the gully did not slow the wolf down. When both wolf and calf were on good footing again and the wolf was around 10 to 15 yards behind, the calf turned sharply right, and the wolf cut the corner and caught the calf. There was no struggle. The first wolf was quickly joined by the second, and both began feeding. The other five

> wolves remained on top of the ridge, unaware of the kill, and the other caribou were gone.

Denali wolf packs hunting caribou must spend a great deal of time searching scattered groups, then maneuvering and positioning themselves in attempts to catch an individual. Tom Meier was radio-tracking caribou on December 7, 1990, not far from where John had seen the Stampede Pack catch the calf, when he was able to watch a pack of three wolves interact with a caribou herd. Tom described the action:

> The wolves were first seen in passing, as we flew along the crest of the Sushana Hills, radio-tracking caribou. The three wolves were moving south, just cresting the top of the ridge. They turned west, following a well-beaten caribou trail that led along the crest. Hundreds of caribou were moving west along this route. The closest herd consisted of about 120, half a mile ahead of the wolves. The wolves continued west, not gaining on the caribou and not hurrying. At one time the caribou spooked and ran a short distance.
>
> After going about 1.5 miles from where we first saw the wolves, the caribou reached a point where in order to continue west, they would have to descend toward the Sushana River. The heavily beaten caribou trail continued down that way, but the caribou herd stopped, milled about, and then moved back east toward the wolves. The lead wolf went around to the side of the group, eventually getting behind them. The other two wolves remained on the trail and briefly chased the caribou when they got near.
>
> We did not see any contact between wolves and caribou. The wolves separated the caribou several times, but they quickly regrouped and continued east. The smallest wolf, which traveled last in line, at one time

appeared to hesitate when several caribou were headed right toward it.

The wolves continued west along the caribou trail down to the Sushana River, then followed the river upstream for 1.5 miles. They ignored five caribou on a bench covered with deep snow on the west side of the river (may not have seen them although they passed within 80 yards). The wolves approached three moose on the river bar, but were rebuffed. We then left to continue radio-tracking caribou.

When wolves finally make a kill or perhaps multiple kills, they may remain for days to feed (plate 10). Meanwhile the caribou move off long distances, and thus the wolves must also travel far and wide searching for them again.

Our radio-collared packs succeeded in killing caribou about 15% of the times they tried while we were tracking them (table 5.1). Of all the caribou the wolves encountered while we watched, they only killed 1% of them. These figures might overestimate successes because of the way we obtained them. We did not routinely follow the wolves while they were hunting; rather our hunting-success figures are based on encounters we saw while homing in on the wolves. Since successful attacks would be more prolonged than failures, we would have been more likely to come upon the wolves during successes.

### Hunting Dall Sheep

In hunting Dall sheep, the wolves course through the mountains, first trying to locate their quarry, then maneuvering to try to catch them along the steep slopes and amidst the pinnacles, where sheep can take refuge. Mile after mile, sooner or later, the wolves find, chase, catch, and kill one or more of them (Murie 1944).

Because of the steepness of the terrain in which sheep escape, it is risky for wolves to pursue them (plate 11). An incident that John Burch ob-

**Table 5.1.** Hunting success rate for Denali wolves[a]

| Prey | Number | | | Success rate | |
|------|--------|------|-------|--------------|--------------|
| | Hunts | Prey | Kills | Based on hunts | Based on prey |
| Moose | 37 | 53 | 7[b] | 19%–38%[b] | 13%–26%[b] |
| Caribou | 26 | 303 | 4[c] | 15% | 1% |
| Sheep | 18 | 186 | 6 | 33% | 3% |

[a] May be biased toward higher successes because successes are more prolonged than failures and thus present a greater chance of being encountered when "spot" tracking wolves rather than following them.

[b] The wolves also wounded 7 moose, which may have died later. Higher figures given for the success rate assume all the wounded moose died.

[c] Of the 4 kills, 3 were newborn calves killed in May.

served illustrates the problem. On April 14, 1989, at noon, while radio-tracking wolves from a Super Cub, pilot Don Glaser and John located eight East Fork wolves 5 miles (8 kilometers) west of Teklanika Campground. The wolves had just consumed an adult Dall sheep and had a lamb cornered on a rock precipice. One or two wolves made several attempts to shinny down a steeply slanting rock toward the lamb, but could come only to within about a half yard or so without sliding off the edge and over a steep cliff.

After about 5 minutes of this activity, a noncollared, light-gray wolf climbed up to the rock and without hesitation shinnied down and fell over the cliff, bouncing once and landing in a boulder field 15 feet (5 meters) farther down the slope. The lamb moved partly up the slanting rock to evade the light-gray wolf and in turn came within range of the other wolves.

One of the wolves grabbed the lamb and pulled it up the rock to the other four, and all five immediately began feeding. Within 3 minutes the lamb was nearly gone, and each wolf was off by itself chewing on its own piece. (The rest of the pack were still feeding on the remains of the first sheep.) After the light-gray wolf fell, it arose and walked very slowly away with its head down, obviously stunned but with no visible injury. It walked over to the remains of the adult sheep and joined the two other wolves.

On investigation of the kill site 2 weeks later from the ground, John found that the first sheep was a 7-year-old ewe, presumably the mother of the lamb. She had moderate jaw necrosis and 17% marrow fat, indicative of near starvation. Hair, stomach contents, and a few small bone fragments were all that remained of the lamb.

John measured the distance the wolf had fallen by dangling a rock with a string over the cliff until it touched the steep slope below. The height of the cliff was approximately 50 feet (15 meters). He found no blood or hair where the wolf landed. From observing the area it seemed that the wolf should have been killed outright, or at least should have shown some visible sign of injury; however, this was not the case. The identity of the light-gray wolf was never certain, but its color was consistent with that of the breeding female.

On several other occasions, Tom Meier and John Burch saw a group of sheep huddling on a rock formation where there was not room for all of them to find a safe spot. Thus, there would be some disadvantage to sheep in large groups because of competition for safe ledges, an interesting contrast to the dynamics of caribou herding.

Our radio-collared packs succeeded in killing sheep about a third of the times they tried (table 5.1), although as indicated earlier, this figure might overrepresent successes.

### Hunting Moose

Moose are one of the wolf's most formidable prey animals, quite capable of killing wolves (Mech 1970; Mech and Nelson 1990a; Weaver et al. 1992). When hunting moose, the problem wolves face is probably not so much finding them as it is testing them and trying to locate one that is vulnerable and can be killed safely. Moose are generally more sedentary than caribou, and thus each

pack probably knows where to find most of the moose in its territory. Chances are even good that they know at least certain of them individually.

However, because moose vulnerability changes throughout the year (see chapter 6), the wolves must stop in on each one and test it periodically until they find one they can kill (Mech 1966a; Peterson 1977; Haber 1977). This activity again takes constant traveling, interrupted only for rest, sleep, and feeding. Although we did not follow the Denali wolves on their moose hunts for very long distances, information from Isle Royale provides insight into the wolves' winter travel routine:

> During 31 days, from February 4 to March 7, 1960, when the entire route of the 16 wolves was known, the animals traveled approximately 277 miles, or 9 miles per day. However, during 22 of those days the wolves fed on kills, and no extensive movement occurred. Thus, in 9 days of actual traveling, the animals averaged 31 miles per day. During the entire study, the longest distance known to have been traveled in 24 hours was approximately 45 miles. (Mech 1966a, 51)

When wolves do find moose, they seem to check each one they come to, sometimes surrounding it for up to 5 minutes (Mech 1966a). Possibly they are testing its pugnaciousness if it continues to stand off the wolves. If it runs upon approach of the wolves or after they confront it, the wolves pursue and attempt to attack it. Even when running, however, moose are formidable and strike at the wolves with both front and hind hooves. Thus, in other studies wolves generally killed less than 10% of the moose they encountered during winter (Mech 1966a; Peterson 1977; Haber 1977).

Denali wolves killed 13% to 26% of the moose they attacked during our study, depending on whether those they wounded eventually died

*Figure 5.8. Even a single wolf can sometimes kill a moose, although it might take several days. (Photo by Thomas J. Meier.)*

(table 5.1). These figures also could be upwardly biased for reasons mentioned earlier.

Sometimes wolves wound a moose but cannot kill it (Mech 1966a; Peterson 1977; Haber 1977), and in Denali our radio-collared packs wounded as many moose as they killed during our surveillance of them (table 5.1). After wounding a moose but being unable to finish it off right away, either the wolves abandon it and at least sometimes return for it (Mech 1966a), or they may remain with it for a long time. Although this situation happens even with large packs, it is probably especially characteristic of attempts involving single wolves.

Our radio-collared breeding male (221) of the East Fork Pack (some 6 to 8 years old) took more than 36 hours to finish off a moose in summer 1987 (figure 5.8). Several park visitors observed the first part of the encounter and reported it to us so we could follow up.

The attack took place on July 9 and 10, 1987, along the main channel of the Teklanika River in the eastern part of the park. The moose was a small yearling male as indicated by its antler growth and tooth-eruption pattern.

A photographer first saw the attack at about 10:15 A.M. on July 9 and thought that the moose had also been attacked earlier. The wolf attacked again between 11:00 and 11:30 A.M. During each assault, it tended to bite at the lower hind legs, haunches, flanks, nose, and throat of the moose.

Observers watched continually from July 9 until the wolf killed the moose at 10:30 P.M. on July 10. For the first 11 hours, the moose stood in the main current of the river while the wolf rested on shore a couple yards from the water. After the third attack, a wound appeared on the moose's left hindquarter about 12 inches (30 centimeters) below his anus; this leg appeared stiff, and the moose favored it. At 7:11 p.m. the moose left the river for the first time and lay down on the bank. At 7:45 P.M. the wolf attacked for the seventh time, and the moose retreated into the river. In the deeper water, the wolf would lose its footing and could only cling to the moose. The wolf would soon let go and swim to shore. The moose would then head to the opposite shore and rest. The moose repeated this maneuver at least six times, and retreating into deep water appeared to be his main defense.

Throughout the first day, the wolf limped on its left front foot, and at times would not use it at all. On the morning of July 10, the foot appeared swollen and bloody, and the wolf frequently ran on three legs. At times, however, he used his injured foot normally.

The moose vigorously resisted attack during the first day, stomping and kicking at the wolf, occasionally pushing it under water. Observers thought the wolf must have been injured. However, except for his front foot, no obvious injury was seen. Throughout the second day, the moose failed to fight the wolf but simply entered the water and dragged the wolf upstream into the current.

At 10:15 P.M. on July 10, the wolf was not in sight. The moose stumbled into the water on his own, fell down, and was swept away while holding his head out of the water. He washed up on a gravel bar 100 yards (meters) downstream. The wolf appeared out of the brush, walking on three legs, and attacked, tearing at an existing wound on the moose's right flank. The wolf made no apparent attempt to kill the animal but simply began feeding.

After about 5 minutes of feeding, the moose's head sank in the water, and it probably drowned. The wolf continued to feed for a few minutes and in doing so tugged the carcass into the current. The carcass swept downstream and out of sight. The wolf crossed the river and walked slowly downstream, out of sight, using all four feet.

The following day, July 11, the carcass lay about 1 mile (1.6 kilometers) downstream, and 221's signal was about a half mile (0.8 kilometers) to the southwest. Approximately 5 to 10 pounds (2-5 kilograms) of viscera and meat, including both kidneys had been eaten. By 5:00 P.M., three wolves were feeding on the carcass.

The wolf had attacked at the Achilles tendon at least three times, although it did not appear to concentrate there. Perhaps an observation like this could account for the idea that wolves "hamstring" their prey (Young and Goldman 1944). The Achilles tendons did show bite marks, but the skin there was not broken. There were many other bite marks where the hair was scraped off but the skin was unbroken. Under the skin on those bite marks, however, the muscles were crushed and bruised, appearing like red jelly. The moose appeared small for a yearling (estimated at 350–400 pounds, or 160–180 kilograms). It had little, if any, internal or subcutaneous body fat, and the fat content of femur marrow was 33%, indicative of malnutrition.

After wolves finally kill a moose, they usually spend longer feeding on it than on other prey because of its larger size. Denali wolf packs of three to nine members spent up to 3 to 4 days feeding, sleeping, and resting around adult moose kills, similar to wolves in other areas (Mech 1966a; Peterson 1977; Haber 1977).

### Hunting Moose Calves

The type of moose that wolves kill most frequently year-round are calves (see chapter 6). Being smaller, calves are easier to kill. During their first year, which generally is about the only time they are vulnerable, they weigh from 25 to 400 pounds (10–185 kilograms). Like most newborns, they are somewhat fragile during their first few days of life.

Contrary to the young of such speedier animals as deer and caribou, however, moose calves are highly dependent for their protection on their mother for much of their first year. Caribou calves and Dall sheep lambs, in contrast, must be nimble and fleet even in their first few weeks just to keep up with their dams as they themselves struggle to evade, avoid, or escape wolves.

On the other hand, moose calves have a formidable ally in their mother. Cow moose are so powerful and aggressive in their defense of their calves that wolves often give up, go on, and seek safer sustenance. When wolves approach, moose calves

*Figure 5.9. The best defense for a moose calf is to remain as close as possible to its mother, which aggressively fights off wolves. (Photo by Layne G. Adams.)*

stick as close as possible to their mother as she charges the wolves and lashes at them with her front hooves. The wolves try to dash in and grab the calf if only for an instant, trying to wound it or grab it away from the cow. The younger the calf, of course, the easier it is for the wolves to disable it. As predator and prey maneuver during the life-or-death contest, it may be difficult for the calf to remain close enough to its mother (figure 5.9).

Moose cows can produce single calves or twins, depending on their nutritional state. The percentage of twin calves varies considerably over the years and in different areas. At some times and places, more than 28% of cows produce twins, whereas at other times and places no twins are born (Pimlott 1959). In Denali, the percentage of moose cows with twin calves in samples of 260, 168, and 529 cows during autumn of 1986, 1987, and 1991 averaged 1.8% (Meier 1987; Meier et al. 1991; Dalle-Molle 1987). By the time of the survey, many calves would already have been lost, so twin births could have been much higher.

Twin calves, while an obvious reproductive advantage, are much harder for the cow to protect.

Thus, by the end of a year, few cows retain both calves. It may seem, then, that there is no value in producing twins. However, having twins may increase the chance that at least one of a cow's calves will survive through the year.

Unlike predation on caribou calves, predation on moose calves continues year-round. Except after winters of extreme snowfall, most caribou calves are safe from wolves if they survive their first month (see chapter 7). Because moose calves are usually vulnerable throughout their first year, wolves get multiple opportunities to attack them. This may mean that chance plays a greater role in moose-calf vulnerability than it does with caribou calves.

Since the main defense for moose calves is their mother's fighting off the wolves, rather than outrunning or outlasting them like caribou calves, circumstances sometimes prevent a moose calf from remaining close enough to its cow during the maneuvering, and it is killed. The age or condition of the cow may have some bearing on the outcome. However, even in autumn when cows are in their best condition of the year, wolves still kill calves.

Moose calves grow quickly, and as they develop, no doubt they become harder and harder for wolves to kill. On the other hand, as they grow, it is increasingly difficult for them to huddle close enough to the cow. Eventually, they grow large enough that their usual defense is to run ahead of the cow as the wolves chase (Mech 1966a). The cow then tends to remain as close to the rump of the calf as she can, striking out at any wolf that tries to attack the calf's rear end. By that age the calf can kick powerfully itself with its front legs; it is the calf's rump that is most vulnerable, and the cow protects that with her front hooves.

It would seem that groups of wolves would have a greater advantage in trying to maneuver around a cow and calf than would a single wolf or pair. However, no data are available on this subject, and generally groups of wolves tend to obtain less food per wolf than do singles and pairs, both for moose (Thurber and Peterson 1993) and for prey in general (Hayes 1995; Schmidt and Mech 1997).

## Defensiveness of Moose Cows

The protectiveness a moose cow exhibits toward her calf would be difficult to exaggerate. Not only does she fight off wolves fiercely (and sometimes hapless humans who accidentally stumble on the pair), but she sometimes continues her defense even after it is too late. In previous reports, some moose cows had been known to protect their dead calves against wolves for up to 48 hours (Allen 1979). In Denali, however, we recorded the most extreme example of this by far, and it is worth describing. The observation was made on February 9–18, 1987, in the headwaters of the Windy Creek drainage 8 miles (13 kilometers) northeast of the town of Cantwell.

On February 9, 1987, at approximately 10:00 A.M., park ranger Norm Simons and his pilot spotted a cow moose defending her two dead calves from four wolves. The calf carcasses were intact with no obvious wounds, and were lying back to back with the cow standing over them.

The next day our pilot saw three wolves nearby but not harassing the cow, and the cow was fending off several ravens from her calves.

On February 11, the wolves were about 1 mile (3 kilometers) upstream of the cow and her two calves. Burch, Meier, and Simons flew in by helicopter and darted and radio-collared two of the seven wolves nearby. They hazed the cow away from her calves, first unsuccessfully with cracker rounds from a shotgun, and then successfully with the helicopter itself, and examined the carcasses.

The two calf carcasses were females; they appeared to have bled to death from wounds by the wolves. Both had bled from bites around the anus, and one had bled from wounds on the neck and the other from wounds to its lower lip. The men collected various specimens and later found that the marrow fat levels of the calves were 65% and 67%, indicating poor condition. After the investigation was completed, the cow returned and continued to defend her calves from the men.

For the next 7 days the two new radio-collared wolves and their companions were located, and the cow and dead calves were checked from the air. On February 12–15, the wolves were not in the immediate vicinity of the cow and were up to 10 miles (16 kilometers) away. The cow, however, stood directly over the calves during February 12, 13, and 14. On the February 15, she was 100 yards (meters) from the calves, and ravens were feeding on them.

On the February 16, six wolves were harassing the cow, which was again standing over her calves and defending them from the wolves. During this observation, the wolves never approached closer than about 70 feet (20 meters) from the cow. The next day, seven wolves were harassing the cow. The cow was standing over one calf facing six wolves while the seventh wolf fed on the other calf behind the cow.

On February 18, the seven wolves were cleaning up the calf carcasses, and the cow was gone. On February 19, the seven wolves were 5 miles (8 kilometers) north of the kill, the calves were completely consumed, and the cow was gone.

Despite such extreme defensiveness by cow moose, wolves do sometimes manage to overcome their defenses and kill the calf. This is probably because the topography, vegetation, and other circumstances during any given encounter are so variable that sooner or later the combination of circumstances will prevent the calf from remaining close enough to its dam to remain protected, as indicated earlier. Also the nutritional condition of a cow changes during the year and may influence her abilities or willingness to defend her offspring. Therefore, the wolves may be able to kill the calf even though they have failed several times in previous months.

The opportunities provided by these varying circumstances are just one more reason wolves keep on the move. Because moose are much more sedentary than caribou, wolves should have little trouble finding each cow-calf pair in their territory. By regularly checking in on them throughout the year, the wolves increase their chances of encountering any given pair when circumstances put them at a disadvantage. This principle probably operates to varying degrees with the wolf's other prey as well. It may just be more obvious with moose cow-calf pairs.

## Wolf Dispersal

Another phase of their life when wolves travel a great deal is during dispersal. Most wolves disperse from the pack in which they were born, usually between the ages of 9 and 36 months (summarized by Gese and Mech 1991). Half the Denali wolves that dispersed did so before the age of 2 years, and another 41% percent between 2 and 3 years of age (figure 2.11).

Dispersal in wolves seems to be a function of both sexual maturation and food competition within the pack. We can infer that maturation is in-

volved, as in many other species (Howard 1960), because the variation in ages at dispersal parallels the variation in ages of sexual maturity. Some wolves begin maturing in their first year (Medjo and Mech 1976), while others remain sexually immature even at 3 years (Mech and Seal 1987).

Food competition plays a role in wolf dispersal in that wolves in food-stressed populations tend to disperse earlier than those where food is more abundant (Messier 1985). What seems to happen is that once new pups are born, the yearlings and older offspring receive less of the food as the adults give preference to feeding the pups. Thus, when food is in relatively short supply, these lower-ranking animals go hungry more often.

These relationships were demonstrated to us dramatically one day when we examined four wolf carcasses from trappers along the northwestern border of the preserve. An adult male wolf and two pups had heavy subcutaneous and internal fat, but the yearling showed no subcutaneous fat and almost no internal fat.

Thus, at some point the 1- to 2-year-old wolves decide to leave the pack to seek food on their own. When food is more abundant, there may be enough for these subordinate wolves, so they can remain in the pack. Nevertheless, as each new litter survives, the pack eventually reaches a size where it becomes food-stressed, and the subordinates then leave.

Denali's East Fork Pack followed this latter trend during 1989 and 1990. Both years experienced deep snow (table 1.1), which made caribou and probably sheep more vulnerable. Thus, the litters from 1988 and 1989 remained with the pack until it reached 29 members in fall 1990 (table 2.2).

Some wolves disperse only short distances, whereas others disperse far. Those that disperse short distances end up in other packs within a few territories of their natal pack as adoptees, or they fill in pack territories that have been vacated by the death of the leaders, or they try to form a new ter-

116

*Figure 5.10. When temporarily sated, wolves often bury their extra food, only to return to it later. (Photo by L. David Mech.)*

ritory wedged in among the existing territorial structure (see chapter 4). Of 18 wolves that dispersed from one pack to another in the study area, 4 later dispersed from the area, 10 others died or were killed, and only 4 (22%) remained in the study area more than 5 years; 1 of them left the area when 5.5 years old.

### Dispersal and Food Shortages

Natural populations of wolves, that is, those not harvested significantly by humans, tend to reach population levels as high as their prey will support. As already discussed, the amount of prey available to wolves varies constantly. The amount depends not only on the number of various prey but, more importantly, on the vulnerability of various prey

(see chapter 6). Because prey vulnerability varies constantly, wolf populations possess several adaptations that help buffer the variation: (1) storing fat, (2) caching food, (3) scavenging, (4) varying litter size, and (5) dispersing.

By storing fat individual wolves can buffer temporary reductions in prey availability or vulnerability, for they can go weeks and possibly months without eating (Mech 1970). The weight of a given wolf can vary by at least as much as 19% (Mech et al. 1984), an indication of the amount of fat it can store.

A similar kind of buffering involves caching food. Wolves cache food when in abundance, and dig up the caches when they need them (figure 5.10). Denali wolves often cached part or all of newborn caribou calves (see chapter 7). Some evidence indicates that wolves may feed on caches even a year old (Mech, in preparation).

Scavenging animals found dead from other causes such as starvation, fighting during the rut, accidents, or kills by other carnivores such as bears also helps individual wolves sustain themselves over periods when prey are less vulnerable. John Burch watched nine wolves of the Highpower Pack snatch pieces of a moose away from a grizzly bear that was killing it on October 11, 1991, some 3 miles (5 kilometers) southeast of Dull Axe Lake. According to John:

> We located the wolves surrounding a bear on what looked to be a dead cow moose. The bear began dragging and rolling the moose over and then the moose began struggling, trying to stand. The bear easily rolled and dragged the moose about 10 to 15 yards into the trees. The whole time the wolves were milling around sometimes approaching the bear to within 10 feet or so. The bear bluff-charged an individual wolf at least twice. The wolves were picking up and eating chunks of the moose that the bear would tear out. When we left, the wolves were leaving the area, the moose appeared dead, and the bear was feeding on it.

Another way wolf populations can adjust to prey availability is through variation in litter size. During this study, average wolf litter size varied from 0.7 to 5.3 per year. Average litter size per pack varied from 1.3 to 7.0 (table 2.3). Within a few months after wolf pups are born, they reach adult size and require as much food as adults, so any reduction in their numbers yields a commensurate reduction in food requirements for the population.

Conceivably direct aggression (see chapter 4) might increase with decreased food and thus be another mechanism of wolf population adjustment. However, we found no relation between

wolf population density in any given year and the rate at which wolves were killed by other wolves (table 2.8).

A final adjustment mechanism in the wolf population is long-distance dispersal. As wolf numbers reach the carrying capacity of their food supply, through annual reproduction, long-distance dispersal becomes a sort of "safety valve." The individuals most prone to disperse, maturing animals 1 to 3 years of age, form as much as 30% of a natural population (Mech 1970).

With the breeders securing enough food for themselves and trying to feed their latest litter as well as possible, any food shortage affects the 1- to 3-year-old wolves the most. Although these maturing wolves themselves are becoming more and more practiced as hunters, any extra food they get they give to their younger siblings, almost as though forced by some social imperative (Murie 1944; Mech 1988a). Furthermore, their parents no doubt usurp whatever food they can that the 1- to 3-year-olds acquire. (This is probably why the 1- to 3-year-olds seldom live independently while still in the pack's territory, although a few of them do as "peripheral" wolves or "biders" [Packard and Mech 1983]).

Most maturing wolves that stay in the territory remain with the pack. Thus, their food supply is continually dominated by the breeding pair. If food competition gets too keen, the subordinate wolves are the first to feel it. They then leave the pack and the territory, and most of them leave the local population (table 2.7).

In a wolf population like Denali's, with negligible human taking of wolves, and some 30% of the animals 1 to 3 years old, there is always considerable potential for dispersal. When because of various circumstances, for example, a severe winter, prey are more vulnerable, the potential dispersers remain with their natal packs longer and take advantage of the abundance of food. The East Fork Pack cited earlier is a good example. When prey is less vulnerable, wolves disperse at a younger age.

Helping a wolf population adjust to its food supply is not really a function of dispersal but rather is more of a side effect. The primary function, of course, is for young wolves to find a space and a mate, and pass their genes on through as many offspring as possible. In addition, dispersal is the primary force behind genetic mixing and outbreeding, as discussed in chapter 4.

### Settling Down

Dispersing wolves are looking for mates and an area with sufficient prey resources (Rothman and Mech 1979). Such an area is either wolf-free or has a low enough wolf density relative to prey numbers that the dispersing wolves can try to "elbow" their way into the existing territorial mosaic and form their own territory (Fritts and Mech 1981). Otherwise, competition would be so great that they might be killed by neighbors (see chapter 4).

When settling a new area, a newly formed pair tends to scent-mark at a much higher rate than do established pairs (Rothman and Mech 1979). If possible, they try to carve out a territory large enough to support not just them but also a litter of offspring. The newly formed Headquarters pair in 1988 used an area of 250 square miles (640 square kilometers), an area as large as the Bearpaw Pack territory, which in 1988 contained 11 members. Eventually, however, the Headquarters Pack increased sevenfold to 14 in fall 1989, and then needed all the space the founding pair had colonized.

Another way in which dispersing wolves settle is to work their way into an existing pack. Little is known about this phenomenon except that usually it is young male wolves that tend to do so (see chapter 4).

### Pack Dispersal

In May 1992, we observed a phenomenon reported only once before for wolves (Ballard et al.

1983). Half the Little Bear Pack dispersed together, and luckily we were busily flying daily for the caribou research (see chapter 7) and were able to track them as they left the study area (figure 3.8). The previous autumn, the Little Bear Pack contained 23 wolves, but over the 1991–92 winter they split roughly into two. All 4 radio-collared wolves, all yearlings or 2-year-olds at the time, ended up in the same group after the split. They continued to use much of the range of the large original pack for the remainder of the winter. On May 19, we located 11 of these wolves, including radio-collared male 459 and females 433 and 435, west of Wonder Lake and outside their territory. We found them several times over the next week as they dispersed together to the southwest. During that time, they left the park, after traveling about 60 miles (100 kilometers) and crossing the territories of two other study packs. In fact, on May 23, they killed a radio-collared member of the McLeod Lake Pack well within its territory.

On June 11, we located the dispersing pack still together and another 100 miles (160 kilometers) farther south, having crossed the Alaska Range in the vicinity of Rainy Pass. Over the next couple of months, we were able to find these wolves only a few times because of the great distance they covered, but male 459 and female 435 appeared to settle in the upper tributaries of the South Fork of the Kuskowim River and in the adjacent Happy River drainage, some 150 miles (240 kilometers) from their home territory (figure 3.8). We last found female 433 on June 16 despite a wide search in July. Female 435 was killed near Styx Lake in January 1994 by a land-and-shoot hunter.

The remaining radio-collared Little Bear wolf that did not accompany the dispersing pack was female 457. However, she also dispersed but did so alone. On June 5, 1992, we found her in the middle of the McLeod Lake territory, the same direction that her dispersing packmates had taken earlier. That was the last time we heard her signal.

The behavior of the dispersing Little Bear Pack was similar to the dispersal of 2, and probably 4, members of a pack of 12 wolves from the Nelchina Basin, south of Denali. These wolves dispersed some 440 miles (732 kilometers) to northeastern Alaska (Ballard et al. 1983).

Both these observations bring to mind the behavior of the Dillinger River Pack of 10 that we radio-tagged in February 1987 along the Foraker River in the west end of Denali (see chapter 3). Within a day after we started studying it, the pack had moved southward, then southwestward out of the park, and we last saw it near the town of Farewell, some 100 miles (160 kilometers) away from where we had found it. Six months later, the radio-collared animal was heard in mortality mode near Lime Village, some 200 miles (320 kilometers) from his capture site.

Conceivably, the behavior of all these packs was similar to that of Burkholder's (1959) pack discussed in chapter 4. Over a period of 6 weeks, that pack of 10 covered an area of approximately 100 miles (160 kilometers) by 50 miles (80 kilometers) and an estimated 700 miles (1,120 kilometers) of lineal distance.

Despite the radio-tagging of about 200 wolf packs in Alaska and the adjacent Yukon Territories (Stephenson et al. 1995), the only packs that have been observed to behave anything like Burkholder's were the Little Bear Pack and the Dillinger River Pack from Denali and the pack reported by Ballard et al. (1983). Unfortunately, we were unable to monitor either of our two packs often enough to determine how similar their movements were to those of Burkholder's pack.

It should be clear from this discussion that wolves and long travel are almost synonymous. Whether it be in dispersing to found a new pack or merely traveling around their own territory, Denali wolves are ever on the go. Ultimately, most wolf travel is dedicated to obtaining food, a process that requires considerable and repeated scanning of their environment. When next we examine the characteristics of the food the wolves eat, it will become even more apparent why travel is so critical to the creatures.

# Patterns of Prey Selection

February 27, 1988, 0902; about 8 mi NE of Park Headquarters. Adult male wolf 980 and at least 3 other Ewe Creek pack wolves had 1 young ram cornered on an isolated outcrop high above Moody Creek; wolves able to move above, below and beside safe area. Sheep several times moved to another spot, and wolves would nearly catch it. Situation remained the same through 3 visits with the plane during next 3 hr.; T. Meier et al.

October 10, 1988, 0940; 2.5 mi E. Savage R. campground. Headquarters Pack of 7 was testing a moose cow, calf, and bull. Cow stood behind the calf and between calf and wolves; bull between cow-calf and wolves. Bull appeared to defend the cow-calf pair from wolves. The wolves just milled around for 10 min, then left; J. Burch.

February 15, 1989, 1200; 4 mi SSE Divide Mt. The 18 East Fork Pack wolves had cornered 7 sheep on some rocks down near the bed of the East Branch of the Toklat. There were 5 wolves in one spot and 2 alone on ledges. All the wolves were concentrating on the 1 most vulnerable sheep, and had it surrounded but could not get to it. Most of the sheep were large rams; the one the wolves were after was young or a ewe. Returned on the 19th—no sign of kill; T. Meier.

May 17, 1989, 1720; 4 mi SW McLeod L. We had been following yearling male 365 from the McLeod L. Pack from 1720 to 1951. He sneaked to within about 40 ft of 2 caribou cows and a calf, all lying, and then rushed them. He went directly to the calf and killed it; D. Mech.

These excerpts from field accounts of Denali wolves hunting show the variety of hunting situations the wolves face. As described in chapter 5, each pack travels far and wide around its territory, searching for whatever prey it can catch and kill. Denali supports a wide variety of prey, each of which has its own characteristics.

Defensive traits of moose, caribou, and Dall sheep, and of male, female, and the young of each of these species differ markedly. Wolves that can learn how best to contend with each will have the

**Table 6.1.** Summer diet of Denali wolves based on scats collected around dens and rendezvous sites, 1986–90

| | | Contents[a] | | | | | | |
|---|---|---|---|---|---|---|---|---|
| | | Moose | | Caribou | | | | |
| Scats | Sites | Adult | Calf | Adult | Calf | Sheep | Beaver | Other[b] |
| 1,677 | 27 | 254 (15) | 198 (12) | 291 (17) | 310 (19) | 26 (2) | 239 (14) | 359 (21) |

[a] Based on number (percentage) of scats containing each item.
[b] Includes ground squirrels (4%), snowshoe hares (3%), birds (3%), marmot (2%), and miscellaneous.

greatest chance of surviving and reproducing. We sought to learn which classes of this wide variety of prey Denali wolves were catching.

From other areas and times, we know that wolves tend to prey on young and older animals and those in poor condition (Murie 1944; Mech 1966a, 1970; Pimlott et al. 1969; Mech and Frenzel 1971; Mech and Karns 1977; Haber 1977; Peterson 1977; Fritts and Mech 1981; Peterson et al. 1984; Ballard et al. 1987; Carbyn et al. 1993). However, most studies documenting these patterns were conducted where there was one primary prey species. In addition, several studies involved both wolves and prey that were also subject to human harvest. In Denali, we were able to examine patterns of selection by wolves on three species of ungulate prey from a system in which neither wolves nor prey were harvested significantly.

Wolves will eat any kind of animal they can catch (Mech 1970), and as indicated earlier, Denali wolves had a wide variety of prey available to them, including smaller animals (see chapter 1). During summer, when prey variety was greatest and the wolves traveled singly most often (see chapter 5), they tended to feed on a greater variety, including several smaller mammals (table 6.1).

In terms of species eaten, the only substantial addition to the summer diet of Denali wolves in general was beaver. The food habits of individual wolves, however, vary considerably. Some wolves may temporarily specialize in catching certain small prey when they are especially available. For

example, in Denali some wolves patrolled the park road during summer, catching ground squirrels.

Nevertheless, even in summer, the majority of the Denali wolf's diet consisted of hoofed prey (table 6.1). This finding is similar to that of other studies and is further evidence that the wolf's niche is that of a hunter of large mammals (Mech 1970).

## Analyzing the Wolf-Kill Data

The main data we gathered on prey killed by Denali wolves were based on the kill remains at which we found our radio-collared wolves when we homed in on them (see chapter 2). However, our intermittent sampling of wolf locations would tend to bias our results toward locating the largest prey, which provide more food and occupy wolves longer (figure 6.1). Therefore, we used two approaches to analyzing our kill data for determining the proportions of moose, caribou, and sheep killed.

First, we examined the observed data directly. Second, we assumed that the time wolves spent on a given age, sex, and species of prey was directly proportional to the weight of that class of prey; we thus adjusted the relative proportions of kill classes accordingly. We did this by dividing the observed number of each age, sex, and species of prey by the relative assumed weight of each prey class to arrive at an adjusted proportion of each kill class. For example, assuming bull moose weigh four times as much as caribou cows, we divided the number of

**Figure 6.1.** *Wolf-killed moose remains are the easiest to find of all prey remains because they are so large and because the wolves remain there longer. (Photo by L. David Mech.)*

**Figure 6.2.** *Wolves often leave few calf remains, so they are much harder to find than remains of adults. (Photo by L. David Mech.)*

bull moose by four. This approach should provide a reasonable estimate of the proportion of different prey classes killed by Denali wolves.

Most of our packs killed both moose and caribou (table 3.1), but our tallies of kills found with the radio-collared packs were probably not a representative sample of the kills made by these packs for several reasons: (1) flying efforts were not distributed evenly over the year or the packs, (2) wolves spend more time at the kills of larger animals, and (3) larger and darker-haired kills such as moose are more visible and identifiable from the air.

Our sample sizes of prey-remains data varied for each type of data we analyzed because not all types of data could be collected from every kill or prey carcass found. For example, some remains lacked leg bones from which we could sample marrow fat.

We performed two analyses of the monthly kill proportions because of strong bias during summer against finding calf kills (figure 6.2) and because we tended to locate certain packs more often than others. In one year-round analysis we excluded calves, and in another, for October through April, we included calves.

**Table 6.2.** Composition of prey (unadjusted for weight) killed by wolves or probably killed by wolves in Denali, October–April

| Species | 1985–86 n | % | 1986–87 n | % | 1987–88 n | % | 1988–89 n | % | 1989–90 n | % | 1990–91 n | % | 1991–92 n | % | Total n | % |
|---|---|---|---|---|---|---|---|---|---|---|---|---|---|---|---|---|
| Moose | | | | | | | | | | | | | | | | |
| bulls | 1 | 14 | 9 | 24 | 4 | 10 | 14 | 18 | 3 | 5 | – | – | 1 | 6 | 32 | 11 |
| cows | 3 | 43 | 14 | 37 | 12 | 30 | 14 | 18 | 3 | 5 | 6 | 14 | 5 | 28 | 57 | 20 |
| calves | 2 | 29 | 6 | 16 | 10 | 25 | 14 | 18 | 6 | 11 | 9 | 21 | 4 | 22 | 51 | 18 |
| sum | 6 | 86 | 29 | 77 | 26 | 65 | 42 | 54 | 12 | 21 | 15 | 35 | 10 | 56 | 140 | 49 |
| Caribou | | | | | | | | | | | | | | | | |
| bulls | 1 | 14 | 4 | 11 | 4 | 10 | 18 | 23 | 10 | 18 | 9 | 21 | 5 | 28 | 51 | 18 |
| cows | – | – | 2 | 5 | 3 | 8 | 5 | 6 | 16 | 28 | 16 | 37 | 1 | 6 | 43 | 15 |
| calves | – | – | – | – | – | – | – | – | 10 | 18 | 2 | 5 | 1 | 6 | 13 | 5 |
| sum | 1 | 14 | 6 | 16 | 7 | 18 | 23 | 29 | 36 | 64 | 27 | 63 | 7 | 40 | 107 | 38 |
| Sheep | | | | | | | | | | | | | | | | |
| rams | – | – | – | – | 5 | 13 | 6 | 8 | 6 | 11 | – | – | – | – | 17 | 6 |
| ewes | – | – | 3 | 8 | 1 | 3 | 6 | 8 | 3 | 5 | 1 | 2 | – | – | 14 | 5 |
| lambs | – | – | – | – | 1 | 3 | 1 | 1 | – | – | – | – | 1 | 6 | 3 | 1 |
| sum | – | – | 3 | 8 | 7 | 19 | 13 | 17 | 9 | 16 | 1 | 2 | 1 | 6 | 34 | 12 |
| Total | 7 | 100 | 38 | 100 | 40 | 100 | 78 | 100 | 57 | 100 | 43 | 100 | 18 | 100 | 281 | 100 |

*Source: Adapted from Mech et al. 1995.*

To determine if any class of prey was killed disproportionately in any given month, we compared monthly proportions of each prey class against the mean of the monthly proportions of the year-round sample (Mech et al. 1995). We performed this comparison for adults only and for adult-and-calf samples.

Despite the biases, the large sample of kills we examined should provide an adequate representation of such information as age, sex, and condition of prey killed.

## The Wolf-Kill Sample

During 1986–92, we found the remains of 294 moose, 225 caribou, and 63 Dall sheep killed or eaten by wolves. Of these, we considered 245 moose, 221 caribou, and 60 sheep as wolf kills or probable wolf kills (hereafter pooled as "kills"). This was our basic sample from which we examined various subsamples for different analyses. We examined remains of 167 moose, 165 caribou, and 49 sheep from the ground to determine species, age, sex, condition, abnormalities, and cause of death.

Overall, moose represented 49% of the kills found, caribou 38%, and sheep 12% (table 6.2). Because of the biases we discussed in the previous section, this sample probably exaggerates the relative numbers of moose taken and minimizes the proportions of caribou and sheep. However, the proportions may more accurately represent the relative biomass of the three prey species consumed.

We judged that about 15% of all moose eaten by wolves (about 40% of the bulls and 9% of cows and calves) were scavenged, so we did not include them in the kill sample. Haber (1977) also found that Denali wolves scavenged considerably on bull moose.

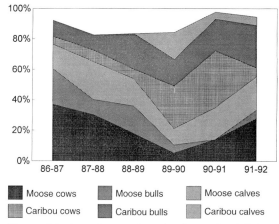

*Figure 6.3. Annual proportions of each prey class killed by wolves or probably killed by wolves in Denali, October–April, 1986–92. (Mech et al. 1995)*

## Annual and Monthly Variation in Prey Proportions

The composition of wolf kills in Denali varied by both year and by month. Moose formed the largest percentage of the sample during the first 4 years of the study, but caribou predominated in winters of 1989–90 and 1990–91 (table 6.2; figure 6.3). As caribou kills increased, actual numbers of both moose and sheep kills decreased. This trend held true both for the proportions of kills in our sample and for the proportions derived after adjustment for weight.

On a monthly basis, our total sample of kills suggested that Denali wolves tended to kill moose calves year-round, newborn caribou calves in May and June each year, older calves in March and April during 1990–92 only, caribou bulls year-round but primarily in July through November, bull moose year-round but primarily in November and December, caribou cows primarily from February through June, cow moose from October through May, and sheep primarily during September through April and especially in December (table 6.3; figure 6.4). Some of these trends could have

resulted from sampling error or bias, but we believe most of them are real.

Wolves took significantly more moose from November through February, more caribou cows and calves in March, and more sheep in December. On a monthly basis, the proportion of caribou (plate 5) taken during August through October did not differ significantly from that of other months (table 6.3). However, bull caribou taken during these months formed the most predominant prey type for any single period of the year (figure 6.4).

The wolves' seasonal concentration on killing various classes of prey was sometimes quite dramatic. For example, on February 7, 1991, we found the McKinley River Pack of six wolves with a group of 17 fresh caribou kills, 11 miles (18 kilometers) northwest of Kantishna. The kills lay in an area of about a square mile (2.5 square kilometers) of rolling hills and lakes, sparsely to heavily wooded with spruce.

Deep snow (40 inches, or 100 centimeters) had restricted the caribou to traveling in deep, heavily compacted trails. Tracks showed that caribou moving even a few yards off these trails were incapacitated and readily killed by the wolves. There were probably still more kills in the area, unseen because of tree cover or snowfall.

We examined 13 of the kills on February 12. Wolves had consumed an estimated 50% to 95% of each carcass (average, 78%). Tooth marks in muscle showed that the wolves had fed on the carcasses even after they were frozen. By April 16, the McKinley River Pack had again dug up several of these kills and fed on them. In May, the pack used two dens located within 0.7 miles and 1.8 miles (1.1 kilometers and 3.0 kilometers) of these kills.

We found 7 other groups of caribou kills (2–5 kills each) in winter 1990–91, most in forested flatlands with deep snow. They were made by the Highpower, Foraker, Chitsia Mountain, Little Bear, Headquarters, and Reindeer Hill packs.

**Table 6.3.** Frequency of wolf kills or probable wolf kills of moose, caribou, and Dall sheep in Denali, 1986–92

| Species | Jan | Feb | Mar | Apr | May | June | July | Aug | Sep | Oct | Nov | Dec | Total | Weighted mean ($\bar{x}$) % |
|---|---|---|---|---|---|---|---|---|---|---|---|---|---|---|
| | | | | | | | *Adults* | | | | | | | |
| Moose | 10 | 23 | 16 | 11 | 6 | 3 | 0 | 1 | 1 | 10 | 14 | 5 | 100 | 36 |
| Caribou | 1 | 14 | 34 | 14 | 11 | 2 | 2 | 8 | 10 | 20 | 9 | 2 | 127 | 53 |
| Sheep | 1 | 10 | 7 | 2 | 0 | 1 | 0 | 0 | 1 | 3 | 4 | 4 | 33 | 11 |
| P[b] | 0.01 | 0.02 | 0.60 | 0.82 | 0.33 | 0.64 | 0.42 | 0.11 | 0.12 | 0.75 | 0.19 | 0.02 | | |
| | | | | | | | *Adults and Calves*[a] | | | | | | | |
| Moose | 14 | 34 | 30 | 19 | – | – | – | – | – | 16 | 20 | 7 | 140 | 55 |
| Caribou | 1 | 16 | 41 | 17 | – | – | – | – | – | 21 | 9 | 2 | 107 | 32 |
| Sheep | 1 | 11 | 8 | 3 | – | – | – | – | – | 3 | 4 | 4 | 34 | 13 |
| P[b] | 0.05 | 0.59 | 0.03 | 0.37 | – | – | – | – | – | 0.07 | 0.85 | 0.18 | | |

*Source: Adapted from Mech et al. 1995.*

[a] *Data are not given for May through September for the adult and calves part of table because of the strong bias against finding kills of young animals during that period.*

[b] *Probability of no significant difference in proportion of prey species in a given month compared with year-round weighted mean proportion.*

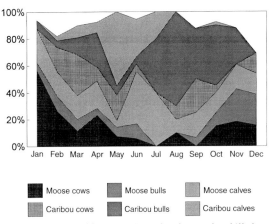

Legend: Moose cows, Moose bulls, Moose calves, Caribou cows, Caribou bulls, Caribou calves

*Figure 6.4. Monthly proportions of each prey class killed by wolves or probably killed by wolves in Denali, 1986–92. (Mech et al. 1995)*

During the previous winter, the McKinley River Pack had also killed a group of 8 caribou near Birch Creek. Ten other groups of 2 to 6 caribou kills were found with the Birch Creek, Foraker, McLeod Lake, Little Bear, and Stampede packs in winter 1989–90.

## Age and Sex Structure of the Kills

Denali wolves killed primarily calves and old moose and caribou (figures 6.5 and 6.6), except during multiple caribou kills (see below). Although our sample of Dall sheep was small, apparently individuals aged 5 years or older were taken disproportionately (figure 6.7). These results parallel those of Murie (1944), Burles and Hoefs (1984), Sumanik (1987), and Hayes et al. (1991) for sheep; Mech (1966a), Peterson (1977), Haber (1977), Fuller and Keith (1980), Peterson et al. (1984), Ballard et al. (1987), Bjorge and Gunson (1989), Hayes et al. (1991), and Gasaway et al. (1992) for moose; and Parker and Luttich (1986) for caribou. Our oldest kills of each species were estimated at 20 years old or younger, 22 years old or younger, and 13 years old or younger for moose, caribou, and sheep, respectively.

Ideally, we would have sampled the Denali

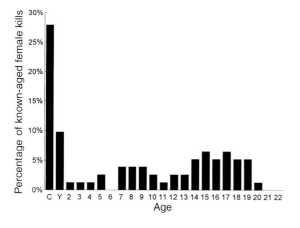

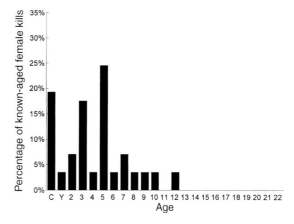

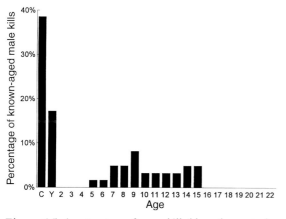

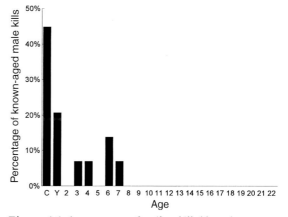

**Figure 6.5.** *Age structure of moose killed by wolves or probably killed by wolves in Denali, October–April, 1986–92; for females and males. (Mech et al. 1995)*

**Figure 6.6.** *Age structure of caribou killed by wolves or probably killed by wolves in Denali, October–April, 1986–92; for females and males. (Mech et al. 1995)*

prey herds to determine their age structure. Then, we could have compared the age structure of the herds to that of the wolf-killed sample, for conceivably the sample merely reflected the age structure of the herds. However, most prey herds consist of a much higher proportion of younger members than we found in our kill.

In fact, a herd with the proportion of old members that our sample had would have been on a very steep decline because of lack of recruitment. Because this was not the case in Denali, we conclude that the old ages of our wolf-killed prey reflect the increased vulnerability of old animals.

Wolves killed cow and bull moose in about the same ratio as they occurred in the population (Meier et al. 1991), but significantly more bull caribou than their proportion in the population (55:100) (Adams et al. 1989). This finding differs from the even sex ratio found by Parker and Luttich (1986) for wolf-killed caribou in Labrador. Samples of the males of each species killed by wolves were younger on average than those of the females (figures 6.5–6.7), although only the male moose and sheep were significantly younger. Ballard et al. (1987) found no significant difference between the sex ratio of wolf-killed caribou and

127

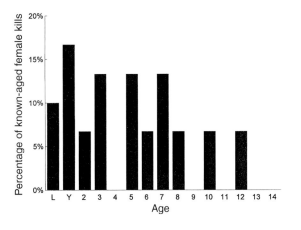

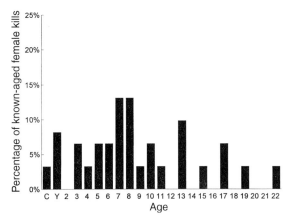

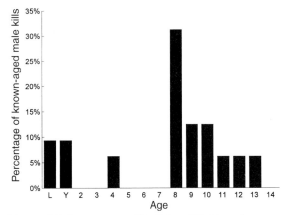

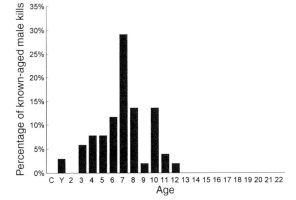

**Figure 6.7.** *Age structure of Dall sheep killed by wolves or probably killed by wolves in Denali, October–April, 1986–92; for females and males. (Mech et al. 1995)*

**Figure 6.8.** *Age structure of caribou killed in multiples; for females and males. (Mech et al. 1995)*

that of caribou surveyed by air in south-central Alaska.

During late winter and spring 1990 and 1991, record amounts of snow fell in Denali (table 1.1), and wolves made several multiple kills of adult caribou. For both males and females, the age distributions of caribou killed during these bouts of mass predation (figure 6.8) were significantly younger than those killed individually and at other times of the year. Contrary to reports from other areas (Kelsall 1957; Eide and Ballard 1982; Miller, Gunn, and Broughton 1985, 1988; Miller, Broughton, and Gunn 1988), Denali wolves re-

turned repeatedly to feed on the frozen carcasses of the multiple kills.

## Nutritional Condition of Wolf-Killed Prey

Ungulates store fat in many locations including the marrow of their long bones. As they lose fat during hard winters when snow makes it difficult to reach food, they use this fat in a regular pattern. The last 2% to 3% of their fat to be used is that in the bone marrow (Dauphine 1971; McCullough and Ullrey 1983). Therefore, if an individual has a low amount of marrow fat, it must be in poor nu-

**Table 6.4.** Mean percent marrow fat of prey killed by wolves or probably killed by wolves in Denali, October–May

| Species | 1985–86 | | 1986–87 | | 1987–88 | | 1988–89 | | 1989–90 | | 1990–91 | |
|---|---|---|---|---|---|---|---|---|---|---|---|---|
| | % (SE) | n | % (SE) | n | % (SE) | n | % (SE) | n | % (SE) | n | % (SE) | n |
| Moose | 58 (10) | 4 | 63 (5) | 30 | 64 (5) | 24 | 71 (4) | 22 | 56 (12) | 8 | 28 (7) | 6 |
| Caribou | 79 (–) | 1 | 48 (13) | 5 | 40 (12) | 6 | 42 (7) | 21 | 59 (5) | 11 | 55 (5) | 20 |
| Sheep | – | – | 93 (–) | 2 | 58 (13) | 5 | 78 (12) | 6 | 88 (–) | 2 | – | – |

*Source: Adapted from Mech et al. 1995.*

**Table 6.5.** Mean percent marrow fat of prey killed by wolves or probably killed by wolves in Denali, 1986–91

| Species | January | | February | | March | | April | | May | | June | |
|---|---|---|---|---|---|---|---|---|---|---|---|---|
| | % (SE) | n | % (SE) | n | % (SE) | n | % (SE) | n | % (SE) | n | % (SE) | n |
| Moose | | | | | | | | | | | | |
| bulls | 58 (–) | 1 | 63 (12) | 6 | 60 (27) | 5 | 62 (–) | 1 | 73 (–) | 2 | 84 (–) | 1 |
| cows | 84 (2) | 7 | 74 (6) | 13 | 62 (24) | 7 | 68 (9) | 6 | 58 (–) | 2 | 74 (–) | 1 |
| calves | 54 (9) | 3 | 67 (5) | 7 | 32 (8) | 10 | 37 (–) | 2 | 10 (–) | 1 | 38 (16) | 3 |
| Caribou | | | | | | | | | | | | |
| bulls | – | – | 33 (12) | 3 | 57 (9) | 9 | 68 (10) | 6 | 52 (–) | 1 | 14 (–) | 1 |
| cows | – | – | 70 (7) | 10 | 62 (6) | 22 | 86 (–) | 1 | 62 (13) | 5 | – | – |
| calves | – | – | 31 (–) | 2 | 45 (7) | 9 | 38 (2 ) | 3 | 21 (2) | 9 | – | – |
| Sheep | | | | | | | | | | | | |
| rams | – | – | 65 (–) | 2 | – | – | 12 (–) | 1 | – | – | – | – |
| ewes | – | – | – | – | 85 (–) | 2 | 56 (–) | 2 | – | – | 20 (–) | 1 |
| lambs | – | – | – | – | – | – | – | – | – | – | – | – |

| Species | July | | August | | September | | October | | November | | December | |
|---|---|---|---|---|---|---|---|---|---|---|---|---|
| | % (SE) | n | % (SE) | n | % (SE) | n | % (SE) | n | % (SE) | n | % (SE) | n |
| Moose | | | | | | | | | | | | |
| bulls | – | – | – | – | – | – | 76 (–) | 2 | 53 (–) | 2 | 41 (15) | 3 |
| cows | – | – | 87 (–) | – | – | – | 69 (6) | 3 | 80 (7) | 4 | 87 (–) | 1 |
| calves | – | – | – | – | 45 | – | 44 (10) | 3 | 52 (–) | 2 | 18 (–) | 2 |
| Caribou | | | | | | | | | | | | |
| bulls | 71 (–) | 1 | 84 (5) | 3 | 85 (2) | 4 | 39 (8) | 12 | 24 (9) | 7 | – | – |
| cows | – | – | 92 (–) | 1 | 85 (1) | 3 | 10 (–) | 1 | – | – | 78 (–) | 1 |
| calves | – | – | – | – | – | – | – | – | – | – | – | – |
| Sheep | | | | | | | | | | | | |
| rams | – | – | – | – | 92 (–) | 1 | – | – | 91 (–) | 2 | 64 (–) | 1 |
| ewes | – | – | – | – | – | – | 90 (–) | 2 | 88 (–) | 1 | 93 (–) | 2 |

*Source: Adapted from Mech et al. 1995.*

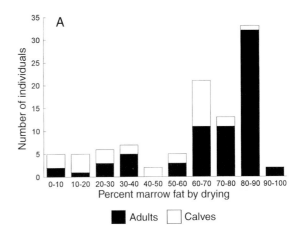

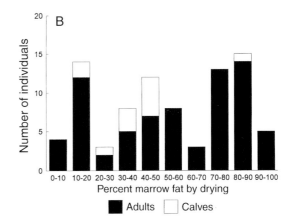

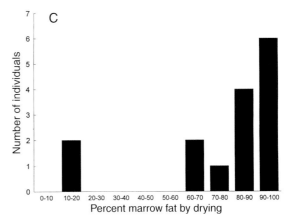

*Figure 6.9. Fat-depleted bone marrow indicating malnu-trition. (Photo by Thomas J. Meier.)*

tritional condition (figure 6.9). If it still has a high amount of marrow fat, it is not necessarily in good condition, for all the rest of its fat could be depleted (Mech and DelGiudice 1985), as will be discussed later. Nevertheless the marrow-fat test is a good one-directional test.

The average marrow-fat content of moose, caribou, and sheep killed by wolves was low during each of the winters (October–April) of the study. Means for moose were lowest in 1990–91 (table 6.4), when snow was deepest (table 1.1). There was less marrow fat in calves of moose and caribou than in adults, less in male caribou during October through May (no January data) than during June through September, and less in bull moose than in cows (table 6.5). Percent marrow fat in 29 caribou killed in multiples during winters of deep snow averaged 66 ± 4% compared with 47 ± 5% for 44 caribou killed individually during all winters. The distribution of marrow fat for each species contained individuals with less than 20% to more than 90% (figure 6.10).

## Skeletal Abnormalities of Wolf-Killed Prey

More than a third of the wolf-killed moose we examined showed necrosis in their jaw ("lumpy jaw," or "mandibular necrosis"), and a third or more had

*Figure 6.10. Percent marrow fat in prey killed by wolves or probably killed by wolves in Denali, October–April, 1986–92; A, moose; B, caribou; C, Dall sheep.*

**Table 6.6.** Incidence of skeletal abnormalities in prey killed by wolves or probably killed by wolves in Denali, October–April, 1986–92

| | Mandibular Necrosis | | Arthritis | |
|---|---|---|---|---|
| | n | Number affected (%) | n | Number affected (%) |
| Dall Sheep | | | | |
| Female | 18 | 8 (44) | 6 | 0 (0) |
| Male | 24 | 13 (54) | 5 | 0 (0) |
| Caribou | | | | |
| Female | 60 | 0 (0) | 43 | 2 (5) |
| Male | 66 | 3 (5) | 52 | 7 (13) |
| Moose | | | | |
| Female | 81 | 29 (36) | 41 | 15 (37) |
| Age 1–13 | – | – | 23 | 0 (0) |
| Age 14–20 | – | – | 18 | 15 (83)[a] |
| Male | 80 | 28 (35) | 52 | 25 (48) |
| Age 1–4 | – | – | 10 | 0 (0) |
| Age 5–15 | – | – | 42 | 25 (60)[a] |

Source: Adapted from Mech et al. 1995.

[a] Different at P = 0.07.

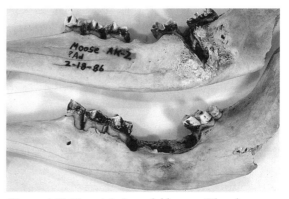

*Figure 6.11. Necrosis in jaws of old moose. (Photo by Thomas J. Meier.)*

*Figure 6.12. Arthritis (left) in moose backbone compared with normal joint. (Photo by Thomas J. Meier.)*

arthritis in their lumbosacral or coxofemoral joints (table 6.6). Similarly, jaw necrosis and arthritis were found in wolf-killed moose on Isle Royale (Peterson 1977); on Kenai Peninsula, Alaska (Peterson et al. 1984); and earlier in Denali (Haber 1977). Arthritis afflicted Denali bull moose as young as 5 years of age, whereas no sign of it was found in cows less than 14 years old (table 6.6).

Our findings contrast with reports that arthritis afflicted moose cows as young as 8 years old on Isle Royale (Peterson 1977) and 6 years old on Kenai Peninsula (Peterson et al. 1984). On Isle Royale, as well as in our study, the incidence of arthritis was higher in male moose (Peterson 1977). This variation may reflect different nutritional histories of individual moose herds (Peterson 1988).

More wolf-killed sheep than moose showed jaw necrosis (table 6.6). Murie (1944) also reported a high rate of necrosis in Denali sheep. We found no arthritis in our small sheep sample, ex-

cept for a severe case in the jaw of a 10-year-old ram where the jaw hinges with the skull. This case nicely illustrated how perilous it is to jump to conclusions about the health or condition of prey killed by wolves. Wolves killed this particular ram within about 50 feet (15 meters) of the road through Denali Park, and one wolf fed on the carcass intermittently all day while the public watched (plate 12). Because the sheep was an old ram with a well-developed, curled set of horns, several people commented on how healthy the creature appeared. Only when we cleaned the skull did the arthritis become apparent, and it appeared quite capable of hindering the ram's ability to chew.

We found less mandibular necrosis (figure 6.11) and arthritis (figure 6.12) in our wolf-killed caribou than in sheep or moose (table 6.6), but the incidence of necrosis in our sample was higher than the incidences reported by Doerr and Dietrich (1979) and others whose work they summarized. Our incidence was higher in male caribou than in females, but not significantly so ($P = 0.14$). Doerr and Dietrich (1979) found significantly more males with necrosis than females.

## Snow and Patterns of Prey Selection

The most striking change in the composition of wolf kills that we saw was the major increase in the proportion and composition of caribou killed beginning the second consecutive winter (1989–90) with above-average snowfall (table 1.1; chapter 7). Although winter 1988–89 was the first year of above-average snowfall during the study, we did not find an increased proportion of wolf-killed caribou cows until 1989–90 and 1990–91 (table 6.2), both of which also had above-average snowfall (table 1.1). This finding may be evidence for a cumulative effect of snowfall on caribou condition (Mech et al. 1987).

The proportion of caribou in observed wolf kills each year, including those we could not sex or age, increased with the snowfall (table 6.2) for that year (Mech et al. 1995). When we examined a subsample of caribou kills that could be sexed and aged and compared them relative to snowfall, the kill of cows varied most with snowfall (figure 6.13). We had not substantially changed the proportion of the time we spent locating various wolf packs or the geographic area of coverage in a way that might account for the switch to caribou during the study.

The occurrence of caribou calves in the sample of winter wolf kills was related to snowfall (table 6.2) during the winter they were *in utero*. Caribou calves were killed by wolves during winters that followed winters of above-average snowfall, whereas no wolf-killed caribou calves were found

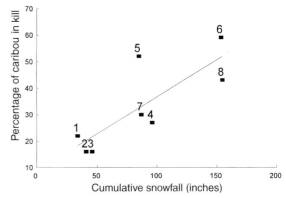

*Figure 6.13. Relationship between snow depth and the proportion of caribou in the total kill of prey by Denali wolves; snow depth accounted for 70% of the variation in proportion of caribou.*

in the winters following a year with below-average snowfall.

This finding parallels the observations of newborn caribou survival in the same herd. Following two winters of below-average snowfall, mortality of calves 30 days old or younger averaged 39%, whereas following three winters of above-average snowfall, the average was 67% (Adams, Dale, and Mech 1995; chapter 7).

We found no corresponding relationship between winter snowfall and the proportion of moose calves killed by wolves. Where moose are the primary prey of wolves, calf vulnerability to wolf predation is related to snowfall (Peterson 1977). In Denali, increased moose calf vulnerability based on snowfall may have been masked by wolves switching to killing more caribou.

## Prey Quality and Understanding Wolf Predation

The Denali wolf-prey system has been minimally affected by human harvesting for two or more decades, unlike most other areas. Thus, our findings should provide a glimpse of the way past wolf-prey systems functioned throughout at least their northern range when only aboriginal people in low densities and with relatively inefficient methods hunted them. The differences between our findings and those of studies elsewhere could be related primarily to the fact that in most other study areas either the wolves, the prey, or both have been harvested or otherwise modified by human activities.

In the Denali system, numbers of moose, caribou, sheep, wolves, bears, and other creatures have been interacting and fluctuating with minimal human disturbance for decades. Caribou increased considerably during the first few years of our study (see chapter 7), a trend that forms an exception to the conclusion that "caribou generally appear unable to survive in areas where there is extensive overlap with wolves and alternate prey species" (Seip 1991, 51).

We do not know the trend in populations of Denali moose and sheep, except that sheep declined regionwide in 1993 (K. Whitten, pers. comm.). Overall, drastic decline was not discernible in either of Denali's moose or sheep populations, and both species remained about as widely distributed as they have been for decades (Haber 1977). A gradual decline in moose was probably under way in the east end of the park during our study, however (V. Van Ballenberghe, pers. comm.).

Except for some of the multiple kills, discussed earlier, wolves consumed their prey as completely as possible, leaving only hair, rumen contents, and bones, most of them chewed. During most of our study, there was no indication, such as incomplete consumption of kills (Pimlott et al. 1969; Mech and Frenzel 1971; Peterson 1977), that weather conditions were especially difficult on prey for prolonged periods.

Under these circumstances, the Denali wolves found enough prey not only to survive and reproduce but to double their numbers (see chapter 8) during a period of widely variable snowfall. They showed a high degree of selectivity in their predation patterns over several different dimensions in

their relationships with prey. The commonality of each dimension, however, was prey vulnerability.

## Vulnerability Factors

Vulnerability took the form of youth, old age, poor condition, and hindrance by snow, and it varied by species, sex, time of year, and snow depth. Calves were especially important prey during summer, when they are weakest; bulls during and after their autumn rut, when they are most stressed nutritionally; and cows in late winter, when snow depth, negative energy balance, and the drain of pregnancy reduce their nutritional state.

Probably the poor nutritional condition of caribou bulls during and after the rut (table 6.4) explains why wolves killed proportionately more bulls than cows. Although cows and calves become more vulnerable primarily during or after winters of above-average snowfall, bulls rut every year. Rutting males are generally in poor nutritional condition due to fighting (figure 6.14) and chasing females rather than feeding (Bergerud 1973; Geist 1974; Clutton-Brock et al. 1982).

Our sample of sheep kills was small and biased. Nevertheless, it is clear that wolves kill sheep year-round, apparently least during summer (table 6.1) and more during late fall (figure 6.4), possibly also a result of the vulnerability of rutting males. Murie (1944) and Haber (1977) also found that sheep were important to wolves in Denali.

As we discussed in our introduction, one of the most salient and important contributions Murie (1944, 123) made involved his analysis of sheep remains. He concluded the following:

> These figures are remarkable because they show that most of the sheep dying belonged to the weak classes. In the absence of predation we would expect the mortality to be distributed among the weak, namely the old, diseased, and the young, but in the presence of a strong predator like the wolf, known to be preying extensively on the

**Figure 6.14.** *Caribou bulls fight and neglect eating during the fall rut and become especially vulnerable to wolves. (Photo by Layne G. Adams.)*

sheep, it is interesting that so few animals in their prime are represented. In the recent material 211 skulls, or 95 percent, were from the weak classes in the population and only 10 skulls, or 5 percent, were from sheep in their prime which were healthy so far as known. The figures for both groups are roughly similar considering the fact that in many cases disease or weakness would not be shown in bony remains.

The same, of course, holds true today. In most cases, we still only had bony remains to examine from the kills. Nevertheless, like Murie, we too found a variety of conditions that probably predisposed the prey to wolf predation.

The incidence of skeletal abnormalities and

other possibly debilitating factors in the general prey population is unknown, and to what degree they contribute to prey vulnerability is open to conjecture. Jaw necrosis can result in abnormal occlusion and tooth loss, and was common in adult moose and sheep taken by wolves. These conditions could greatly affect the condition of creatures that must take hundreds or thousands of bites of food each day.

Arthritis of the lumbosacral joint (between the sacrum and sixth lumbar vertebra) appears to be related to age in moose, severe arthritis being common in animals 15 years and older. Not only might arthritis be indicative of a poor nutritional history (Peterson 1988), but it could also hinder a moose's movements. Because such movements are

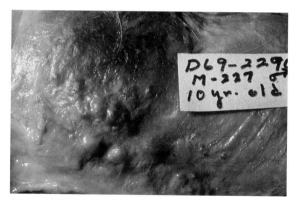

*Figure 6.15. Hydatid tapeworm cysts infect the lungs of most older ungulates and predispose them to predation. We did not find carcasses in Denali intact enough to examine for this parasite. (Photo by L. David Mech.)*

important for a moose to fend off wolves, any hindrance to them could reduce the animal's defense.

Neither we nor other workers have found many skeletal abnormalities in the remains of caribou eaten by wolves, although Murie (1944) mentioned finding jaw necrosis. However, caribou are subject to several parasites that could be important. These include hydatid tapeworm (*Echinococcus granulosis*) cysts (figure 6.15) in their lungs (Crisler 1956), which can reach a size and number capable of severely debilitating an animal (Mech 1966a). These would not have been evident in the bony remains we found of caribou killed by wolves.

Other parasites whose importance to a caribou's defense is unknown but could be great include the warble fly (*Oedemagena tarandi*), whose larvae and pupae live in great numbers under the caribou's skin, and the nostril fly (*Cephanomyia nasalis*), whose larvae load the caribou's nose. Unfortunately, any indications of these parasites are lost when wolves eat the soft tissues, so it is difficult to assess their effect.

Another affliction that may affect caribou but that we found no sign of is injury or disease of the hooves. Crisler (1956, 346) indicated that in an-

other part of Alaska "at least half of the kills that we observed involved crippled or sick caribou, whose incidence is in the neighborhood of 1.8 per cent among stragglers and even lower among the main herds."

The mean ages of female prey animals the wolves killed were older than those of males. Arthritis did not afflict cow moose until much older than bulls, which suggests that the arthritis may have helped predispose older individuals to predation.

### Effects of Deep Snow

Although Denali wolves were able to survive and increase during a year of below-average snowfall, their predation patterns did change during winters of greater snowfall, and their numbers increased dramatically thereafter (see chapter 8). Above-average snowfall in Denali helped predispose the prey, especially caribou, to wolf predation. Deep snow had a direct effect on reducing prey condition and mobility and thus on increasing predation by wolves, as has been found elsewhere (Mech and Frenzel 1971; Mech and Karns 1977; Peterson 1977; Haber 1977; Nelson and Mech 1986b). This fact probably helps explain the multiple kills of younger caribou cows that our wolves made during springs of unusually deep snow.

We also found evidence of an indirect effect of snow depth on caribou calves that had been *in utero* during the periods of unusually deep snow. They were predisposed to wolf predation during the next summer (see chapter 7) and winter (table 6.2), similar to findings in other wolf-prey systems (Mech and Karns 1977; Peterson 1977; Mech et al. 1987, 1991).

### Nutritional Condition and Vulnerability

The most important common denominator predisposing Denali prey to being killed by wolves was probably nutritional condition, indicated by the low marrow fat content (figure 6.10) in all of the prey species, ages, and sexes of our wolf-kill sample (table 6.4). Considering that some individuals must have been predisposed by physical frailties not apparent in the bones, which were usually all that could be examined for most kills (Murie 1944; Mech 1970), and that such animals would not necessarily show low marrow fat (Mech and DelGiudice 1985), the low average percent fat we found is striking. This is especially true given that our values are probably artificially high because of dehydration.

In caribou, femur fat less than 70% indicates an individual whose weight has declined to about its limit (Dauphine 1971), with total body fat less than 5% (Huot and Goudreault 1985). Adult caribou cows in good condition possess 11% to 14% total body fat (Dauphine 1971; Huot and Goudreault 1985), and bulls 31% or more (Dauphine 1971), with marrow fat more than 70%. Starvation has been documented in adult moose at an average marrow fat level of 52% (SE = 15.3) (Ballard et al. 1987).

Nevertheless, there is still confusion, or at least lack of agreement, about the actual meaning of these figures. Several workers believe that marrow fat must reach much lower levels before indicating that an animal is near death. For example, Stephenson and Johnson (1972), Franzmann and Arneson (1976), Peterson et al. (1984), and Hayes et al. (1991) used 20% marrow fat in adults and 10% in calves as indicators of starvation. Although there is value in being conservative, we believe that using such low levels ignores starvation physiology and may lead to erroneous conclusions.

### Starvation Physiology

Ungulate marrow fat less than 70% to 87%, depending on the species, is a direct indicator of low total body fat, but by the time the marrow fat is as low as this threshold, the great majority of body fat has already been lost (Dauphine 1971; Huot and Goudreault 1985; Watkins et al. 1991; Holand 1992).

As ungulates lose fat stores, they also lose protein, or muscle mass (Leibholz 1970; Paquay et al. 1972; Hovell et al. 1987; Torbit et al. 1985; DelGiudice et al. 1990). In adult white-tailed deer, for example, the correlation between weight loss and protein (muscle) loss was 0.91 (DelGiudice et al. 1990).

At maximal work loads, such as when running from wolves, it is muscle glycogen that forms the major source of fuel (Froberg et al. 1971; Hultman and Nilsson 1971), so with less muscle mass, less energy is available. Furthermore, blood glucose, which also is important to a running animal, in starved individuals falls to about one-third of its usual level, and insulin, which fosters glucose use, drops to one-tenth (Smith et al. 1983, 542).

Thus, we believe that marrow-fat percentage should be viewed not so much as a fat indicator but as an indicator of depletion of fat, muscle, and energy, and any level below the threshold indicates an animal in marginal condition. While it certainly is true that some individuals do not actually die until their marrow is almost depleted, loss of vigor and vitality is a matter of degree rather than an all-or-none phenomenon. Additional stressors such as fighting, plowing through snow, or being chased by wolves would probably raise the marrow-fat threshold at which individuals in marginal condition would perish. This relationship could explain the starved moose with a mean of 52% marrow fat (Ballard et al. 1987).

Given these considerations, we believe that most of our wolf-killed moose and caribou were in poor condition, although how they compared with the rest of their population is unknown. Because such individuals would have lost considerable muscle mass as well as fat, these animals would have had little energy left to withstand chases by wolves.

The marrow-fat content of Denali wolf-killed prey was consistently low despite relatively low snow depths in some years. There seemed to be no relationship between percentage marrow fat in our wolf kills and the snowfall, except that the marrow fat of our moose kills was lowest during the winter of deepest snow (tables 1.1 and 6.2).

The preponderance of low marrow fat despite low snow depth during three of the seven years of the study indicates that the unharvested Denali prey herds must include a certain proportion of individuals that cannot secure enough food even under average environmental conditions. Our data indicate that such individuals are primarily the oldest and the youngest, and the bulls around the rut. This situation is probably typical of ungulate populations.

Wolves can depend on such vulnerable members of prey populations, along with the annual crop of young, which are generally more vulnerable, to sustain their own numbers during most years. When snowfall or other weather factors become extreme and increase prey vulnerability, wolf populations can increase (Mech 1977b; Peterson 1977) to make use of a sudden increase in resources such as the caribou during our study.

# The Caribou Calving Season: A Scramble for Survival

"Eight-eight, Tango, Alpha; this is the Flagship. We're in upper Birch Creek with some action for you," the helicopter radio squawked.

"What's up, Brad?" Layne Adams replied.

"Well, we found five of the McLeod wolves mixing it up with nine caribou cows. We can see a couple dead calves, but there could easily be more."

It was May 22, 1988. Biologist Brad Shults, assisting Layne Adams with the caribou research, and Don Glaser, pilot of Super Cub 4627Y (aka "the Flagship"), were making their daily rounds over Denali. They were radio-tracking young caribou calves, a few expectant cows, and the seven McLeod Lake wolves, whose territory included the western half of the calving ground (see chapter 3).

"We're on our way and about 20 minutes out," Layne replied, and they immediately diverted the helicopter to further investigate.

While circling and waiting, Brad and Don noticed another site about 2 miles (3 kilometers) away where several calves had been killed, probably the night before. From the Super Cub they could see four scattered along a snowy ridgeline at about 5,000 feet (1,500 meters) elevation. Tracks showed that wolves had chased the caribou down the ridge.

The helicopter landed there first. Layne and Tom Meier quickly found five calf carcasses along a 400-yard (-meter) stretch. Since it was snowing, visibility was poor, so there could have been more. Except for one, the calves had been mostly consumed. Two golden eagles were busily cleaning up what remained.

Next, the men headed to where Brad and Don had observed the wolves. The Super Cub was circling over a broad, rounded, and sloping ridge at about 4,800 feet (1,450 meters) elevation. Brad radioed that four of the wolves had headed back toward their den, 8 miles (13 kilometers) north. A radio-collared young adult male was busily burying a calf in a snowbank.

Once out of the helicopter, Layne and Tom searched an area of about 500 by 200 yards (meters). Nine frantic caribou cows also milled around, searching hopelessly for their missing young. The body count quickly climbed to nine calves. Five of them were battered but whole, and three were missing only some entrails. The carcass buried by the wolf was about half eaten.

The events of that May afternoon encompass many facets of the common view of wolf predation on caribou calves. The 14 dead calves were all younger than 2 weeks old. Their short lives ended during the annual spring calving season, which is critical for caribou. Caribou deliver their vulnerable young into an environment teeming with an array of predators ready to partake of "easy" food. The herd's future depends on enough young surviving this predation gauntlet.

Young caribou calves do not seem to present much challenge to wolves, and reports of multiple kills of calves by wolves are common (Murie 1944; Crisler 1956; Miller et al. 1985; Adams, Singer, and Dale et al. 1995). Further, because calves are so easy to kill, wolves commonly dispatch more than they immediately use, leaving uneaten carcasses in their wake. However, as is often the case with ecological events, a complex reality lurks not far behind a simplistic facade. We were fortunate enough to be able to investigate this apparent "surplus killing" (Kruuk 1972) in Denali.

## Background

The Denali Caribou Herd is small by Alaskan standards, numbering 2,300 to 3,100 during our study (plate 13). However, the herd is of special interest to wildlife managers and researchers because it and associated moose, sheep, and predators are largely unaffected by human harvest. Therefore, this herd and its community provide a unique comparison with harvested herds throughout Alaska and Canada.

Initially, the interest in conducting caribou research at Denali resulted from a major decline in herd size during the late 1960s to early 1970s. The Denali herd was estimated at about 9,500 in the early 1960s but declined to 1,000 by the mid-1970s (Adams et al. 1989). Concurrent declines in several other Alaskan caribou herds were equally dramatic (Klein and White 1978).

The causes of these declines have been widely debated and include severe winters, heavy wolf predation, overpopulation, and overharvest (Davis et al. 1980; Gasaway et al. 1983; Van Ballenberghe 1985; Bergerud and Ballard 1988; Valkenburg and Davis 1988; Eberhardt and Pitcher 1992). But unlike for the other herds, human harvest was not a factor for the Denali herd (Adams et al. 1989).

High neonatal calf loss is common in caribou herds that share ranges with large predators. Commonly half the calves born die before 6 months of age (Bergerud 1980). The Denali herd was no exception. While caribou numbers were falling, early calf losses were important in the herd's dynamics. During midsummers 1967–83, ratios of calves to "cows" (including young bulls indistinguishable from cows during surveys) averaged only 18:100, even though caribou pregnancy rates usually exceed 70%. Therefore, well over half the calves could have died by midsummer (Adams et al. 1989). Range conditions and the nutritional status of Denali caribou (Boertje 1981) indicated that cows should have been able to produce the characteristic high numbers of calves.

The role of predators in the early calf losses was suspected but unclear. Wolves were known to be important caribou predators and were commonly believed to be the primary cause of high calf losses. Wolf control programs in Alaska and the Yukon had resulted in increased survival of caribou calves (Gasaway et al. 1983; Farnell and McDonald 1988), and in the high-latitude barrens of Canada, many wolf-killed calves were found in searches of calving grounds in June (Miller and Broughton 1974; Miller, Gunn, and Broughton 1985, 1988; Miller, Broughton, and Gunn 1988). Because wolves can easily kill calves, they were suspected of doing so throughout the calving season.

Bear predation had been documented, but no one knew whether it was important. After many years of observation in Denali, Murie (1981, 135) viewed the grizzly bear as "a carnivore that cannot

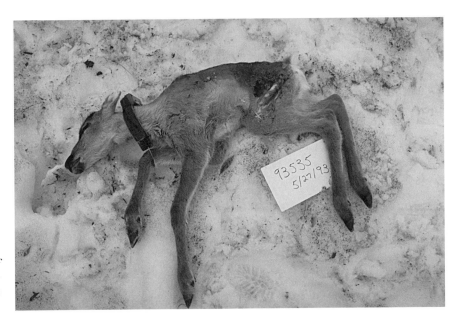

*Figure 7.1. Remains of a newborn calf killed by an eagle. (Photo by Layne G. Adams.)*

capture enough prey for subsistence." He believed that bears were "too slow to capture caribou, moose, or mountain sheep except for offspring a day or two old." However, in 1973, biologists in Idaho affixed radio-collars to newborn elk calves and discovered that black bears were significant predators of elk calves (Schlegal 1976). Similar studies in Alaska and Canada documented the importance of grizzly and black bear predation on moose and caribou calves (Ballard et al. 1981; Schwartz and Franzmann 1991; Whitten et al. 1992; Page 1985).

The importance of smaller predators was also unknown (figure 7.1), although lynx and golden eagles are important predators of young caribou calves in other areas (Bergerud 1971; Whitten et al. 1992).

## Caribou Defensive Strategies

Caribou employ an array of temporal, spatial, and social strategies that minimize predation on their vulnerable newborn calves, but it was unclear what Denali's small herd would do or how successful these strategies would be. For example, calves are produced synchronously during a short period each spring (Skoog 1968; Dauphine and McClure 1974); in Denali, 75% are born in only 15 days (Adams and Dale 1998). Although this pattern probably evolved because of the short northern growing season (Rutberg 1987), one effect is a glut of calves that may overwhelm the capacity of predators to find and kill them all. Could a small herd produce enough calves to have this effect?

The spacing strategies that caribou employ to minimize predation on calves vary with caribou abundance, as well as the abundance and distribution of predators and alternative prey (Bergerud and Page 1987). At one extreme, low-density woodland caribou that share habitats with wolves and bears as well as other ungulates (primarily moose) "space out" during calving to reduce chances of predators finding them. They may be more dispersed during calving than any other time (Fuller and Keith 1981; Brown et al. 1986).

These caribou also select calving areas, such as mountains, shorelines, and islands, that are harder for predators to search, and they avoid habitats used by other large prey (Bergerud et al. 1984,

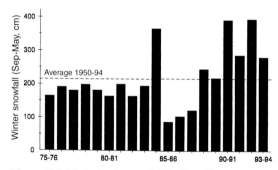

*Figure 7.2. Variation in snowfall in Denali*

1990; Bergerud 1985; Edmonds 1988). They hide in dense forests or areas of patchy snow and limit their movements to minimize detection (Bergerud and Page 1987).

The large barren-ground herds, on the other extreme, "space away" from wolves during calving (Bergerud and Page 1987). Cows about to calve migrate hundreds of miles to open tundra that lack other ungulates and thus support few wolves. These herds produce tens or even hundreds of thousands of calves, which drastically swamp the few predators.

Many caribou herds, like Denali's, fall somewhere between the two ecotypes discussed earlier. At first it was unclear what strategies Denali caribou would employ to beat predators during calving. We knew that some Denali caribou aggregated on a calving ground (plate 14), but they could not "space away" from predators. At low populations, did they produce enough calves to really swamp the predators on the calving ground? Did some caribou employ the woodland "spacing out" strategy? If so, what were the relative trade-offs of these two strategies?

## The Caribou Research

In 1984, the National Park Service embarked on a study at Denali to address some of these issues. Initially Francis Singer led the research, which was aimed at determining the causes and extent of calf

mortality in the Denali Caribou Herd and the causes of annual variation in the losses. In 1985, Singer transferred to Yellowstone National Park, and Layne Adams assumed responsibility for the project.

With the wolf study starting in 1986, the value of concurrent intensive research on wolves and caribou became apparent. The calf mortality study was expanded into a broader investigation of caribou population ecology, focusing on calf production and survival, and wolf-caribou relationships.

Luckily, we also experienced a wide range of winter snowfalls (figure 7.2) that improved our understanding of how winter weather can influence wolf-caribou interactions. At first, winters were relatively mild with low snowfalls; for example, the 34-inch (86-centimeter) snowfall during winter 1985–86 was less than 50% of the park's 60-year average. Below-average snowfalls had been the rule for about 15 years. In winter 1988–89, however, that pattern ended, and the next 5 consecutive years had above-average snowfall, the longest stretch of severe winters in over 30 years. Winters 1990–91 and 1992–93 were extreme, with nearly 13 feet (4 meters) of snow falling each winter.

## A Focus on Calves

To study caribou calf mortality in the park, we had to gather basic information like calf sex, weight, and birth date, and timing and causes of deaths. This required capturing calves within a few days of birth ("neonates") and radio-collaring them. Luckily, such calves are easy to catch, and using experience from a similar study (Whitten et al. 1992), the caribou project began radio-collaring calves in 1984.

In May 1984–86, we searched the known calving range of the Denali Caribou Herd, using a helicopter or Super Cubs or both, for newborn calves to capture (figure 7.3). By 1987, we had

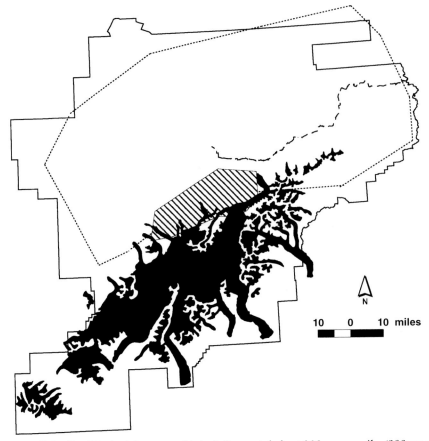

*Figure 7.3.* The Denali Caribou Herd calving ground (stippled) occupied about 300 square miles (800 square kilometers) in the central part of Denali. Dotted line represents herd range; dashed line, park road.

about 30 radio-collared cows (see chapter 2) to monitor daily for locating calving caribou and determining the timing of births. We captured any calves we could ("ad lib") as previously, but we also radio-collared the calves of the radio-collared cows.

After a year of closely monitoring expectant caribou cows, we realized that the calves caught opportunistically may not very well represent the calf population as a whole. Early in the calving season, we caught many calves, but as calving peaked, those radio-collared were beginning to die. Thus, we were busy locating them and figuring out what killed them. That left less time for catching more

calves during the calving peak, when most of them were being born.

Also, the final 25% of calves are born over the last 2 weeks of May, based on our radio-collared cows (Adams and Dale 1998), and these calves are hard to find among the multitude of older calves. So with ad-lib captures, we were sampling too many early-born calves and not enough later ones.

## Cow-Calf Relations

At the same time, we realized that we could learn a lot by capturing the calves of our radio-collared cows. We could amass complete histories of the reproductive attempts and successes of each cow,

*Figure 7.4. An important part of the research was to radio-collar the calves of radio-collared caribou cows and follow the survival of both. (Photo by L. David Mech.)*

learn about their calving habitat selection, and relate calf survival to maternal characteristics such as age (Clutton-Brock et al. 1982; Ozoga and Verme 1982, 1986; Mech and McRoberts 1990a) and nutritional condition (Verme 1962; Clutton-Brock et al. 1982; Peterson 1977; Mech and Karns 1977; Mech et al. 1991).

To our knowledge, this type of study based on newborn calves and their mothers had only been conducted on one other free-ranging ungulate population, the red deer (*Cervus elaphus*) of the Isle of Rhum, Scotland (Clutton-Brock et al. 1982). Our work could make a good comparison to it because Rhum was basically predator-free, and its deer lived at extremely high densities.

Thus, in 1988, we began radio-collaring only calves of radio-collared cows (figure 7.4). However, to study factors affecting the onset of breeding, we also captured 10 to 15 10-month-old cows each year. Added to the 34 cows we initially radio-collared in winter 1986–87, our radio-collared cow sample was heavily weighted to younger animals.

Many characteristics of ungulate calf production and survival, including habitat selection at birth, pregnancy rate, birth dates, and birth weight, are related to maternal age (Dauphine 1976; Thomas 1982; Clutton-Brock et al. 1982; Ozoga and Verme 1982, 1986; Mech and McRoberts 1990b). Therefore, we needed a subsample of radio-collared cows that reflected the age structure of cows in the herd (Adams, Dale, and Mech 1995).

*Figure 7.5. To catch a newborn caribou calf, a person is dropped off by helicopter to chase it down. (Photo by Thomas J. Meier.)*

Starting with the 34 cows we radio-collared from throughout the herd that presumably represented the herd's age structure, each year we added yearlings from the samples radio-collared at 10 months of age. We based the number of "recruits" each year on the ratio of female calves to cows in the herd the previous fall and randomly selected them from the radio-collared yearlings. Once included, these females remained in the age-simulated sample until death. This sample would increase and decrease in concert with the population by design (Adams, Dale, and Mech 1995). To keep the age-structured sample size large enough during the herd's decline, we added 11 cows caught from throughout the herd in 1991 and 10 more in 1993.

Our caribou calf research had two distinct but overlapping phases. During 1984–87, with ad-lib calf captures, we determined the timing, extent, and causes of mortality (Adams, Singer, and Dale 1995). From 1987 on, with the captures of calves born to our radio-collared cows, our data on those topics were improved because they reflected the age structure of cows in the herd. In addition, we began studying the habitat selection of expectant cows and the movements of wolves around the calving ground (Adams, Dale, and Mech 1995). The following results cover both phases during 1984 through 1991.

## Capturing Caribou Calves

Our method of capturing calves was straightforward. When we found a cow and calf, we landed the helicopter as close as possible, usually within a few yards, and dropped someone off to grab the calf (figure 7.5). Usually the capture was routine, especially for newborn calves, which had little coordination and weighed 15 to 20 pounds (7–9 kilograms). Calves 2 to 3 days old gave the calf catcher a good run, and the occasional older calf got away.

Sometimes we located calves in terrain so steep, or swamp so thick, that we could not land close enough. In those cases, we dropped off two people within 100 to 200 yards (meters) to set up an ambush. The helicopter then slowly herded the cow and calf into the arms of the hidden capture team.

Of the many hundreds of calf captures, a few nonroutine ones stand out, and they fall into two categories. First, sometimes the terrain or snow conditions added a bit of spice, leaving vivid memories. Keith Baird, a veterinarian who assisted in 1986, followed a scampering calf off a dry tundra bench onto a snowfield at full speed. The calf stayed on top of the snow, but Keith's 200-pound (90-kilogram) frame sank to the armpits. The calf, about 30 feet (10 meters) ahead, noticed Keith's predicament, turned around and walked back to check Keith out before taking off to catch up with its mother.

Likewise, we can never forget the look on assistant Doug Waring's face after he dove at an agile calf running across a snowbank that turned out to be a small but deep pond! Somehow Doug regained his composure, extricated himself from the snow, ice, and water, put on an incredible burst of speed, and caught the calf!

### Protective Cows

Even more exciting were the second category, memorable captures involving the rare cows that were more protective of their calves than most. Most often a cow would stand or run around from 15 to 150 feet (5–50 meters) away while we radio-collared and examined its calf. Rarely, however, a cow would stay to guard her calf. Usually we could tell by both her look and her defiance as the helicopter approached that we were in for some action.

A few of the cows were protective each year and became notorious. We anxiously awaited the day they bore their calves and joked about who would be the "lucky" person on the capture crew that day. Usually we put two people out of the helicopter for those cows, one to ward off the cow and one to handle the calf. Generally we captured the calf, but occasionally it was a stand off. The cows weigh 250 to 300 pounds (115–135 kilograms) and when irate, can be a challenge for a human being.

Early in the study, capture-crew member Brad Shults was forced to stand behind a lone 5-foot-tall (1.5-meter-tall) spruce, with an irate cow and her calf on the other side. Whenever Brad moved, the cow would charge with her antlers poised to skewer him. She only lost interest in Brad as the helicopter approached to pick him up after failure to radio-collar the calf.

The next year, Dave Mech, with a struggling calf under his arm, had to grab the antlers of a butting cow and deflect her several times until Bruce Dale arrived to help keep her away.

It is also common for these protective cows to rear up and "box" at a person with their front hooves. Layne Adams once reached out to grab a calf of one of these notorious cows standing a couple of yards uphill. Layne said:

> The cow reared up to let me have it. With her advantage uphill of me, she seemed 10 feet tall! She came at me with both front hooves flailing, and I heard one whistle by my left ear. At that point, discretion became the better part of valor. I let her calf go and waited for Bruce to come to the rescue. The three of us (me, the cow, and her calf) politely waited the 20 seconds it took Bruce to pile out of the helicopter. Once outnumbered, the cow backed off, and we were able to handle the calf with her almost breathing down our necks.

Usually, these close encounters ended with a radio-collared calf and no one the worse for wear. We have taken a few bumps and bruises, however. The scariest encounter involved our first attempt at capturing the calf of a cow we later dubbed "the Psycho-Cow." We were unable to get to her until her calf was a few days old. Thus, we dumped out catchers Patty Del Vecchio and Ken Stahlnecker. However, between high winds and steep terrain, we could not maneuver the helicopter as close to the cow and calf as usual.

Initially, Patty, Ken, the cow, and the spry calf ran around in circles, but as they sorted themselves

*Figure 7.6. In less than 2 minutes, the biologist weighs and examines the calf and attaches a mortality collar, then releases the calf to return to its mother. (Photo by Layne G. Adams.)*

out, Patty ended up trying to distract the cow while Ken tried for the calf. When Patty approached, the cow charged with antlers poised, then reared to box at her. Short in stature but tall in attitude, Patty held her ground, shouting and waving her arms. However, after a few seconds of hoof-to-hand combat, Patty lost her footing in the slippery rubble and fell!

In a split second, the cow was on her. From the helicopter we could see that Patty, who had rolled onto her stomach, was being stomped into the tundra. After several flurries of hooves, the cow saw that her calf had evaded Ken, and she broke off the attack. Fearing the worst, we swooped in with the helicopter to retrieve Patty and Ken. It turned out that, other than a few bruises and scrapes, Patty was fine.

Over the next year, we all agreed that the Psycho-Cow attacked because Patty was too short to take seriously! We even had Patty believing it, until the next year, when the Psycho-Cow showed she was not very impressed with any of us, regardless of size.

## Handling Calves

Each calf-catcher wore clean rubber gloves to minimize scent transfer among calves and the possibility of calf rejection by the cow. Also, we kept the radio-collars in bags of spruce boughs and moss to minimize contamination by human scent. Once we had a calf in hand, we followed a brief routine in handling it.

First, we radio-collared the calf. The collar weighed about 5 ounces (130 grams), including a small radio-transmitter affixed to a band of 1-inch-wide (2.5-centimeters-wide) elastic. The transmitter pulse rate would double if the calf held still for more than 1 hour, and thus allow us to detect deaths (or long naps on occasion!). The collar could be easily stretched over the calf's head. As the calf grew, the elastic stretched, and three expansion folds opened to allow for more growth. After a year, a special seam opened so the collar could fall off.

Once we radio-collared a calf, we weighed it (from 1986 on) and quickly examined it for sex, any obvious abnormalities, hoof development,

*Figure 7.7. Layne Adams (left) and Brad Shults examine a freshly killed caribou calf for cause of death. (Photo by Bruce W. Dale.)*

and umbilical cord dryness (figure 7.6). Both hoof and umbilicus traits, along with posture, degree of coordination, and behavior of their radio-collared mother over the previous few days aided us in estimating the calf's age (Adams, Dale, and Mech 1995).

Capturing the calves took about 30 seconds from the time the helicopter touched down, and handling took less than 2 minutes. The handler then pointed the calf toward its waiting mother and sprinted away to be picked up by the helicopter. Unfortunately, when calves are younger than 2 days old, they are programmed to follow whatever is close to them, normally their mother. Thus, often the calf would run after the handler as he or she headed to the helicopter.

Once, John Burch ran to the helicopter, closely pursued by a confused calf, which was closely pursued by its worried mother. As Mom caught up with her calf, she came within mere inches of Burch, so just for good measure she hooked him in the butt with her antlers! Then she ran off with her calf in tow.

## Monitoring for Mortality

We aerially located each radio-collared calf daily during May to keep track of their survival. This was not an especially pleasant task, because with the characteristic high losses of calves, the "morts" (short for mortality signal) came fast and furious. Usually the person in the Super Cub picked up the mortality signals, but occasionally they would find a calf being consumed by a predator. In any case, the plane radioed the calf's location and what they saw to the helicopter.

The helicopter crew, in addition to capturing calves, served as the project coroners. If a predator was eating a radio-collared calf, we left them alone. When the fast pulse led to a blood spot or a nondescript hillside or shrub thicket, we headed there right away.

Once on site, we got to play Sherlock Holmes, looking for clues to the calf's cause of death (figure 7.7). More often than not, determining this was easy because there were tracks in the snow or a characteristic predator scat. Also, bear kills were usually obvious because bears cover the scraps of a

*Figure 7.8. Wolves often bury an entire calf, or half a calf after eating the other half. (Photo by Layne G. Adams.)*

kill, even if only bone chips, by scraping up big piles of moss or ground cover over them. These monuments of their predatory prowess are characteristic and impossible to miss.

### Wolf Kills or Bear Kills?

Wolves also commonly bury or cache remains of their kills, but they are much more meticulous than bears. Whereas bears cover a few bone chips with moss scraped up from a few yards of ground, a wolf usually buries only something of value, like half or all of a calf (figure 7.8). Wolves must also intend to hide the remains, because they dig a hole in the substrate, whether it is snow, moss, or mud, place the carcass in the hole, and then carefully cover it.

Other than in snow, it is often hard to detect a wolf cache until one is right on top of the covered carcass. Occasionally, we have been awed by the extremes wolves have gone to in hiding a carcass. In one case, we recovered an entire calf buried in the mud under a small flowing stream. We have found several calves submerged in the edges of moss-choked ponds in the area's spruce bogs.

Without these obvious and characteristic clues, we had to look harder to determine a calf's cause of death. If a carcass was left, we could often determine the culprit from the wounding pattern. Bears usually mangle the carcass, leaving its limbs attached by skin. Wolves tend to bite calves along the back and top of the head and often leave only the front or rear half, at least at first (figure 7.8). A thorough search of the ground and shrubs around the kill scene commonly turns up a few carnivore hairs, although spotting them amidst the calf hair is not easy. Sometimes we only found a bloody collar or a few bone chips and could not identify the predator.

Most of the calves that die do so during only a few weeks in May. Thus, we monitored the calves daily throughout May to obtain a good picture of the timing and causes of mortality. After May, we monitored the calves about weekly in June and bimonthly for the rest of the year. The deaths we found after May we investigated as soon as we could bring in a helicopter, generally after a few weeks, and usually we could not be sure of the cause.

Another facet of our calf-mortality research was to monitor the wolves that lived around the calving ground to compare what we learned from the radio-collared calves with what we observed the wolves doing. Starting in 1988, we located those wolves daily.

This flurry of fieldwork each May provided information on (1) the timing of calving and sizes of calves, (2) the movements and habitat selection of expectant caribou cows, (3) the extent, timing, and causes of calf losses, and (4) the activities of wolves on the calving ground. With this suite of data, plus our other wolf and caribou information from throughout the year, many pieces to the puzzles of caribou calf survival and wolf-caribou relationships came together.

## Calf Survival

Caribou calves in Denali began appearing May 4 to May 15 in any year. If the cows were in good nutritional condition during the fall breeding season, they tended to calve earlier than when in poorer condition (Adams and Dale 1998). Once calving began, the number of calves increased rapidly: 75% were born during the initial 15 days, and the last 25% were strung out over the ensuing 15 days (Adams and Dale 1998).

From 1986 through 1988, newborn calves averaged 17.6 and 20.0 pounds (8.0 and 9.1 kilograms) for females and males, respectively (Adams, Singer, and Dale 1995; Adams, Dale, and Mech 1995). With the high-snowfall winters beginning with winter 1988–89 (figure 7.2), birth weights declined, reaching bottom by 1991, when both sexes averaged only 14.7 pounds (6.7 kilograms).

The differences in appearance were just as striking as those in birth weights. In the early years, the newborn calves were husky and well rounded, but by 1991, they were leggy and boney. From 1991 to 1994, average birth weights increased to 15.4 and 17.6 pounds (7 and 8 kilograms) for females and males, respectively, still 2 pounds (1 kilogram) shy of the earlier weights.

In general, most calf deaths occurred within 15 days after birth. Of the 350 calves we monitored during 1984–91, 155 never made it beyond 15 days of age (tables 7.1 and 7.2). The proportion dying by this age varied among years from 29% in 1984 to 71% in 1991 (Adams, Singer, and Dale 1995; Adams, Dale, and Mech 1995).

Calf losses tapered off after the first 2 weeks. During 1987–89, when calves were heavier on average, only 10% to 18% of those surviving the first 15 days died during the rest of the year. However, in 1990 and 1991, when calves were lighter, many died throughout summer, and 76% of the survivors had died by fall (table 7.2).

The magnitude and variation in losses of radio-collared calves were corroborated by results of the helicopter surveys we conducted in late May through early June and in late September to determine calf:cow ratios in the entire herd (Adams et al. 1989). During 1986–89, fall calf:cow ratios were 30–40:100, but sank to 6–17:100 during 1990–93.

Predation accounted for nearly all the deaths of young calves. Of the 155 monitored calves that died prior to 15 days during 1984–91, we knew of only 5 that died of other causes, including 2 drownings, and 3 stillbirths (tables 7.1 and 7.2). For another 8, we knew the radio-collared cows were pregnant, but we never saw their calves. Probably some of these were stillborn and others died by predation.

Wolves were a major source of caribou calf mortality, accounting for at least 55 (35%) of the early deaths (Adams, Singer, and Dale 1995; Adams, Dale, and Mech 1995). Surprisingly, grizzly bears killed more calves, at least 64 (41%) of the neonates that died. An additional 15 deaths (10%) were caused by either bears or wolves. Thus, wolves and bears took nearly equal numbers of calves and were by far the most important causes of their deaths.

The remaining 8 predation deaths were caused by smaller predators, including golden eagles (6),

**Table 7.1.** Ages and causes of deaths of caribou calves radio-collared as neonates in Denali, May 1984–87

| Age class (days) | Cause of death | 1984 n = 41 | 1985 n = 55 | 1986 n = 56 | 1987 n = 74 |
|---|---|---|---|---|---|
| 1–15 | Grizzly bear | 7 | 12 | 10 | 13 |
| | Wolf | 1 | 8 | 9 | 10 |
| | Unknown large predator | 4 | 5 | 1 | 2 |
| | Golden eagle | | 3 | | 1 |
| | Wolverine | | 1 | | |
| | Drowning | | | 1 | |
| | Perinatal mortality | | | | 1 |
| | Total deaths[a] | 12 (29%) | 29 (53%) | 21 (38%) | 27 (36%) |
| 16–30 | Grizzly bear | | 2 | | |
| | Wolf | | | 1 | |
| | Unknown large predator | | 1 | 3 | 4 |
| | Total deaths[a] | | 3 (12%) | 4 (11%) | 4 (9%) |
| 31–60 | Wolf | | | | 2 |
| | Golden eagle | | | | 1 |
| | Undetermined | | | 2 | 2 |
| | Total deaths[a] | | | 2 (6%) | 5 (12%) |
| 61–150 | Grizzly bear | | | 1 | |
| | Fall into glacial crevasse | | | | 1 |
| | Undetermined | | | 1 | 3 |
| | Total deaths[a] | | | 2 (7%) | 4 (11%) |
| 151–365 | Total deaths | – | – | – | – |

*Source: Adapted from Adams, Singer, and Dale 1995.*

[a] *Number in parentheses is percent mortality during the period.*

wolverines (1), and coyotes (1). Losses to these animals occurred only in 1985 and 1991 following severe winters when the calves were lightweight and much snow remained during the calving season, thus increasing the vulnerability of calves.

## Calf Age versus Predator Type

Although similar in magnitude, predation by grizzly bears and wolves differed in other ways. The rate at which grizzlies killed calves declined quickly as the calves got older, and it was rare for a bear to kill a calf more than 10 days old (figure 7.9). Therefore, bears killed calves roughly in proportion to the availability of young, vulnerable individuals.

Wolf predation, on the other hand, showed no trend with age for calves less than 15 days old (figure 7.9). After 13 days, wolf kills dropped off. Also, wolves mostly killed calves during the middle of the calving period, primarily for a week shortly after the peak of calving (Adams, Singer,

**Table 7.2.** Caribou calf production and mortality for radio-collared cows in Denali

| | | 1987 | 1988 | 1989 | 1990 | 1991 |
|---|---|---|---|---|---|---|
| Cows monitored[a] | | 29 | 38 | 45 | 40 | 40 |
| Calves produced | | 23[b] | 33 | 35 | 28[c] | 28 |
| *Mortalities* | | | | | | |
| *Age class (days)* | *Cause of death* | | | | | |
| 1–15 | Bear | 2 | 6 | 10 | 3 | 3 |
| | Wolf | 4 | 5 | 3 | 9 | 10 |
| | Stillbirth | | 1 | | 1 | 1 |
| | Undetermined perinatal | 1 | | 2 | 2 | 3 |
| | Unknown large predator | | 1 | 2 | | |
| | Coyote | | | | | 1 |
| | Eagle | | | | | 2 |
| | Drowning | | | 1 | | |
| | Total deaths[d] | 7 (30%) | 13 (39%) | 18 (51%) | 15 (54%) | 20 (71%) |
| 16–30 | Wolf | | | | 1 | |
| | Unknown predator | 1 | 1 | | 4 | 1 |
| | Unknown cause | | | | 1 | |
| | Total deaths[d] | 1 (6%) | 1 (5%) | | 6 (46%) | 1 (13%) |
| 31–120 | Wolf | 1 | 1 | 1 | 1 | |
| | Unknown predator | | | | 3 | |
| | Accident | | | 1 | | 1 |
| | Unknown cause | 1 | | 1 | | 4 |
| | Total deaths[d] | 2 (13%) | 1 (5%) | 3 (18%) | 4 (57%) | 5 (71%) |
| Calves surviving 120 days[e] | | 13 (57%) | 18 (55%) | 14 (40%) | 3 (11%) | 2 (7%) |

*Source: Adapted from Adams, Dale, and Mech 1995.*

[a] *Cows from an age-justified sample of radio-collared cows for each year that were > 2 years old.*

[b] *This sample is a subset of the 1987 sample in table 7.1.*

[c] *29 calves were produced, but one died due to study activities.*

[d] *Number in parentheses is percent mortality during the period.*

[e] *Number in parentheses is percentage surviving to 120 days of age.*

and Dale 1995; Adams, Dale, and Mech 1995) (figure 7.10).

Grizzly bears and wolves differ in several ways that we believe lead to their differences in predation on caribou calves. Grizzlies are four to eight times more abundant than wolves in Denali (Adams, Singer, and Dale 1995), are generally solitary, and live in areas concurrently with many other bears. Further, grizzlies emerge from their dens in late April to early May in the same mountainous habitats caribou choose for calving.

All this means that many bears instantly detect

the beginning of caribou calving, since it happens on their doorsteps. Then they quickly learn to locate calves still young enough for them to kill. However, as calving season progresses, the proportion of calves less than 10 days old drops rapidly, and calves quickly become much less vulnerable to bears.

Wolves are less abundant and live in territorial packs (see chapter 4). In most years, only one or two packs had access to the calving ground, and like their neighbors, they were busy killing adult ungulates throughout winter in areas far from the calving ground. Further, as we will detail later, caribou cows chose calving habitats difficult and unlikely for wolves to search. Also, initially calves were few and far between and less profitable for wolves to search for.

As more calves were born, however, and they began to group up, they became both more detectable and profitable to wolves. Thus for about 1 to 2 weeks following the peak of calving, the calving-ground wolves concentrated on killing calves (plate 15). Then, as the increasing proportion of older calves made it harder to locate the young, still vulnerable ones, losses of calves to wolves declined. Also, moose calves began appearing shortly after caribou calving peaked and may have replaced caribou calves as the most profitable prey for wolves.

### Factors Affecting Calf Vulnerability

During 1984–89, wolves killed on average 12% to 17% of the calves we radio-collared each year before they reached 15 days of age, but in 1990–91, these losses jumped to 34% on average. As we noted, calves in those years were extra small, and unlike in other years, a high proportion died over summer.

We found no direct information that in any given year calf survival was related to birth weight, contrary to studies of other ungulates (Verme 1962; Clutton-Brock et al. 1982; Nelson and Woolf 1987; Kunkel and Mech 1994). However,

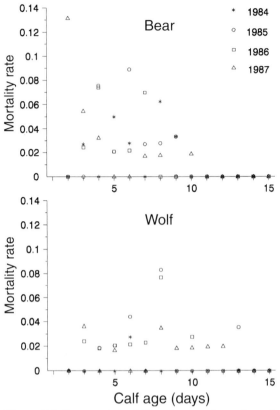

*Figure 7.9. Bears tended to kill newborn caribou calves primarily when only a few days old, whereas wolves killed them at about the same rate through about 13 days of age. (Adams, Singer, and Dale 1995)*

as annual mean birth weights of our calves declined from 1986 to 1991, more calves died by 15 days old, as well as through the summer.

Birth weight is only one of several possible indicators of inferior prenatal nutrition. Others include stunting, delayed development of motor skills and hearing, and marked learning deficits (Verme 1963; Zeman 1967; Stephan et al. 1971; Bresler et al. 1975; Zamenhof and Van Marthens 1977). Any of these factors could have contributed to the high and prolonged vulnerability of our caribou calves to predation following severe winters.

As mentioned earlier, even eagles will kill young calves, especially after severe winters, when they are more vulnerable (figure 7.1). Bruce Dale

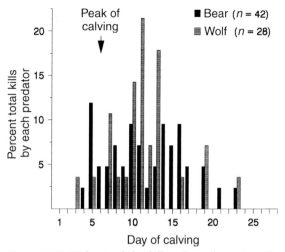

*Figure 7.10. Wolves tended to kill caribou calves primarily during the peak of calving and the week after. (Adams, Singer, and Dale 1995)*

once watched an ambitious golden eagle circling a herd of 30 caribou in Denali and described its attack as follows:

Calves stood under their mothers as the eagle made its passes. The caribou started to run down the hillside, leaving the calves less protected. The eagle swooped in and grabbed a calf in the middle of the back with its talons, but the calf fell under the eagle, rolled and got free. The eagle caught another calf as it ran down the gentle slope. For a brief second, the calf was actually airborne as the eagle lifted it to set its talons deep into the calf.

The eagle and calf then came to a stop with the calf laying on its stomach. We could see the eagle working its talons on the back of the calf. At one point the eagle rapped the calf in the head with its beak as the calf struggled to get free. The group of caribou was standing nearby, and after a few seconds the cow nearest the eagle and calf took a few steps toward them, hesitated, then made a run at the eagle, which immediately flew off and circled. The calf jumped up and went

back to the group with its mother. Although it appeared unhurt, the calf surely suffered serious injuries and may eventually have become eagle food.

In some years, a calf's birth date influenced its chance of surviving. Following low-snowfall winters, calves born within 2 to 3 days of the peak or median calving date had 50% better survival than those born earlier or later (Adams, Singer, and Dale 1995). During that short period, about half the calves are born, so the improved survival probably reflects the swamping effect.

Here is how it seemed to work. The first calves quickly caught the attention of bears. Also, early calves were in nursery bands (figure 7.11) when wolves began hunting calves, and were thus more detectable when most wolf predation occurred than calves born during the peak. Late-born calves came after predators had already keyed on caribou calves and were noticeably smaller than the abundant older calves, so they would have been vulnerable. In years following high-snowfall winters, survival was low regardless of birth date.

## The Value of Defensive Strategies

Denali caribou cows employed both spacing strategies described by Bergerud and Page (1987). The first strategy, used on average by about half the caribou, was to utilize a calving ground encompassing about 350 square miles (900 square kilometers) (table 7.3). The area consisted of open, rolling terrain with low shrub tundra at the lower elevations (650–1,050 yards or meters) to the north, and steep mountains with alpine tundra, rock, scree, and glaciers at higher elevations (1,050–1,850 yards or meters) to the south, right up against the rock and ice of Mount McKinley (plate 14).

Caribou rarely used these areas during winter, and very few, if any, moose or sheep wintered there (Adams, Dale, and Mech 1995). Thus, there was no reason for wolves to patrol it. The eastern half

*Figure 7.11. Cows and calves soon join others to form large "nursery" herds, which help spread predation risk and reduce profitability for wolves hunting them. (Photo by Layne G. Adams.)*

of the calving ground in particular was nearly devoid of prey during winter, and wolves that tried to live there often did not fare well. Thus, by using this area, the cows could "space away" from wolves, and from the other ungulate prey that could attract wolves, as much as possible.

The proportion of cows using the calving ground varied among years depending on the snowpack in May (Adams, Dale, and Mech 1995) (table 7.3). When there was little snow, about 60% of cows calved there, and of those, 85% used the mountainous areas. When the May snowpack was deep, an average of 38% of the cows calved on the calving ground, and they tended to use the lower elevations (51%), presumably because the mountains were less accessible.

In the second strategy, the cows not using the calving ground scattered, or "spaced out," throughout the rest of the herd's range. This included the spruce bogs in the northwestern part of the park (figure 1.3), the high mountains on the south side of the Alaska range and east of Mount McKinley, and virtually everywhere in between. Like the cows on the calving ground, they tended to calve at lower elevations and use forested areas in years with a deep spring snowpack (table 7.3).

Was there any difference in survival of calves born to "spaced away" or "spaced out" mothers? As it turned out, it was really a matter of picking your poison! During 1987–91, slightly more calves born on the calving ground survived than calves scattered elsewhere (53% and 45% survival to 15 days, respectively), although the difference was not statistically significant.

**Table 7.3.** Calving distribution and habitat selection of radio-collared caribou cows in Denali during May

|  | 1987 | 1988 | 1989 | 1990 | 1991 |
| --- | --- | --- | --- | --- | --- |
| Snow conditions during calving season | shallow | shallow | deep | shallow | deep |
| **AJCS Cows**[a] |  |  |  |  |  |
| Monitored | 29 | 38 | 45 | 40 | 40 |
| Calves produced | 23 | 33 | 35 | 29 | 28 |
| **On calving grounds** | **14 (61%)** | **21 (64%)** | **15 (43%)** | **15 (52%)** | **9 (32%)** |
| Mountains | 13 | 18 | 8 | 11 | 4 |
| Lowlands | 1 | 3 | 7 | 4 | 5 |
| **Dispersed** | **9 (39%)** | **12 (36%)** | **20 (57%)** | **14 (48%)** | **19 (68%)** |
| Mountains | 5 | 10 | 11 | 10 | 11 |
| Forests | 4 | 2 | 9 | 4 | 8 |
| **Calving elevation (m)** |  |  |  |  |  |
| < 600 | 4 | 1 | 9 | 4 | 12 |
| ≥ 600–900 | 2 | 6 | 12 | 5 | 5 |
| ≥ 900–1,200 | 9 | 6 | 9 | 7 | 2 |
| ≥ 1,200–1,500 | 5 | 17 | 4 | 11 | 4 |
| ≥ 1,500 | 3 | 3 | 1 | 1 | 2 |
|  | 23 | 33 | 35 | 28[b] | 25[b] |

Source: Adapted from Adams, Dale, and Mech 1995.

[a] AJCS = Age-Justified Cow Sample, or a subset of radio-collared cows selected to approximate the age structure of the herd.

[b] Calving elevations not determined for 1 and 3 perinatal losses in 1990 and 1991, respectively.

On the calving ground, fewer calves were killed by wolves (13% on versus 29% off), particularly in 1990–91, when calf survival was poorest (16% on versus 45% off). However, they stood a greater chance of being killed by a bear (22% on versus 12% off). Thus, by aggregating on a calving ground, caribou limited their losses to wolves but may have increased them to bears.

## Calving Ground and Wolf Territories

The calving ground lay partly in the territories of one or two wolf packs during 1987–91. The western half was in the territory of the McLeod Lake Pack, which commonly denned near the calving ground's northwestern edge. These wolves generally hunted north of the calving ground in lowland spruce forests before and during the onset of calving.

The tenure of packs with access to the eastern half of the calving ground was highly unstable. Packs changed every year during 1987–91 (see chapter 4). In 1987, the Clearwater Pack controlled this area, but they denned 14 miles (24 kilometers) to the north, where the caribou had wintered. They spent much of the May calving season well north of the calving ground but did swing through the area late in May. After September 1987, they avoided the part of the territory that included the calving ground.

We suspected that other wolves were attempting to colonize the area during winter 1987–88 but were unable to verify that until we found a young male disperser from the Clearwater Pack and his mate at a den on the calving ground in May 1988. This pair, known as the Pirate Creek Pack (see appendix 2), produced seven pups and continued to inhabit the area through November 1988. In late November, the adult female, which was the only pack member with an active radio, died of starvation, and the fates of the others remain unknown.

By late winter 1988–89, the Clearwater Pack was again using the eastern half of the calving ground and denned just 4 miles (6 kilometers) north of it in May 1989. However, moose and beavers were common near their den, and we found them on the calving ground only 1 out of 39 radio locations during May 1989.

In winter 1989–90, these wolves inhabited the same small territory that the Pirate Creek wolves had used. Areas to the north previously used by the Clearwater wolves had been usurped by the Little Bear Pack. In December 1989, we found the radio-collared Clearwater breeding male and two pups dead, apparently starved, and his mate and four other pups were never seen again (see chapter 3).

We knew of no resident wolves using the eastern part of the calving ground during May 1990 or 1991. However, we saw two wolves there on June 1, 1990. We also radio-collared one there on May 28, 1991, but it left the area by June 6. We doubt that other undetected wolves used that part of the calving ground in those years because the only wolf-killed calves were associated with those wolf sightings. Snow-tracking before and after the 1990–91 calving seasons confirmed the lack of resident wolves.

In years with shallow snowpacks during May and caribou calving high in the mountainous terrain, we rarely located radio-collared wolves in this terrain before the peak of calving but found them there regularly after the peak (Adams, Dale, and Mech 1995). These observations corroborated the delayed onset of wolf predation we noted from calf deaths. With deep snow, caribou calved lower on and near the calving ground, and we found wolves in their midst throughout calving. However, regardless of snow conditions, those wolves preyed primarily on adult caribou and moose before the peak of calving. From about the peak until early June, we observed our wolves with only caribou calf kills.

## The Importance of Calf:Wolf Ratios

From 1987 to 1991, our wolf population doubled (see chapter 8), but caribou increased only 30%. Thus, at first it looked like caribou calves would be exposed to more wolf predation, and that could partly explain the increased losses of calves to wolves in 1990–91. In 1987, about 25 caribou calves were born per wolf in the study area, but that ratio declined to 18 calves per wolf by 1990–91 (Adams, Dale, and Mech 1995). Further, this decline was strongly correlated inversely with the increasing wolf density. With so few calves per wolf, it would only take each wolf killing a calf every 2 to 3 days in May, an apparently easy task, to eliminate half the calves available. Once again, the initial glance was deceiving.

A rangewide estimate of calf:wolf ratios presumes that caribou and wolves are distributed similarly. However, caribou are notorious for being clumped, especially at calving, with many calves born on the calving ground (plate 14). Wolves are also clumped, into packs that have limited territorial ranges. As noted, up to two-thirds of Denali's caribou calve within only one or two wolf pack territories.

Thus, we calculated calf:wolf ratios for each year that took into account differences in their distribution at the scale of the wolf pack territory. First we calculated calf:wolf ratios for each pack

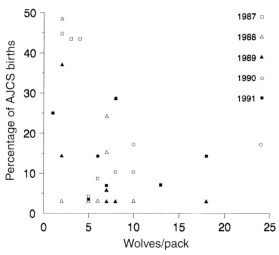

*Figure 7.12. The proportion of Denali caribou that produced calves in territories of various-sized wolf packs (Adams, Dale, and Mech 1995).*

## Persistence of the Wolf-Caribou System

What are the important messages from all these observations? First, lots of calves were killed each year, primarily by bears and wolves. Those losses, however, varied widely among years, and much variation could be explained by the amount of snow during the winter prior to calving. After winters of low snowfall, calves were heavier and their survival was relatively good, with about half surviving to their first birthday. In those years, cows gained some survival advantages for their calves from synchronous calving and congregating on the calving ground. Beyond that, luck played a big role in determining who lived or died.

When winter snows were above average, calves were lighter at birth on average, and their survival was poor, down to about 10% because of high losses from the calving season throughout summer. Losses to wolves of the calves born off the calving ground were especially high.

How significant were calf losses to the caribou population? A good benchmark with which to compare the calf losses is the number of calves needed to replace the adults that die over the year. When winter snowfall was below average, survival of our cows averaged about 95%. Therefore, recruitment of about 10 calves per 100 cows (5 of each sex, assuming equal calf sex ratios), or 13% of calves born, would be sufficient for the cow segment of the herd to remain stable.

As we noted, following mild winters, fall ratios were 30 to 40 calves per 100 cows, and the herd grew moderately. Even with the loss of about half the calves to predation, reasonable levels of herd growth were assured.

With above-average snowfall, cow survival sank to about 80%, requiring survival of 40 calves per 100 cows, or 53% of calves born, for the herd to remain stable. However, following those severe winters, calf survival was poor, with fall calf:cow ratios of 6 to 17 per 100; the herd declined dra-

based on the total number of calves born, the proportion of births to our age-structured sample of caribou cows within each pack territory, and the number of wolves in each pack. Then for each year, we multiplied the calf:wolf ratio for each pack by the proportion of calves born in its territory and summed the products.

When spacing in relation to wolf territories was accounted for, the number of calves born per wolf ranged from 103 in 1991 to 156 in 1988 and 1990. These ratios were six times larger on average than the simple rangewide ratios of calves to wolves. Furthermore, the spacing-corrected ratios did not decline with increasing wolf abundance as they did rangewide. Therefore, through their spacing strategies during calving, caribou buffered the impact of a doubling wolf population, resulting in no increase in calf exposure to wolf predation (figure 7.12) (Adams, Dale, and Mech 1995). We noted this effect largely because many cows calved in the eastern half of the calving ground, where wolves were especially scarce. There, the ratio averaged 270 calves per wolf.

matically. Therefore, low calf survival in those years contributed greatly to the declines (figure 7.13).

The caribou calving season constitutes a condensed version of the annual struggle for existence that faces both predator and prey. During May, wolves are faced with the challenges of supporting the new pups, which represent the pack's future, and must exploit whatever prey resources are available, including caribou calves, to meet their needs. The caribou herd's productive-aged cows, upon emerging from the lean winter season, must produce calves and try to maximize the chances of those calves surviving, especially through their first couple of weeks. The winter snows tip the balance toward one participant or the other by influencing the nutrition of caribou cows and their calves, and hence the vulnerability of calves to predation, and even the habitats available to caribou for this high-stakes game of hide-and-seek.

About a week after the mass calf kills we described earlier occurred, we revisited the sites.

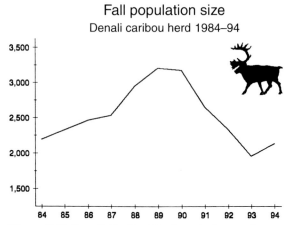

**Fall population size**
Denali caribou herd 1984–94

*Figure 7.13. Denali Caribou Herd population trend*

There was little evidence of the calves that had died—a bone chip here, some blood-stained snow, a small shred of hide there. However, the area was crisscrossed by wolf, grizzly bear, and wolverine tracks. The "surplus killing" had become important fuel for the entire carnivore community.

# The Denali
# Wolf-Prey System

The game of hide-and-seek between caribou and wolves that we described in the previous chapter typifies the basic nature of most predator-prey interactions in Denali and elsewhere. In such relationships, continual contests and perpetual see-sawing take place everywhere. Whether it be a moose fighting off a pack of wolves or a wolf producing a larger litter of pups in the face of a flush of food, the games go on. None of the players are conscious of it; they merely respond as programmed by eons of evolution. Genetic lines that did not respond are long gone.

Perhaps it is this constant pressure between predator and prey—predators kill enough to eat, but enough prey escape to reproduce—that has become popularly known as the "balance of nature." Like the ambiguous patterns in clouds or clusters of stars, the balance-of-nature notion means different things to different people.

Nevertheless, the concept has become a mainstay of popular arguments with explicit predictions for the influence of human disturbance on community diversity, population abundance, and population stability. The balance of nature is frequently referred to as a force or characteristic that

results in stable and abundant populations of predators and prey in the absence of human disturbance.

The Denali wolf-caribou relationship is a good illustration of the dynamics of populations and why stability or balance at a variety of levels should not be considered inherent in natural systems. In fact, scientific definitions of the balance of nature are hard to come by (Pimm 1994), and the concept has largely been discarded in favor of examining more-concrete biological processes.

With wolf-prey systems, the specific questions to be answered are (1) how many wolves are there in an area? (2) what is their trend in numbers? (3) how many prey? (4) what is their population trend? (5) what are the relationships between predator and prey numbers? and (6) what other factors influence these relationships?

The complexity of predator-prey relations also dictates that we fully explore the mechanisms by which numbers change. It is through these mechanisms that the effects of some basic perturbation cascade among various species and trophic levels (McLaren and Peterson 1994). By examining this process, we more fully understand the wolf-prey system.

## Wolf-Prey Relations

The general relationship between wolf numbers and their ungulate prey can be seen in Keith's (1983) synthesis of wolf-prey studies. The gist was that the more food there is in an area, the more wolves. Keith found a linear relationship between wolf density and the weight or biomass of ungulate prey. The relationship held up as data from more recent studies were incorporated into the analysis (Fuller 1989).

This intuitive correlation can be interpreted in several ways. It is not necessarily cause and effect. Moreover, it could support the contradictory theories that prey numbers determine wolf numbers or, conversely, that wolf numbers determine prey numbers. These competing theories drive many wolf controversies (summarized by Mech 1995c). The relationship also speaks to the notion of the balance of nature, that is, that left alone, wolf numbers would seek a level appropriate to the prey base.

Upon examination, however, it is easy to see that wolf-prey numerical relationships are only very general in nature, that much remains to be explained. Certainly, some of the variation is attributable to simple sampling error. Dale et al. (1995) explained some of the variation by pointing out that, to the wolf, not all ungulate prey species are equal. These authors showed that the abundance of prey species shown as "preferred" in the wolf diet had a larger influence on wolf density than did other prey types.

It further follows that the abundance of certain classes (e.g., sex or age) within a prey species could also disproportionately influence wolf numbers, as well as could a long list of other factors. It becomes apparent that this numerical relationship between wolves and their prey is very general and not sufficient to predict year-to-year changes in wolf numbers.

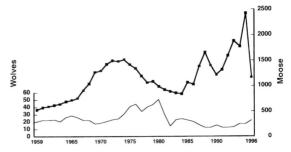

*Figure 8.1.* The wolf (bottom) *and moose population trend on Isle Royale (Peterson et al. 1998).*

An example of a wolf population trend that is useful to examine is provided by the Isle Royale wolf-moose studies. An island national park in Lake Superior, Isle Royale is the site of the longest running study of wolves and their prey (Mech 1966a; Jordan et al. 1967; Peterson 1977, 1995; Allen 1979). The wolf-prey system there is much different than Denali's.

Unlike the numerous predators found in Alaska, the wolf is the sole large predator on Isle Royale—bears are conspicuously absent. Likewise, moose are the only ungulate prey on the island. Except for the minor contribution of beavers in summer, life and death for the Isle Royale wolf depends on the availability of moose. The insular nature of Isle Royale also influences the wolves. Long-distance dispersal, a dominant population mechanism in Denali, is unknown on Isle Royale because of its great distance (15–20 miles, or 24–32 kilometers) from the mainland.

The Isle Royale moose and wolf populations have fluctuated greatly over time (figure 8.1), and there is little correlation between wolf and moose numbers in any given year. Only after three decades of investigation has it become apparent that there was a strong correlation between wolf numbers and the number of moose 9 years old and older (Peterson et al. 1998). Isle Royale wolf numbers were related not to numbers of prey but to

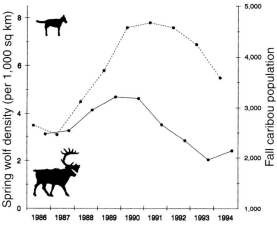

*Figure 8.2. The Denali wolf and caribou population trend*

the vulnerable-prey biomass (Packard and Mech 1983).

## Denali Wolf-Prey Dynamics

That wolf populations can be dynamic over short periods in more complex predator-prey systems is dramatically evident from our study. When we began in 1986, the Denali wolf population was relatively low (figure 8.2). Its productivity also appeared low, based on fall counts of only a few litters (table 2.3). Caribou were increasing slowly (Adams et al. 1995b), and moose numbers seemed to be stable (Meier 1987; Meier et al. 1991). Wolves preyed primarily on moose (table 6.2).

Then, in winter 1988–89 the situation changed abruptly. Wolf numbers nearly doubled in 2 short years (table 8.1). After peaking, wolves began to decline nearly as rapidly.

The mechanisms by which wolf numbers changed dramatically provide insights into the life of the wolf as well as into the relationships between the wolf and its prey. Productivity, mortality, and dispersal are the possible mechanisms of wolf population change. As these parameters fluctuate, so too does the population. The obvious question then is, what causes changes in rates of productivity, dispersal, and mortality?

### Pup Production

During the beginning of our study, pup production appeared low. Although we were able to sample litter sizes in only 3 packs in 1986 and 10 in 1987, the most pups per pack we observed then was 5, whereas in 1988 we began to see up to 12 pups per pack, including double litters (see chapter 4). A pack that had 2 pups in 1987, and another with 4 in 1987 each included 12 in 1988 (table 2.3).

Differences in the number of offspring produced by most mammals are generally related to the nutritional condition of females at breeding and during pregnancy (Sadleir 1969), which in turn must reflect the food supply of the population. This principle almost certainly applies to wolves (Boertje and Stephenson 1992).

Female wolves gain weight from September to January and maintain their highest weights through the March breeding season and gestation period (Seal and Mech 1983). This weight increase appears to be due to increased fat accumulation (Hillis 1990). Thus, the amount of fat may help regulate the number and survivability of offspring produced. If females are in poor condition, fetal resorption is probably one of the mechanisms that help adjust litter sizes in wolves (Rausch 1967; Hillis 1990).

Wolf pups do not begin to emerge from the den until about 3 weeks of age (Young and Goldman 1944). Even after they do emerge, it is difficult to be certain of anything but the minimum number unless one makes many sightings of each litter (plate 16). Thus, it would have been difficult to gather precise information on the sizes of litters that Denali wolves produced. That would have required invading their dens or time-consuming monitoring of many remote dens.

### Early Pup Survival

Our best pup counts were from the air during autumn, a measure of net productivity, that is, the

**Table 8.1.** Wolf densities for Denali National Park and Preserve

| | Late winter (approx. 15 March) | | | | Early winter (approx. 1 October) | | | |
|---|---|---|---|---|---|---|---|---|
| Year | Packs | Wolves | Area (km²) | Density (1,000 km²) | Packs | Wolves | Area (km²) | Density (1,000 km²) |
| 1986 | 4 | 26 | 7,380 | 3.5 | 4 | 22 | 8,180 | 2.7 |
| 1987 | 8 | 37 | 12,125 | 3.1 | 9 | 70 | 13,150 | 5.3 |
| 1988 | 14 | 69 | 15,355 | 4.5 | 14 | 122 | 14,670 | 8.3 |
| 1989 | 13 | 98 | 16,810 | 5.8 | 11 | 127 | 15,240 | 8.3 |
| 1990 | 10 | 106 | 13,930 | 7.6 | 11 | 136 | 13,930 | 9.8 |
| 1991 | 13 | 111 | 14,275 | 7.8 | 13 | 137 | 14,275 | 9.6 |
| 1992 | 15 | 103 | 13,620 | 7.6 | 15 | 120 | 13,620 | 8.8 |
| 1993 | 12 | 68 | 9,900 | 6.9 | 12 | 93 | 9,900 | 9.4 |
| 1994 | 10 | 61 | 11,145 | 5.5 | – | – | – | – |

number of pups produced and surviving (table 2.3). Nevertheless, for 23 pack years, we were able to make reasonably good May-June pup counts. A comparison of them with our autumn counts indicated that our average pup survival over summer was 91% or greater. Comparable summer pup-survival figures from other high-latitude areas are 97% from an area south of Denali (Ballard et al. 1987), and 76% on Alaska's Kenai Peninsula (Peterson et al. 1984). In the High Arctic, pup survival through early August (nine litters from one pack) was 100% (Mech 1995a). Probably these high young-pup survival rates result from the plethora of young prey available during summer, in Denali including ground squirrels, marmots, beavers, and hares (table 6.1).

With such high numbers of pups produced and surviving, it should not be surprising that the main determinant of our wolf population changes was the number of pups produced. Some 80% of the variation in annual percent spring-to-spring change in the Denali wolf population (table 2.4) can be explained by the annual percent pup production (average annual litter size in fall [table 2.3] divided by average spring pack size [table 2.4]). Presumably, then, the increased pup production we observed during the early years of the study reflected a better food supply starting during

winter 1987–88 and continuing for the next 4 years.

### Female Weights and Pup Production

The weights of the female wolves we captured for radio-collaring did seem to reflect a better food supply. The 12 females we captured in winter 1985–86 and 1986–87 weighed an average of 72.5 ± 2.7 (SE) pounds (32.9 ± 1.2 kilograms), whereas the 58 we caught during the next 6 years averaged 82.5 ± 1.4 (SE) pounds (37.5 ± 0.63 kilograms). These two samples might not be strictly comparable because of possible differences in proportions of adults and younger wolves. However, when we compared only yearling and adult wolves during the same periods (6 versus 35 individuals), those during the latter period averaged 13 pounds (6 kilograms) heavier.

Why was the food supply better beginning in winter 1987–88? The only difference we could find was that snowfall that winter measured 45 inches (121 centimeters), whereas during the two previous winters it measured 33 and 39 inches (86 and 103 centimeters) (table 1.1). Even though 45 inches (121 centimeters) is below average, it may have been deep enough in some areas to have increased prey vulnerability (see chapters 6 and 7).

Certainly the snow in 1987–88 would have

impeded prey more than during the previous 2 years. Furthermore, the two preceding winters might have been so mild that even usually vulnerable prey may have been able to survive. Then, when snow got deeper the next year, they may have finally become vulnerable.

In any case, by winter 1988–89, snowfall greatly exceeded the average, wolves preyed more on caribou, which suddenly became vulnerable, wolf weights maximized, more and larger litters were born, more pups survived and tended to remain longer with the packs, and the wolf population increased.

### Dispersal

The Denali wolf-dispersal rate also changed between the low- and high-density phases of our wolf population. Whereas during 1986 and 1987 an average of 52% of our radio-collared wolves dispersed, that number dropped to 27% for the next 4 years (table 2.7). Not only were more pups produced, but those that were produced remained with their packs longer.

We discussed wolf dispersal in chapter 5. Suffice it to say here that dispersal rate increases in times of low wolf food supply, and decreases with better food supply. Production of pups does the opposite. As expected, then, the dispersal rate of our radio-collared wolves was negatively related to litter sizes; the degree of relationship was about 60%.

### Wolf Mortality

The average annual rate of mortality of our radio-collared wolves from all causes (27%) was relatively low (table 2.8), considering that the average pack containing 6.7 wolves in spring produced an average of 3.8 pups per year by fall, a 57% annual increase. While our sample of wolves on which the mortality rates were derived was probably not completely representative of the Denali population at large (see chapter 2), our results should generally reflect the actual proportions of deaths

to various causes. Also, it is safe to conclude from our estimates that mortality was not the primary determinant of our wolf population change. As indicated earlier, most mortality of our radio-collared wolves was caused by natural factors, primarily other wolves (39%–65% of total mortality); only 14% was human-caused, mostly as wolves ventured outside the park and preserve (see chapter 2). This estimate of human-caused mortality amounted to less than 4% of the Denali population per year.

Our estimated rate of human-caused wolf mortality in Denali is the lowest of any large wolf population that has been studied anywhere except Isle Royale, the national park island in Lake Superior, which is closed and uninhabited for 8 months of the year. In an area adjacent to Denali, humans accounted for an estimated 80% of wolf mortality during years just preceding this study (Ballard et al. 1987).

Conversely, our rate of wolf mortality inflicted by fellow wolves was one of the highest reported, at least partly because human-caused mortality was so low. The natural state of a wolf population seems to include high natural-caused turnover.

### The Role of Disease

Disease can cause a high mortality rate in wolves. For example, rabies might at certain times and places influence Alaskan wolf populations (Davis et al. 1980), but rabies is virtually nonexistent anywhere near Denali. Serologic surveys of captured wolves across the state indicate that wolves in Alaska harbor numerous infectious and parasitic diseases (Zarnke and Ballard 1987). Nevertheless, severe outbreaks resulting in population declines have not been observed.

It is important to note that such occurrences might be difficult to detect because serologic testing only indicates exposure rates. Thus, we can only estimate the proportion of a population that has been exposed to a pathogen and survived. Estimates of mortality due to the pathogen cannot be made via blood samples. Still, large numbers of radio-tagged wolves should reveal most important disease-caused mortality. Neither this study nor other wolf studies in interior Alaska have found any sign of disease seriously affecting wolf populations.

The main type of disease-caused mortality that would not show up in radio-tagged wolves would be that affecting pups too young to radio-tag. A new disease that has precisely that effect is canine parvovirus (CPV), and circumstantial evidence indicates that CPV might be having some effects on wolf populations in the lower United States (Mech et al. 1986; Johnson et al. 1994; Wydeven et al. 1995; Mech and Goyal 1995). Furthermore, wolves on Alaska's Kenai Peninsula, where CPV seroprevalence in the population is high (Bailey et al. 1995), have unusually low summer pup survival.

Wolves in the interior of Alaska have also been exposed to CPV (Zarnke and Ballard 1987), and in a sample ranging from 9 to 30 Denali wolves per year whose blood we collected from 1986 to 1993, CPV-serum-antibody prevalence varied from 5% to 50% (R. Zarnke, pers. comm.). However, none of the 70 dead radio-collared wolves we examined from in and around Denali showed any sign of having died of the disease.

The possibility remains that some young pups in Denali may have died from CPV. Although Denali wolf-pup production (table 2.3) was as high as in most populations (Mech 1970), in the cases of three female wolves in the northeast corner of the park, we found evidence of entire litters being lost. In all three cases, we saw no pups in fall; yet one of the females appeared pregnant when examined in May, another had placental scars when killed the following January, and all three occupied dens during the period when pups are born. Nevertheless, there is no evidence that

CPV or any other disease was seriously affecting Denali wolf numbers.

## Wolf Population Turnover

The Denali wolf population during our study was productive, converting moose, caribou, sheep, and various smaller creatures to wolf pups at a relatively high rate. On the other hand, its members died off at an estimated average of 27% per year. This rate could be somewhat low because the age structure of our wolf sample was probably older than the age structure of the population (see chapter 2), and younger wolves tend to have lower survival (Van Ballenberghe and Mech 1975).

Our radio-collared wolves dispersed from the study area at an average rate of 21% per year. This estimate probably reasonably portrays the actual dispersal rate for the Denali population because our sample of wolves of dispersal age (1–3 years old) was reasonably representative of the population (see chapter 2).

The average time ("tenure") that our radio-collared wolves spent in Denali was about 4 years (table 8.2). However, because we selected older wolves to study rather than pups, and because older wolves tended to remain longer in Denali (table 8.2), this figure probably overestimates the average tenure of wolves in Denali. Our wolves 1 year old and younger remained in Denali an average of less than 2 years.

Since pups comprised about half the Denali population in winter (see chapter 2), by the end of the following winter, an estimated average of half the Denali wolves were gone (table 8.2). When the population was stable (only 2 years during this study), this loss would have been replaced by new pups and immigrants. When the population increased, relative amounts of dispersal, mortality, pup production, and immigration tipped in favor of adding wolves. When it decreased, the combination of these factors did the opposite.

**Table 8.2.** Estimated ages (years) of wolves live-captured in Denali National Park and Preserve, 1986–94, and their known tenure in the study area based on radio-tracking

| Age (yr) | Mean capture age (yr) | N | Mean additional tenure (yr)[a] | Mean ± SE total tenure in Denali[a] |
|---|---|---|---|---|
| 0–1 | 0.8 | 26 | 1.1 | 1.7 ± 0.1 |
| 1–2 | 1.7 | 37 | 1.4 | 2.9 ± 0.2 |
| 2–3 | 2.7 | 25 | 1.3 | 3.8 ± 0.3 |
| 3–4 | 3.6 | 17 | 2.1 | 5.7 ± 0.5 |
| 4–5 | 4.6 | 4 | 1.9 | 6.5 ± 0.9 |
| 5–6 | 5.9 | 3 | 3.3 | 9.1 ± 1.2 |
| 6–7 | 6.8 | 2 | 2.8 | 9.7 ± 0.3 |
| 7–8 | 7.4 | 2 | 0.5 | 7.9 ± 0.1 |
| 8–9 | – | 0 | – | – |
| 9–10 | 9.5 | 3 | 1.6 | 11.1 ± 0.6 |
| 10–11 | 10.8 | 1 | 0.6 | 11.4   – |
| | | | | |
| 0–10 | 2.6 | 120 | 1.5 | 4.0 ± 0.2 |
| 3–10 | 5.2 | 32 | 2.0 | 7.2 ± 0.5 |
| | | | | |
| 0–2 | 1.7 | 88 | 1.3 | 2.8 ± 0.2 |
| 3–4 | 3.8 | 21 | 2.1 | 5.9 ± 0.4 |
| 5–6 | 6.3 | 5 | 3.1 | 9.3 ± 0.7 |
| 7–10 | 9.0 | 6 | 1.0 | 10.1 ± 0.7 |

[a] *This does not include 8 wolves alive when this analysis was conducted (early 1997). Addition of those animals would increase mean additional tenure and mean tenure in Denali by an estimated 3–6 months for wolves < 5 years old at capture.*

## Prey Vulnerability and Wolf Population Change

The ultimate cause of change in most animal populations is the availability of food (Lack 1954). Certainly, the abundance of prey affects wolf food availability but the simple abundance of prey animals alone does not completely explain wolf numbers, nor year-to-year changes in wolf numbers. As discussed in chapter 5, wolves must search extensively for prey that they can kill, prey that are vulnerable. Such prey translate into wolf food.

What makes prey vulnerable? It has been said that wolves kill the very young, the very old, the sick, and the unlucky (plate 12). Vulnerability itself cannot often be measured; rather it is a proba-bilistic consequence of other factors such as nutrition, accidents, age, weather, weather-nutrition interactions, and other intrinsic or environmental circumstances.

Obvious examples of nutrition influencing prey vulnerability are populations that have outgrown their food supply, or those that because of unusually deep snow are hindered in getting to their food. A larger than normal proportion of those populations will exhibit the negative consequences of poor nutrition. Poor nutrition can cause physiological symptoms such as small size, weakness, or disease that would make it easier for wolves to find, catch, and kill an animal.

Less obviously, poor nutrition could cause behavioral deficiencies that might affect vulnerability, such as reduced vigilance or foraging far from escape terrain. Vigilance in detecting predators might be reduced if malnourished animals forage in smaller groups to avoid competition for food or spend less time looking around. Dall sheep in poor condition, for example, may have to forage far from the safety of cliffs and rocks.

The low survival of newborn caribou calves discussed in chapter 7 is an example of intrinsic vulnerability. Although the extent of their vulnerability from year to year is influenced by maternal nutrition, their basic vulnerability is inherent in being newborn. Similarly, bulls weakened by rutting efforts and concurrent inattention to feeding are more vulnerable to predation (see chapter 6).

Conversely, adult caribou cows are extremely resistant to predation. During October 1986–September 1996, annual survival of cows 1 year old and older averaged 88%, based on over 440 caribou-years of monitoring (L. Adams, unpublished).

### Snow and Prey Vulnerability

Environmental conditions can also affect vulnerability. Very deep snows may physically impede the ability of prey, especially caribou and sheep, to escape wolves. Or sometimes combinations of factors like vegetation, topography, and weather may result in extreme vulnerability of one or more animals for short periods.

In Gates of the Arctic National Park in Alaska's Brooks Range, a single wolf was seen feeding on at least 11 caribou carcasses at the base of a steep cliff, illustrating how such a combination of factors can work. A clear picture of what happened was etched in the snow above (B. W. Dale, pers. comm.). The 11 caribou had been walking along the ridge. A wolf approached from the opposite side and gave chase. The caribou fled, but the wolf must have been on an intercepting course because some of the caribou ran down a little couloir to a ledge 15 feet (3 meters) below while the rest headed to a cornice just above the others. The cornice must then have given way beneath the excited caribou, sending all tumbling a few hundred feet to their death. Tracks showed that the single wolf had approached the overhang, likely peered down to the bounty below, and made its way safely around the cliff, via a 3-mile (5-kilometer) detour, to the site where, one imagines, the wolf happily savored its solo feat.

A single wolf killing 11 caribou in a single attack is rare. However, it illustrates how topography and snow resulted in prey being extremely unlucky and therefore vulnerable. While arguments to the contrary could be made, probably at least some of the caribou were in good condition. This type of mortality is termed *additive* if the animals would have otherwise survived to reproduce without unduly decreasing the survival of other herd members through competition for resources.

Additive mortality is contrasted with *compensatory* mortality (Errington 1967), wherein prey taken by predators would have died anyway before reproducing, or had they survived, would have lowered survival of associates through competition for limited resources. Learning whether mortality is additive or compensatory is fundamental to understanding the effects of wolves on prey populations. Viewing wolf predation this way gives greater insight to the concept of prey vulnerability and illustrates the importance of vulnerability in wolf-prey dynamics.

Snow, however, is probably the factor that most consistently affects ungulate vulnerability (Stenlund 1955; Pimlott et al. 1969; Mech and Frenzel 1971; Peterson and Allen 1974; Peterson 1977; Mech and Karns 1977; Mech et al. 1987, 1991). Furthermore, snow conditions bring several direct and indirect effects that predispose prey to wolf predation (Mech 1990).

### Direct Effects of Snow on Prey Vulnerability

Deep snow can both impede the escape of animals chased by wolves and hinder the prey's daily acqui-

*Figure 8.3. Herbivores spend most of their time eating and searching for food. Deep snow hinders ungulates from finding and eating enough food. Because they are pregnant over winter, deep snow can make both the adults and eventually their prenatally undernourished offspring vulnerable to wolves. (Photo by L. David Mech.)*

sition of food. At certain depths, depending on the prey species, snow may hamper pursuing wolves more than the prey (Kelsall 1968). However, at other depths and consistencies, snow hinders prey more than wolves (Mech and Frenzel 1971). This can happen regardless of prey condition, although obviously a weakened animal would flounder more in the snow.

The hindrance by snow of ungulate feeding takes longer to affect prey and is more insidious. Most ungulates in the north gain weight into fall and lose it over winter, just the opposite of wolves. The extent of ungulate weight loss depends on temperature and snow conditions (Mautz 1978), and caribou may even maintain weight over winter if conditions are good. Nevertheless, during espe-

cially snowy winters, it is hard for all prey animals to get to, find, and eat enough food.

It takes deeper snow to hinder moose than it does to hinder other ungulates, and their winter food of twigs and branches is easier to reach. Hard, deep snow can even make more browse available to them. On the other hand, because of the moose's size, it must find and eat much more browse than smaller species need (figure 8.3). It takes less snow to affect the shorter-legged caribou and sheep. Both try to find food by frequenting windblown areas where they can move more easily and uncover the ground plants they graze on. Nevertheless, severe winters can be especially hard on their nutrition.

In winter 1988–89, both caribou and Dall

sheep in Denali became dramatically more vulnerable to predation. Adverse weather, including deep snows, not only nutritionally stressed many adult caribou but even hampered the escapes of prime-age caribou from pursuing wolves. This was evidenced by the much younger average age of both male and female caribou taken by wolves in multiple-killing episodes during deep snows (see chapter 6).

The marrow fat of caribou killed by wolves in usual situations averaged 47 ± 5% (*n* = 44), whereas the mean of the multiple-kill sample (*n* = 29) was 66 ± 4% (chapter 6). This finding indicates that although the caribou that wolves killed in multiples were still in poor condition, they were in better shape on average than those killed under more normal conditions.

The difficulties of fleeing through the deep snows may have replaced the differences in nutritional condition among individuals as the primary determinant of vulnerability, resulting in a wolf kill that more closely approximated the age and condition of the caribou herd as a whole. Just the fact that 40% of the adult caribou we found killed by wolves were taken during multiple-killing sprees during deep snows shows how important snow conditions are to caribou vulnerability.

*Indirect Effects of Snow on Prey Vulnerability*
Snow conditions also cause a variety of indirect effects on prey vulnerability (Mech 1990). Ungulates are pregnant all winter. Thus, winter weather not only affects the nutritional condition of the females but also of their fetuses (Verme 1962, 1963; Skogland 1990), which in turn affects their vulnerability to wolves (Mech et al. 1991).

Again, Isle Royale is a good case in point (Peterson 1977). From 1959 through 1969, moose aged 1 to 7 years old formed only 13% of those killed by wolves. After a series of deep-snow winters that affected the nutrition of pregnant cows, and thus the development of their calves, these age classes comprised 53% of the wolf kills.

In our study, wolves did not kill caribou calves during winter until after a previous winter of above-average snow (see chapter 6). In other words, the only winters in which wolves killed calves were those following severe winters during which the calves were fetuses.

This prenatal-nutrition effect can even persist for an additional generation such that, for example, white-tailed deer fawns whose grandmothers were poorly nourished are more vulnerable to wolves, even though their mothers were well-nourished (Mech et al. 1991). Although most of the details about the workings of this third-generation effect are based on studies of laboratory animals (Zamenhof et al. 1971; Bresler et al. 1975; Zamenhof and Van Marthens 1978), some evidence has been found in deer that animals with poorly nourished grandmothers were lighter weight (Mech et al. 1991).

An additional indirect effect of snow conditions is the "cumulative effect." Some evidence indicates that the effects of consecutive winter weather can accumulate in ungulates (Mech et al. 1987; Feldhamer et al. 1989; McRoberts et al. 1995; cf. Messier 1991, 1995). The idea here is that deep snow, for example, during one winter can have a stronger effect on animal condition if it immediately follows one or two other winters of deep snow.

Denali data tend to support the cumulative effect of snow conditions. The first winter of above-average snow during our study was 1988–89. Nevertheless, the proportion of caribou that wolves killed did not begin to increase until winter 1989–90 (see chapter 6). Both 1988–89 and 1989–90 had almost twice the snow of the previous winters (figure 7.2).

## Wolf Numbers and Caribou Vulnerability

The increased vulnerability of caribou was followed by decreased dispersal of wolves from packs and from the study area (table 2.7). Wolf numbers also rose because of increased pup production

**Figure 8.4.** *Above-average snowfall in winters 1990–91 through 1993–94 reduced caribou calf survival and recruitment into the herd, resulting in a decrease in population. (Photo by Layne G. Adams.)*

through increased litter size and multiple litters, as mentioned earlier. In addition, new packs proliferated through a variety of mechanisms. Whole packs split in two; singles, pairs, and trios budded off to form new packs; and dispersers from other areas successfully settled and raised pups (see chapter 4).

Within the range of the Denali Caribou Herd, wolf numbers nearly doubled. In addition to increasing the vulnerability of adult caribou to wolves, adverse weather through 1993 affected caribou reproduction (figure 8.4) and calf survival (see chapter 7). The herd crashed, and the wolf population soon began declining (figure 8.2). Notably the wolf population's decline was not as drastic as the caribou's decrease, reflecting the wolf's dependence on other prey as well as caribou.

Thus, it appears that in Denali winter weather greatly influenced the populations of wolves and caribou. This finding parallels similar findings about the Isle Royale wolf-moose system (Peterson 1977) and the northeastern Minnesota wolf-deer system (Mech 1977a,b, 1990; Mech and Karns 1977). The implications for stability within and among populations, and for the popular notion of the balance of nature are obvious.

Knowing that weather conditions assert such a profound effect on predator-prey systems makes one ponder the ultimate causes of weather changes. No doubt they arise far beyond the shadow of the Mountain, perhaps in El Niño in the equatorial Pacific. However, they are beyond the scope of our work, and certainly beyond anything anyone can do something about.

Nevertheless, it is reasonable to wonder how often a series of such unusual winter weather occurs. Should such weather patterns be considered rare? Not according to the joking comment of Jack Whitman, a biologist stationed just west of Denali in McGrath, who recently referred to the "seventeenth consecutive abnormal winter" for the area.

Despite Whitman's quip, just as there is some weather that is detrimental to caribou, so too must there sometimes be favorable weather. Its effects should be opposite those of severe weather. When we began our study, wolf numbers were down, pup production was low, and dispersal rates were high. The Denali Caribou Herd was growing. How was the weather then?

The weather preceding the caribou crash consisted of nearly a decade of below-average snowfall (figure 7.2). Wolves killed few caribou cows (see chapter 6), newborn calf survival and survival through summer were relatively high, and the herd increased (see chapter 7). Wolves were not flourishing, but they were surviving by preying primarily on moose and a scattering of other prey classes, depending on the season.

## The Wolf as an Opportunist

Individual wolves in their daily lifestyles are opportunists. They put on many miles per day seeking opportunities to take advantage of, whether those be in the form of newborn caribou calves, aging moose, or hungry sheep that venture too far from steep, rocky havens. If the wolves can kill their neighbors and take over more territory, that helps too. If necessary, they can take off, abandon their home, and try to make a better living hundreds of miles away.

Just as individual wolves are opportunists, so too are wolf populations, and for that matter, so is the wolf as a species. Wolf populations are adapted to hanging on at low densities when prey availability or vulnerability is low. But in a sense they are merely waiting, poised to rapidly and effectively exploit any increases in prey abundance and vul-

nerability brought on by changes in weather or other factors.

Such a lifestyle requires wolves to be well adapted to surviving lean times. When in good condition, they can probably last months without eating (Mech 1970). As indicated in chapter 5, they also make use of old kills and the caches around them (Murie 1944; Cowan 1947). Anyone who has followed wolves any distance knows that they rarely pass up a chance to dig up an old kill, even after all edible parts are seemingly long gone.

Single wolves and pairs can utilize small prey for extended periods to survive (L. D. Mech, unpublished). Hares, beavers (Voigt et al. 1976), and miscellaneous small prey can provide enough energy for survival. To reduce energy needs, wolves sometimes curl up for days (figure 8.5), traveling little in favor of rest and sleep (Mech 1977b).

A pack of wolves lacking the resources to successfully rear pups may choose to remain within a territory rather than disperse (Mech 1995a), for each season brings new opportunity. Food may become abundant because of the onset of the rut, changes in prey migration routes, increases in vulnerability, or even a bumper crop of young prey animals.

The very cold winter of 1995–96 in central Alaska with low snowfall resulted in deep freezing of rivers, ponds, and lakes. The thickening ice forced many beavers to leave their lodges to forage because their carefully stored stick caches froze in. Their choice was to risk starvation within the lodge or risk being eaten or killed while venturing overland. The result was an increase in vulnerable prey for wolves in many parts of interior Alaska.

When prey becomes available, wolves have mechanisms for rapid exploitation. Pup production can increase dramatically by greatly increased litter sizes and increased survival of those pups. Subadult and young adult wolves may remain with the pack, taking advantage of the opportunity

*Figure 8.5. When prey is less vulnerable, one of the ways that wolves respond is by reducing their activity. (Photo by L. David Mech.)*

to grow large, healthy, and more experienced before setting forth on their own.

In addition, adoption of young adults or strange wolves into the pack may result in more than just temporarily increased pack size. The pack may produce two, or perhaps even three, litters of pups by different females in a single year (see chapter 4). Survival may increase as competition decreases and as wolves take less risks for food. All together, these mechanisms make wolves highly adapted for rapidly exploiting increases in prey availability.

## Short-Term versus Long-Term Prey Exploitation

An increase in prey availability due to greater vulnerability, rather than higher numbers, may result in lower prey availability in the longer term. That is, prey may become so vulnerable that wolves may kill many prey in a short time. Thus, wolves could have a significant effect on the number of prey available the following years by killing more in 1 year than can be reproduced.

In Denali, the caribou population crash means

fewer caribou for years to come. This "boom-and-bust" economy might result in reduced productivity for Denali's wolves for many years. However, consider the short tenure of breeding wolves in the population (table 8.2; chapter 4) and the low chances for young wolves to secure a breeding slot in their home territory. From that perspective, it is easy to understand why natural selection would favor wolves that exploit the changes to the fullest and increase the number of offspring produced over that brief tenure.

The high dispersal rates common to wolf populations reveal the strategy employed by wolves to maximize their genetic fitness: raise as many pups as possible as fast as possible to an age where they have acquired the physical size and experience to hunt on their own. These young animals then disperse to find new territories, breeding opportunities, and genetic combinations (figure 8.6).

Considering the role of wolf dispersal in maximizing fitness, the ephemeral nature of vulnerable prey, the wolf's average short breeding tenure, and the effective mechanisms for exploiting food abundance, we would expect wolves to

*Figure 8.6.* Most wolves disperse as loners far from their natal packs and try to find new areas in which to breed and raise their own packs. (Photo by Thomas J. Meier.)

kill as many prey as possible. There is little for wolves to gain by being prudent about resources within the territory.

## The Role of Moose in the Wolf-Prey System

By 1994, moose again had become the primary prey for wolves in Denali. What happened to the moose population in the interim when wolves were more abundant and caribou became their primary prey? Our investigation lacked adequate funding to fully address this question. Ecological theory, however, provides some intriguing possibilities and illuminates the importance of just such an investigation for understanding complex predator-prey systems.

Two contrary predictions can be made regarding the fate of the moose population when the secondary prey species, caribou, suddenly becomes more vulnerable. As we have seen, wolf numbers may increase in response. More wolves hunting the countryside may put more pressure on the moose population, even if the adverse weather does not increase moose vulnerability.

Such a scenario is entirely possible. Snows may be deep enough to influence caribou but not deep enough to affect the longer-legged, browsing moose. When one species is negatively affected indirectly by the presence of another of the same trophic level (i.e., both herbivores in this case), it is termed *apparent competition* (Holt 1977). In this case, the moose are exposed to greater risk simply

*Figure 8.7. Many unanswered questions about wolves will someday be answered through new technology such as this experimental GPS collar, which records actual routes used by animals; see figure 5.5. (Photo by Layne G. Adams.)*

because wolves have increased due to increased caribou vulnerability.

The second prediction one can make is that the wolf increase affects the moose oppositely. It is the consequence of an ecological process known as *prey switching*. In this scenario, the increased wolves take fewer moose because caribou are more profitable. Reduced moose predation could result from wolves being more selective when they test moose or from changes in the habitats that wolves search for prey. In other words, wolves may spend more time in caribou country than where moose are likely found.

Sorting between these two theories requires information about the absolute numbers of each prey type killed rather than just the proportions. Such data are difficult to obtain because of the many biases associated with finding the remains of vastly different-sized prey. Hopefully, new technology (figure 8.7) or methodology will soon be developed to meet this challenge because the implications for distinguishing between these two outcomes may be enormous.

It is also important to consider that, while

having contrary consequences, the two hypotheses are not mutually exclusive. Considering the many vagaries of vulnerability, the issue becomes very complex indeed.

## Speculations about Wolves and Moose

What speculations can be made from what we have observed so far? A few relevant facts come to mind. First, estimates of total moose numbers remained about the same between 1987 and 1991 (Meier 1987; Meier et al. 1991). However, moose may have increased since 1991 (K. E. Stahlnecker, unpublished). Clearly, not enough moose surveys have been conducted, but they are very expensive (figure 8.8). Furthermore, surveys alone cannot explain the causes underpinning any changes in population trend.

Second, our indices to numbers of moose killed by wolves (see chapter 6) suggest that more moose may have been killed in 1988–89 but fewer during 1989–92, although because of the biases discussed earlier, this interpretation must be guarded.

Finally, a last qualitative argument can be

*Figure 8.8. Moose censuses must be done from the air and thus are very expensive. (Photo by L. David Mech.)*

made. Wolves quickly and efficiently exploited an increase in caribou vulnerability. It seems reasonable to assume that they would also continue to exploit the vulnerable portion of the moose herd. Nevertheless, this remains an interesting and important topic to be studied for understanding the complex wolf-prey system in Denali. How long does it take a wolf population raised on killing caribou to learn how to take advantage of moose?

Thus, we really cannot say what the net effect of wolves on moose numbers has been during our investigation.

As the Denali Caribou Herd declined, the number of vulnerable individuals followed suit. Fewer caribou were available to the wolves. Also, weather improved, further decreasing the number of vulnerable caribou. As a result, the wolf population also began to decline (figure 8.2). In just a few years, the particular boom we documented for wolves was over in Denali.

By 1994, the wolf population performed at an intermediate level, unlike the lean years when we began our study and the boom years of 1988–90. Presumably now the wolves will produce fewer pups, multiple litters will become less common, wolves will disperse at a younger age (Messier 1985), and interpack strife may cause more mortality (Mech 1977b). Territory sizes may well expand, and fewer packs will split and bud.

Where is the balance? At the level of Denali's wolves and spatially dynamic prey like caribou, we must understand that such wide fluctuations are the natural condition, the natural result of natural processes. Both predator and prey are adjusted to these fluctuations and readily survive them. Possibly the only semblance of balance in such a system could be that fleeting moment when the system swings away from one extreme and heads toward the other.

# Wolves in Perpetuity

Almost six decades ago, Adolph Murie stood along the East Fork River deep in the heart of Mount McKinley National Park. High above him the sprawling earthen hues of Polychrome Mountain revealed a geologic history of millions of years. As Murie scanned the hills for sheep or wolves, no satellites whisked across the skies. No busloads of tourists rumbled by. Not even a park ranger intruded on the scene.

Sixty years before that, only Athabascan Indians prowled that area. No park road gave easy access. Only sheep ruts cut diagonally across the mountainsides, and caribou trails meandered miles along the braided rivers, over the tundra, and through the mountains.

But the East Fork River looked the same then as it does now. And Polychrome Pass too. And some miles beyond it, connecting the earth with the clouds and casting its mammoth shadow over the area, stood the massive mountain of rock, snow, and ice that the Indians called Denali, "the High One."

Scattered over the landscape all those many years ago during both periods were the wolves and the moose, the sheep and the caribou, the grizzly bears, the marmots, the eagles, and the ground squirrels. Probably little different from today, they plied their lives with ancient habits peculiar to their kind but profoundly successful.

None of the creatures sported radios in Murie's day or before. Their lives, therefore, were much more of a mystery then than now. Nevertheless, all these unique components of the Denali ecosystem, and all the other parts as well, interact today like they did when the Athabascans hunted among them or Murie watched them. The difference is that today we know much more about those interactions than we did before.

Like everywhere else, the Denali ecosystem is comprised of multitudes of interacting food chains including those involving eagles, lynx, foxes, wolverines, bears, coyotes, and the prey of each as well as many other birds, mammals, and various invertebrates. In Denali, many of these chains interact with the wolf-prey chain in a complex web of life and death.

It is the wolf-prey chain, however, that in a certain sense dominates Denali both in the way human beings perceive the park and also in terms of scale. Wolf prey are the largest creatures of

Denali, and the full-time ecological "job" of wolves is to kill them. In doing so, wolves provide food not only for themselves but also for most of the smaller carnivores and scavengers.

Because wolves and their prey are large, it is easier in some ways to study them than to investigate food chains involving smaller creatures. Thus, an understanding of the life of the wolf and its prey in Denali lends insights into the functioning of the rest of the food web. All types of prey depend on plants, which in turn are affected by the basic physical conditions of soil and climate. All carnivores exist in lower numbers than their prey, and so must circulate about and scan their prey for likely targets. Thus, although the specific workings of the various food chains may vary, they share basic elements.

Denali's wolf-prey system functions today as it did in Murie's day and in the Athabascans' day. Wolves scan every fertile area of the park, avoiding only the sterile ice, rock, and snow of the Mountain.

Picture the park from space: Perhaps it is summer, and individual wolves, some in twos and threes, are trotting up the river bars, along the ridges, across the tundra, fanning out from their dens of pups.

In the East Fork area, a wolf makes its way along the Toklat River, another heads over Sable Pass, and a small group checks out the Wyoming Hills north of the den. To the northwest, Little Bear Pack members spread over the Kantishna Hills, some coursing the barren tops while others pick their way through the tangled willows and alders of their steep valleys. Way off to the southwest, the wolves of the McLeod Lake Pack inspect the myriad ponds reflecting nearby Mount McKinley, head over the eskers, and lope steadily across the flats.

Yard after yard, mile after mile, the wolves cover the area. What they do not see, they hear; what they do not hear, they smell. If they miss some spot today, they may hit it tomorrow, or the next day. Or some fellow pack member may check it out. Although their quest is always food, their other interests include signs of friends and enemies. Thus, as each wolf circulates about the region, it hesitates often, sifting the scents, sounds, and sights for any clue of interest.

Feces and urine yield cues about what other wolves have passed and when. If strange, they may need more investigation and perhaps some scouting about for the maker. Or maybe they require retreat. Signs from packmates may indicate that the area has been hunted recently, or that a fresh kill lies nearby.

If a traveling wolf runs into a packmate, the two will usually socialize for a few seconds and travel together awhile. When they spot an enemy, they may give pursuit, or they may turn tail. Foxes, wolverines, lynx, coyotes, or other competitors are promptly chased. Bears give the wolves pause, and unless a meaty carcass is involved, the wolves are usually content to back off. When some difference in motivation besets each of the traveling companions, they will go their separate ways, only to meet again sometime or someday back at the den.

Meanwhile, the moose, the caribou, and the sheep of Denali busy themselves with eating. Bite after bite, they munch their way over or through the vegetation. Each frequents its own type of area and chews its own kind of food. The moose prefers the willows, wrapping its tongue around each fresh shoot, pressing it against the roof of its mouth, and stripping off the leaves. Small bands of sheep search the rocky crags for grasses and sedges, and in between, any shrubby willows they can find. Caribou herds frequent the park's high, open slopes, not only to avoid the variety of insects that harass them but also to exploit the hills' profusion of lush grasses, sedges, herbs, willows, and dwarf birches.

As these herbivores feed, they move slowly over the area, picking and choosing their plants but constantly chewing as they go, and only occasionally looking up, unless some troublesome cue alerts them. Thousands of bites are needed to fill their rumens and build their bodies over the summer. When the animals stop grazing or browsing and rest, they bring up their food again in cuds, chew it more thoroughly, and swallow it again, this time for good.

The adult females whose new offspring still survive have an even stronger need to concentrate on feeding during this brief period of plenty. Their nursing young will drain them more of their energy than will anything else. With the breeding season coming again soon, followed by the cold and snow of winter, they must take full advantage of this short opportunity to replenish themselves. Otherwise, they will get no other chance.

These Denali herbivores outnumber the wolves by about 60 to 1. Thus, we can imagine from 70 to 140 wolves (depending on year and season) wandering over the park day after day, one pack here and another there, moving among the moose, sheep, and caribou. Each time a wolf locates prey, it must try to turn the encounter to its own advantage. Many times that is not possible, and the wolf must go on.

During summer, the most opportune types of encounters for wolves are usually those involving the young of their prey, especially moose calves. If the winter has been especially snowy, caribou calves may be more profitable. Now and then a wolf may find an old or weak adult ungulate it can kill, or a carcass washed up on a river bar. Beavers, marmots, ground squirrels, hares, and other small prey fill in as the wolves come upon them.

Then back to the den or rendezvous site each wolf heads with stomach or jaws full, excitedly approaching the breeding female and her litter of perhaps six pups. They in turn rush the provider frantically and instantly usurp its bounty. Numerous such trips are made, and the pups grow quickly. By about October, they are usually large enough to join the adults in their hunts, and the pack travels as a group.

Bull moose have been fighting for females some weeks already, ignoring food and everything else in a desperate attempt to pass on as many of their genes as possible. They are growing weak, and the wolves will dispatch the older ones. Caribou bulls, too, are trysting and fighting and providing additional food for the wolves. One to 2 months later, Dall sheep rams will fall into the same pattern.

By the end of December, the sun has reached its nadir, light is low, and bitter cold pervades Denali. Snow has covered the park for as many as 3 months already in some years. During others, strong arctic highs hold off the storms, and snow is light. The difference will determine whether or not wolves can depend on female prey during the next few months, especially caribou. If not, they must continue finding moose calves and what miscellaneous older or weaker moose, caribou, and sheep remain.

The number of wolves during the next years may turn on this difference. Caribou herds drift far and wide across Denali's vastness at this time. If snow is light, and food is found in many places, the herds circulate among these areas, warding off the worst ravages of winter's scarcity and making discovery by wolves less probable. Windblown ridges expose the lichens, mosses, and remaining grasses and sedges that caribou seek. The less the creatures have to hunt and dig for these dry strands, the more of their precious fat reserves they can shunt to their developing fetuses. The better too the caribou can resist the inevitable attacks by wolves.

Such resistance may then translate into increased dispersal by the wolves' maturing young. As prey become harder to catch, the yearling and 2-year-old wolves must yield to their parents as they feed the developing pups. One by one, then, the maturing wolves break away from their natal group. A few will visit neighboring packs and somehow work their way into one. Most will head far outside the park toward mates and what could be "greener pastures" but what may end up being their demise.

Even most of the wolves that remain, however, will survive for very limited periods. In 1 year or 2, the pups will be in the same positions their older siblings are and will also depart. The adults will breed again and probably produce pups. However, at any time as they make their way around their territory, they may suddenly be confronted by their neighbors. If so, a fight to the death is probable. One or both breeders may be killed, and some of the younger wolves as well. If the young wolves are not killed, they may languish and die without the adults to provision them.

In any case, some wolves will triumph and survive a while longer. They will continue their travels over their territory, marking it as they go, and howling frequently to warn their neighbors. If the breeders still find food scarce, they may produce only a few pups that spring, or maybe none. The winter weather's fickleness has had a pervasive effect on their life, and they may be lucky to even survive.

On the other hand, if snow is deep, a different set of effects may cascade through the system. Moose and sheep will find it harder to feed and will weaken sooner. Travel will be harder, more restricted, and more energy-depleting for caribou. The ever-scanning wolves may find the herds sooner, and certainly they can catch and kill the caribou more easily.

The timing is perfect, for the wolves are now fattening up for their own reproduction. A bonanza of vulnerable prey due to deep snows primes the wolves for a productive year. So, too, the lack of competition allows the maturing pack members to remain longer, and the packs build up.

With either scenario, spring brings change. Not only do the sheep and moose in their new freedom from the restricting snows begin to gorge again and immediately start replenishing their lost reserves, but the caribou, too, drift back toward their calving ground in the shadow of the Mountain near the center of the park. The wolves, suspending their own nomadism, begin to dig their dens.

Just as the wolves are whelping, the caribou begin to calve. A sudden burst of easy prey becomes available. How easy and how big a burst depends again on the preceding snows. If light, the calves may provide only a 2-week feast, but if the snows are deep and long, some calves may be available throughout the year. Moose calves come next, and similar workings affect their vulnerability.

So on and on the Denali system churns, year after year and decade after decade. Winter storms come and go, some more severe, some less. At times herbivore numbers wax; at other times they wane. Wolves respond accordingly and add their effects to the process. They flourish for awhile, and their dispersers probe the outside world. Some find mates and spread Denali genes far and wide; the others perish. Then, when conditions change, Denali wolves wait, their full potential to expand on hold. There will be another day.

In the shadow of the Mountain, there will always be another day.

# Dispersal of Wolves from Study Packs, Denali National Park and Preserve, 1986–94

Following is a list of wolves that dispersed from our study area and for which we had reasonably complete data when the list was compiled. Our various dispersal analyses were based on these wolves and on others, but because not all kinds of data were available for all dispersed wolves, slightly different samples were used for different analyses.

| Wolf no. | Sex | Pack | Age (mon) | Dispersal Date | Location | Distance (km) | Direction | Fate[a] |
|---|---|---|---|---|---|---|---|---|
| 151 | F | Clearwater | 29 | Oct 86 | Styx River | 240 | SW | H |
| 213 | F | Clearwater | 19 | Dec 86 | Macomb Plateau | 320 | E | H |
| 215 | M | East Fork | 13 | Jun 86 | Tanada Lake | 352 | ESE | H |
| 217 | F | East Fork | 79 | Dec 90 | Kantishna Hills | 40 | WNW | W |
| 219 | F | Headquarters | 22 | Mar 87 | Kavik River | 696 | N | H |
| 231 | M | Headquarters | 17 | Oct 86 | Chulitna River Pack | 48 | S | H |
| 233 | F | Alma Lakes | 25 | Jun 86 | Lake Minchumina | 72 | W | H |
| 237 | M | Sushana | 34 | Mar 87 | Totek Hills Pack | 40 | N | H |
| 239 | M | East Fork | 16 | Sep 87 | Slide Creek/Wood River | 136 | ENE | H |
| 250 | M | Clearwater | 28 | Sep 87 | Pirate Creek Pack | 24 | S | |
| 301 | M | Birch Creek | 36 | Oct 91 | Bearpaw, Old Minto | 168 | NE | H |
| 311 | M | Last Chance | 20 | Oct 90 | Last Chance Pack | 128 | ENE | C |
| 315 | M | McKinley River | 47 | Apr 89 | Chitsia Mountain Pack | 40 | NE | |
| 321 | F | McKinley River | 39 | Aug 88 | Foraker Pack | 32 | W | N |
| 330 | F | Ewe Creek | 14 | Jul 88 | Usibelli + beyond | 80 | E | |
| 337 | F | Highpower | 11 | Apr 88 | Kuskokwim River area | 48 | NW | U |
| 347 | F | Birch Creek | 32 | Jan 91 | Birch Creek N Pack | 16 | N | H |
| 363 | M | Clearwater | 34 | Mar 89 | Clearwater Pack | 40 | NE | N |
| 367 | F | McLeod Lake | 36 | May 91 | McLeod West Pack | 32 | SW | |
| 369 | F | Birch Creek | 56 | Jan 91 | Birch Creek N Pack | 16 | N | W |
| 379 | M | McKinley River | 35 | Apr 89 | Chena Hot Springs | 288 | NE | H |
| 381 | M | Ewe Creek | 24 | May 89 | Snodgrass Lake | 96 | SE | H |
| 385 | M | Highpower | 24 | May 91 | Foraker River Pack | 32 | E | H |

| Wolf no. | Sex | Pack | Age (mon) | Dispersal | | Distance (km) | Direction | Fate[a] |
|---|---|---|---|---|---|---|---|---|
| | | | | Date | Location | | | |
| 395 | M | East Fork | 24 | May 90 | Mulchatna River | 576 | SW | H |
| 397 | M | Stampede | 24 | May 90 | McKinley River Pack | 64 | W | |
| 399 | F | Stampede | 12 | May 90 | George Parks Highway | 32 | E | H |
| 407 | M | McKinley River | 27 | Sep 90 | Chilchukabena Pack | 32 | N | W |
| 409 | F | McLeod Lake | 24 | May 91 | McLeod West Pack | 32 | SW | N |
| 415 | M | Last Chance | 24 | May 91 | Black Rapids Glacier | 120 | ESE | H |
| 423 | F | Dry Creek | 25 | Jun 88 | Reindeer Hills Pack | 80 | SSW | H |
| 433 | F | Little Bear | 24 | May 92 | Styx River | 256 | SW | |
| 435 | F | Little Bear | 36 | May 92 | Styx River | 256 | SW | H |
| 437 | M | Little Bear | 37 | Jun 91 | Stampede, Ferry | 64 | NE | H |
| 441 | M | Foraker | 23 | Apr 91 | Slippery Creek Pack | 48 | NE | N |
| 453 | F | McLeod Lake | 24 | May 92 | McLeod West Pack | 32 | SW | U |
| 457 | F | Little Bear | 24 | May 92 | Foraker River + beyond | 80 | SW | |
| 459 | M | Little Bear | 24 | May 92 | Styx River | 256 | SW | |
| 463 | F | Chitsia Mt. | 25 | May 93 | Lower Toklat River | 112 | NNE | W |
| 469 | M | East Fork | 35 | Apr 92 | Totatlanika Pack | 96 | NE | U |
| 481 | F | McLeod Lake | 23 | Apr 92 | Ferry + beyond | 160 | NE | |
| 489 | M | McLeod Lake | 36 | May 92 | Susitna River | 176 | E | |
| 509 | M | Savage | 32 | Jan 93 | Tatlanika Pack | 64 | ENE | U |
| 531 | M | Turtle Hill | 23 | Apr 93 | Tangle Lakes | 240 | E | H |
| 545 | M | Jenny Creek | 13 | Jun 94 | Headquarters Pack | 24 | SE | H |
| 547 | M | Lone/disp | 35 | Mar 94 | Seventy Mile River | 360 | ENE | H |

[a]H = human-killed; W = wolf-killed; U = unknown; C = capture-related; N = unknown natural mortality.

# *Pack Histories*

The following histories cover the Denali wolf packs we studied other than those discussed in chapter 3.

## Chulitna River Pack

Gray male wolf 231, after dispersing from the Headquarters Pack in October 1986, paired with a white-backed female in the Chulitna River drainage southeast of Denali. The 2 occupied a 390-square-mile (993-square-kilometer) area in winter 1986–87, southeast of the George Parks Highway and outside Denali.

The Chulitna pair produced 5 black pups near the East Fork of the Chulitna River in 1987, 3 of which survived into winter 1987–88. In autumn 1987, we found many bones of sheep, caribou, and moose around the den, all of which were plentiful in the area.

In March 1988, 4 of the 5 Chulitna Pack members, including both adults, were killed by illegal aerial gunning. Skinned carcasses of 2 adults and 2 pups were found on a lake 2 miles (3 kilometers) outside the park. At least one criminal conviction was obtained in the case. No wolves used the Chulitna den in 1988, but the Windy Creek Pack used it in later years.

## Ewe Creek Pack

The Ewe Creek Pack territory covered less than 390 square miles (1,000 square kilometers) in northeastern Denali and outside but eventually shifted eastward entirely outside the park (figure 4.1). This pack consistently frequented more mountainous terrain than any other pack we studied, and it apparently killed proportionately more sheep (table 3.1). It also had access to moose in the Dry Creek, Moody Creek, and Healy River valleys, and to occasional bands of caribou from the Denali, Delta, and Yanert herds.

Track surveys in winter 1984–85 had indicated a pack of 6 to 8 wolves north of Mount Healy (Dalle-Molle and Van Horn 1985). Six wolves were seen in the Dry Creek–Ewe Creek area in October 1986. At least 1 wolf, a pup, was legally snared in that area by residents during winter 1986–87.

We radio-collared adult male 980 near the Savage River in late August 1987 and learned that the pack consisted of 5 adults and 3 pups in fall

1987. Its range extended south to the park road corridor, where we once saw these wolves chasing the Headquarters pair. This pack also frequented the Healy dump, and at least 1, a female pup, was legally caught there by a local trapper.

In December, we found breeding male 980 alone in the upper Sushana drainage, dragging a trapper's snare and 4 feet of the lead wire. We darted him and removed the snare. The wolf appeared in good shape and had gained 22 pounds (10 kilograms) since we had caught him 3 months earlier. In May, he died in an illegal snare, left out after the season closed, just outside the park boundary on the Savage River.

Female pup 330, radio-collared only a month earlier, was caught in another snare nearby but broke loose. In June she was still carrying the snare on her leg, so we darted her and removed the snare. Although 330 recovered from that injury without a limp, she never rejoined the pack but dispersed eastward. The pack, containing 5 wolves, was located again in October by snow-tracking, and we radio-collared yearling females 341 and 343.

A male pup was legally caught by a local trapper in Bison Gulch in November, and the pack dropped to 4. We radio-collared male pup 381 and female pup 383 near Moody Creek in March 1989. An adult female caught and killed by a local trapper in December 1988 near Otto Lake may have been the breeding female of the Ewe Creek Pack. Yearling female 341 was trapped by a local trapper on the Healy River in March. Yearling male 381 dispersed to the southeast in summer 1989 and was shot near the Susitna River in January 1990.

There was no evidence of denning or pup production in the Ewe Creek Pack in summer 1989, and the pack in fall 1989 consisted of females 343 and 383 and an unknown third animal. They were not found west of the park road after June 1989. Female 383 was killed by wolves on Moody Creek in winter 1989–90.

This death left female 343 and male 405, which we radio-collared in March 1990. This pair denned near Garner in 1990 and produced at least 3 pups but were seen with only 2 pups through the remainder of the winter. In May 1991, 343 denned in the Cripple Creek area, but we never saw any pups. We did not follow the pack closely after they shifted outside the park. Four to 5 wolves were seen in the pack in late winter 1991–92, but only 3 in winter 1992–93. Both 343 and 405 were last radio-located in March 1993. Male 405 was shot by ADFG wolf-control personnel in October 1994.

## Last Chance Pack

Male wolf 311, originally from the Clearwater Pack, spent a year with the Headquarters Pack (see chapter 3) and then paired with a female in the Nenana Canyon area just outside Denali. His mate and a pup may have been trapped near Healy in fall 1990. In early February 1991, 311 was found in the Cody Pass–Last Chance Creek area with 3 other wolves. On March 13, 1991, we re-collared 311 and radio-collared male pup 415 and adult female 425, which wore an old ADFG radio-collar.

From 425's known history, it appeared that 311 had joined an existing pack. Unfortunately, 311 died as a result of his capture. He was found dead 4 days later, 1.5 miles (2.4 kilometers) from where he was released. A kidney abnormality had made him unable to metabolize the tranquilizing drug.

Wolves 415 and 425 and 2 others remained in the territory and were located only intermittently because of their distance from our study area. Male 415 dispersed 75 miles (120 kilometers) east-southeast and was road-killed at Black Rapids Glacier along the Richardson Highway in early June 1991. Female 425 was found killed by wolves in upper Coal Creek in mid-February 1992, ending our contact with the pack.

## Pirate Creek Pack

This was a short-lived pack, an offshoot of the Clearwater Pack, that occupied a 155-square-mile (400-square-kilometer) area south of the McKinley Bar. The territory, which contains the core of the Denali Caribou Herd calving range, contains few prey in winter. Male wolf 250 of the Clearwater Pack had paired with another wolf and was occupying the southern part of the Clearwater territory when his signal was last heard in November 1987.

In May 1988, we discovered a pair of wolves raising a litter of pups in this area, south of the McKinley Bar. One wolf, presumably male 250, was wearing a nonfunctional radio collar. We radio-collared the female, 339, near the den in July 1988. The pair raised 7 pups and appeared to be carving out a territory among the Clearwater Pack territory, the McLeod Lake Pack territory, and the Alaska Range.

We found wolf 339 dead in late November 1988. Necropsy by John Blake of the University of Alaska showed evidence of starvation and duodenal ulcers. The fate of 250 and the pups is unknown, but we saw no more sign of them in the territory. In May 1992, wolves again inhabited this area (the Turtle Hill Pack).

## Alma Lakes Pack

The Alma Lakes Pack, followed only in 1986, occupied a 980-square-mile (2,500-square-kilometer) area, half in and half out of the park and preserve in the Bearpaw and Kantishna River drainages. The territory supports relatively few moose, no sheep, and probably few caribou. Beavers may be important in summer, and salmon are present in the Kantishna and Bearpaw Rivers. The entire territory was subject to subsistence trapping, and a local trapper reported catching 3 black pups from this pack in winter 1985–86.

The pack consisted of 1 gray and 3 black wolves when first seen in the Alma Lakes area near the north edge of the park in April 1986. We radio-collared 2 black yearling wolves, male 229 near Chitsia Creek on April 8, and female 233 near John Hansen Creek on April 21. For the first 6 months of monitoring, the Alma Lakes Pack restricted its activities to the southeastern part of its territory. From October to December 1986, it was found only in the northernmost part of the territory.

Wolves 229 and 233 were always alone when located from May to October. Female 233 dispersed 25 miles (40 kilometers) southwest in late June and occupied 310 square miles (800 square kilometers) south of and including Lake Minchumina until being shot in the community of Lake Minchumina about November 20. She apparently had been scavenging around the community and various cabins in the area.

No evidence of reproduction was seen in this pack. Both radio-collared wolves appeared to be away from the pack all summer, but those seen in fall appeared to be the original pack, without female 233. Male 229 was last found on December 30, 1986; no signal from his collar has been heard since then.

## Windy Creek Pack

The Windy Creek Pack occupied an area of up to 350 square miles (900 square kilometers) in the Windy Creek, Jack River, and Chulitna River drainages along the southeast corner of the park. This area contained high densities of moose and intermittent high densities of caribou, which this pack preyed on (table 3.1), and some sheep.

In February 1987, a cow moose was seen on upper Windy Creek, fending off wolves from the carcasses of her two dead calves for 10 days (see chapter 5), after which the Windy Creek Pack finally ate them. We radio-collared 2 members of this pack, males 243 and 245, near the carcasses.

Seven wolves were present in the pack in February, decreasing to 6 by March. During the previous winter, track surveys had indicated at least 11 wolves in this area, but 3 of them were poached inside the park in March 1985 (Dalle-Molle and Van Horn 1985).

Three pups were seen in summer 1987 at a den near Little Windy Creek, and apparently all survived to fall. Five adults remained with the pack into the fall, including both radio-collared animals. The Windy Creek Pack occupied a relatively small area during the first 10 months we monitored it, mostly in the Windy Creek and Cantwell Creek drainages south of the Alaska Range.

The pack made two known forays north into the Alaska Range, and in December 1987 we found them 15 miles (25 kilometers) southeast at Caribou Pass, south of the Denali Highway, where many caribou of the Nelchina Herd were wintering.

Although we located wolf 245 near the den area in summer 1988, we saw no pups in fall. The pack appeared to spend more time outside Denali, in the Jack River and Chulitna River drainages, than it had in 1987. The signal from male 243 was last heard in April 1988, and he presumably dispersed or was killed. The pack contained 5 wolves in winter 1988–89.

We radio-collared breeding female 377 in the Yanert River valley in March 1989, the only time we found the pack north of the Alaska Range. In summer 1989, the pack produced 5 pups at the den near Little Windy Creek, and the pack contained 8 wolves in fall 1989 and spring 1990. They denned some 20 miles (32 kilometers) farther south in 1990 than previously, using a den occupied by the Chulitna Pack in 1987 and by other packs in previous years (W. Ballard, pers. comm.). Six pups were seen at that den.

The Windy Creek Pack then began spending little time as far north as Windy Creek. We found no evidence that other wolves were occupying that area except for two known visits by the Headquarters Pack, which in itself may have suggested a vacancy there. We last heard female 377 in August 1990, her radio collar apparently having failed.

In November 1990, we saw 17 wolves in the Windy Creek Pack, suggesting that the pack may have produced two litters. We radio-collared female pup 413 then but later in winter failed to locate her or the other radio-collared pack members.

In early June 1991, a wolf that looked radio-collared and fit female 377's description was seen suckling at least 3 pups at the Chulitna River den. This was the last record we have for the Windy Creek Pack.

## Dillinger River Pack

We found this itinerant pack of 10 wolves along the Foraker River in February 1987 and radio-collared adult male 249. The pack soon moved southward, then southwestward, and never returned to the park. The entire pack was last seen near Farewell, about 100 miles (160 kilometers) from 249's capture site. In December, after not finding 249's signal for 6 months, we heard it in mortality mode near Lime Village, 200 miles (320 kilometers) southwest of his Denali capture site. We were unable to investigate the cause of death, although we suspect humans.

## Bearpaw Pack

The Bearpaw Pack occupied 250 square miles (644 square kilometers) northwest of the Kantishna Hills along the Bearpaw River and Moose Creek in central Denali during 1987 and 1988. The Alma Lakes Pack had occupied this area in 1986. In April 1987, we radio-collared male 259 and female 261, both estimated as yearlings, from a pack of at least 5 black and gray wolves in the Flume Creek area.

This pack was afraid of our aircraft and occupied densely forested country, so observations were difficult. We did make a reliable count of 10 wolves in December 1987, however, and at least 3 black pups were alive in November. A minimum of 5 pups had been produced, because 2 black and 2 gray pups had been seen at the den in July 1987.

Radio-collared male wolf 259 was killed by

other wolves in January 1988, and female 261 was killed by McKinley River Pack wolves on March 1. Another wolf, female 313, was radio-collared that day, as were 2 members of the McKinley River Pack. Wolf 313 was killed by wolves 3 weeks later, leaving the Bearpaw Pack without a radio-collar and with 5 or fewer wolves.

The McKinley River Pack continued to use the Bearpaw Pack territory through winter 1987–88, and after that the area was occupied by the new Chitsia Mountain Pack, made up of former McKinley River wolves (see chapter 3) and possibly 1 remnant member of the Bearpaw Pack.

Each time we located the Bearpaw wolves during summer and fall, except near the den, they were feeding on salmon (probably dog salmon) carcasses along streams. Moose were also present in moderate numbers in the territory.

## Chilchukabena Pack

This short-lived pack was formed when McKinley River male 407 joined 2 other wolves on the northwest edge of the McKinley River territory in fall 1990. They occupied some 200 square miles (500 square kilometers) south of Chilchukabena Lake in northwestern Denali.

We radio-collared black female 439 from this pack in March 1991. The pack produced 3 pups in summer 1991 and consisted of 6 wolves in autumn. Male 407 and Chitsia Mountain male 461 were killed by wolves 200 yards (meters) apart in March 1992 (see chapter 3). The pack produced at least 3 pups in summer 1992, but female 439 was killed by unknown natural causes in December 1992, ending our monitoring of this pack. We saw these wolves feeding on moose four times and on salmon once.

## Slippery Creek Pack

The Slippery Creek Pack was an offshoot of the Foraker River Pack, formed in spring 1991 when Foraker male 441 paired with a female on the east edge of the Foraker territory. They occupied a ter-

ritory of 275 square miles (700 square kilometers) of lowland forest, with a low density of moose and caribou.

This pack produced 3 pups in 1991, and the pack consisted of 5 wolves in fall. In March 1992 we saw only 3, and we radio-collared adult female 495. Two pups were seen in summer 1992, and male 441 died of unknown natural causes that summer. By fall, female 495 was consistently alone and was killed by wolves in December 1992.

## Highpower Pack

We monitored the Highpower Pack from March 1988 until summer 1993. However, because its territory lay on the extreme western edge of Denali far from our base, we did not monitor these wolves closely. Their 550-square-mile (1,400-square kilometer) territory lay in the Highpower Creek drainage, mostly in the preserve. The area contains a low density of moose and caribou, and the pack fed on both (table 3.1).

We first radio-collared 2 wolves from this pack along the Herron River west of Castle Rocks in March 1988. The 135-pound (61-kilogram) male, 325, was the heaviest wolf we handled. Genetic evidence suggested that he had come from the Bearpaw Pack. The female, 337, soon dispersed beyond the Telida Mountains and 3 years later died there of unknown causes.

In summer 1988, this pack produced 5 pups and in fall the pack consisted of these 5 plus 3 adults. We radio-collared male pup 357 in October, but then found him dead and eaten in the Telida Mountains, outside the pack territory, in January 1989. The next year, the pack bore at least 3 pups as indicated by a pack count of 10 in fall. In November 1989, we radio-collared male pup 385.

The next summer, we saw 5 pups with the Highpower Pack, and the pack totaled 12 wolves in early winter 1990–91. We replaced the collar on adult male 325 in March 1991. Then yearling male 385 dispersed to the Foraker River Pack in April (see chapter 3). The Highpower Pack still included 10 members in spring 1991, and 11 in fall, including 3 pups.

The pack produced 3 pups again in 1992 and consisted of 10 wolves that fall. We last located wolf 325 alive in fall 1992, and found him dead of unknown natural causes in July 1993. No further attempt was made to monitor this pack.

## Castle Rocks Pack

This was another short-lived pack, consisting of a new pair and their pups, which lived in a small, 195-square-mile (500-square-kilometer) area in the White Creek drainage. There they lived primarily on moose. We radio-collared the breeding pair, female 333 and male 335, south of Castle Rocks Lake in March 1988, and they produced 6 pups that spring. Female 333 limped badly in early winter, and the pack's movements were restricted to a very small area.

Both 333 and 335 were killed by neighboring wolves in November 1988 and their carcasses consumed, probably by their starving pups. When we were retrieving the carcass, we heard a wolf howling nearby, probably indicating that at least 1 pup was still alive. The McLeod Lake Pack was in the area at the time these wolves were killed.

## Swift Fork Pack

We radio-collared adult male 353 and adult female 355 from the Swift Fork Pack in October 1988 near the toe of the Chedotlothna Glacier. They were large, pale-colored wolves that looked a great deal alike. Their estimated territory (based on only 10 radio locations), west of the Herron River, covered only about 120 square miles (300 square kilometers) but probably represented just a portion of the pair's actual range. It contained moderate populations of moose, caribou, and sheep. Female 355 was killed by wolves in February 1989, and male 353 died of unknown natural causes in May 1989.

## Tonzona River Pack

We discovered a pack of 5 wolves in the Boulder Creek area west of Denali in March 1991 and radio-collared female pups 443 and 445. No more than these 2 wolves were observed through summer, and we found no evidence of denning, but the pack again numbered 5 in January 1992. Both 443 and 445 were legally shot by a land-and-shoot hunter at that time. During the 8 months we monitored the pack, it used a territory of 490 square miles (1,250 square kilometers), including areas occupied earlier by the Swift Fork Pack and later by the McLeod West Pack.

## Yanert Pack

This pack probably occupied the Yanert River valley east of Denali throughout the study, but we did not radio-collar any members until March 1991. We had reports of several wolves from this pack being shot earlier in the winter. Then we radio-collared male pup 417 and male yearling 419 from among the 10 remaining members. Wolf 417 disappeared from the pack in April 1991. We saw no evidence of pup production in summer, and only 5 wolves remained in the pack that fall.

The next year at least 6 pups were produced, and the pack reached 18 wolves in fall 1992. A year later there were 27 in the pack. Male 419, which we thought was the breeding male, was legally trapped in March 1994 on Moody Creek, and several other wolves were taken from the area during 1993–95 by ADFG wolf-control activities. The Yanert Pack territory covered at least 195 square miles (500 square kilometers).

## Reindeer Hills Pack

In March 1991, we radio-collared 2 wolves from a pack of 9 in the Reindeer Hills east of the southeast corner of Denali National Park and Preserve. They were yearling male 421 and adult female 423. Wolf 423 was wearing an old ADFG collar, having been captured as a pup north of the Alaska

Range in March 1987. We did not monitor them enough to completely delineate their territory, but all their locations were east of Denali and north of the Denali Highway.

Male 421 (and maybe the entire pack) may have had some association with the Yanert Pack. We saw 421 and Yanert wolf 419 together (sleeping) among a group of 5 wolves in early April 1991, and 421 was found in the Yanert Valley twice more. Three pups were seen with female 423 in early June 1991 at a den near the upper Nenana River. The pack numbered 14 wolves in fall 1991. Male 421 was shot in March 1992. The pack numbered 7 wolves in fall 1992. Female 423 was shot in March 1993.

## Turtle Hill Pack

We discovered the 3 members of the Turtle Hill Pack in May 1992 in an area south of the McKinley Bar formerly occupied by the Pirate Creek Pack and radio-collared adult male 4520. The pack produced 5 pups in summer 1992 and numbered 8 in fall. We also radio-collared adult male 505 in September 1992, but he was killed by wolves 2 months later.

In winter, few prey inhabit the 235-square-mile (600-square-kilometer) Turtle Hill territory, and the pack spent much of winter 1992–93 outside its territory, traveling as far as Flume Creek in the Kantishna Hills, some 35 miles (55 kilometers) north.

Keeping active radio collars working in this pack was especially difficult. We radio-collared adult female 529, female pups 527 and 537, and male pup 531 in March 1993. Male 531 then dispersed to the Tangle Lakes area 150 miles (240 kilometers) away and was legally snared in December 1993. Female 527 produced 3 pups in summer 1993 but was killed by wolves in September. Female 527 disappeared in November. Male 4520's radio collar failed after May 1994. Female 537's collar was chewed off in September 1994. We radio-collared adult male 9405 in September, but

he soon dispersed east to the Ferry area. Only female 535 wore an active radio collar in the Turtle Hill Pack into 1995.

## Savage Pack

We first found this pack of 3 adults and 2 pups in September 1992, living in the northeastern corner of Denali used earlier by the Ewe Creek Pack. Its 135-square-mile (345-square-kilometer) territory fell primarily outside the park boundary. We radio-collared adult female 501 and adult male 509 in September, but 509 dispersed to the Tatlanika River area in December. In March 1993, we radio-collared adult male 511. The pack produced 4 pups that summer and numbered 8 animals in fall. Male 511 was shot along the George Parks Highway in October 1994; female 501 remained active in the territory until February 1996, when she was killed by wolves near Dry Creek.

## Thorofare Pack

In May 1992, we radio-collared lone yearling wolf female 499 on the Thorofare Bar in central Denali. By July she had paired with another wolf, male 515, which we radio-collared in March 1993. The pair produced 5 pups that summer and formed a pack of 7 by fall. Male 515 died in an avalanche in November 1993, and 499's signal disappeared about then; the fate of the pups is unknown. The Thorofare Pack occupied a territory of some 175 square miles (450 square kilometers).

## Jenny Creek Pack

We discovered this new pack living in the Jenny Creek–Savage River area of eastern Denali in summer 1993. In November, we radio-collared adult male 539, and in March, male pup 545. Male 539 died in an avalanche in winter 1993–94. Pup 545 briefly joined the Headquarters Pack and was killed, apparently by humans, in November 1994; we found his collar along the George Parks Highway.

## Stampede Pack

We studied this pack intermittently from fall 1988 until the end of the study. We applied the name "Stampede Pack" to the successive packs we found between the lower Clearwater Fork and the lower East Fork of the Toklat River. However, because several wolves moved in and out of the area, there may not have been continuity between successive packs there. The Stampede territory was a 390- to 470-square-mile (1,000- to 1,200-square-kilometer) area of mostly open tundra.

Since the demise of the Sushana Pair of wolves in 1987 (see following section), this area had received only intermittent visits from the surrounding Ewe Creek, East Fork, Clearwater, and Totek Hills packs. With moderate populations of moose and caribou, the area seemed capable of supporting more wolves.

We radio-collared breeding female wolf 349 and male 351 while they were with their 5 pups in October 1988 on the upper Sushana River. These wolves appeared to be a new pack, wedging its way into the space among the four pack territories. In 1989, 6 pups were seen in summer, and 10 wolves total in fall. Both 349 and 351 were killed in an avalanche in February 1990 (figure 2.14).

We continued to see 7 wolves in the territory, and radio-collared male 397 and female 399, both pups, in March. We found no evidence of denning in 1990. Male 397 dispersed west and joined the McKinley River Pack (see chapter 3), and female 399 was shot along the George Parks Highway near Healy, northeast of Denali. We saw 3 wolves in the Stampede Hills in December 1990, which probably represented the remainder of the Stampede Pack.

In March 1991, we radio-collared adult female 427 and adult male 429. They stayed together through March, but 429 then moved eastward. We saw 427 occasionally with a new companion during summer. She localized at a den on the lower East Fork River, but we never saw pups.

In September 1991, 427 began traveling with Little Bear male 437 until mid-October 1991. Then male 437 also moved off and was killed by humans near Ferry in January 1992. Female 427 took up with yet another male in October 1991, which we then radio-collared, adult male 455. In mid-January 1992, 427 was killed by a local trapper on the lower Sushana River. Placental scars indicated that she had had pups in 1991, but they must have died during summer.

Meanwhile, male 429 began ranging north of the Stampede Pack's territory. After 427's death, we found 429 and 455 together with 4 other wolves, and later 8 others, probably the old Totek Hills Pack. Male 429 died of unknown causes along the Toklat River in spring 1992. Male 455 lost his radio collar in the Myrtle Creek area.

In spring 1992, we radio-collared female 475 near Wigand Creek. She appeared to den and have pups, but if she did, they had perished by fall. We captured her companion in March 1993 and discovered he was male 455. No evidence of pup production was seen in 1993, and the pack was comprised of 3 wolves that fall. A year later, we re-collared female 475 and male 455, and we radio-collared yearling male 9407. Male 455 died of unknown natural causes along the Toklat River in August 1995.

## Sushana Pair

Both members of this pair (female 235 and male 237) were captured in December 1986 at Sushana Lakes. During winter 1986–87, they occupied an area of 190 square miles (482 square kilometers) in the northeast corner of the park and outside. We found 235 dead under ice in the lower Teklanika canyon in March, apparently having fallen into an open hole after being attacked by other wolves.

We then found 237 with a black wolf, and they eventually moved north and joined, or rejoined, the Totek Hills Pack. The rest of his history is recorded with that pack in the following section.

## Totek Hills Pack

The Totek Hills Pack occupied an area of more than 550 square miles (1,400 square kilometers) just north of Denali between the Toklat and Teklanika Rivers. Their territory extended slightly into the park and into the range of the Denali Caribou Herd, but the pack seemed to subsist primarily on moose (table 3.1). The 1985 wolf survey done before this study began had located a pack of 5 black and 7 gray wolves in this area (Dalle-Molle and Van Horn 1985).

After 237 joined this pack, we found in fall 1987 that it included 8 black and 7 gray wolves. At least 4 of them were pups. The highest count in winter 1988–89 was 7. Ten wolves were seen in the pack in early winter 1989–90, indicating that pups probably were produced in summer 1989.

We last located 237 in March 1990. His radio collar probably failed some time after that, but he remained in the territory, probably as the Totek Hills Pack breeding male, until he was legally snared near Toklat Springs in March 1994.

## Lone Wolf 389

We found the tracks of a single wolf around a sheep kill and a scavenged moose in the Somber Creek area in extreme western Denali in November 1989 and captured male wolf 389 on the Chedotlothna Glacier. This is the same area where the Swift Fork pair of wolves lived. Wolf 389 appeared to be living alone, and in 1990 he drifted southwest to the Pingston Creek area and beyond.

## Lone Wolf 411

We captured wolf 411 in November 1990, and he traveled widely in the study area, from Ferry to the Straightaway Glacier and back to the Yanert Valley. He was snared in December 1991 in the upper Totatlanika River.

## Lone Wolf 447

Male wolf 447 was captured on the caribou calving grounds (Turtle Hill area) in late May 1991. We located him alone seven times in the calving grounds, the last time in early June 1991.

# *Timelines*

The following timelines summarize the radio-tracking tenures and fates of the collared wolves in each of the packs we studied. The bottom row of figures for each gives the pack sizes.

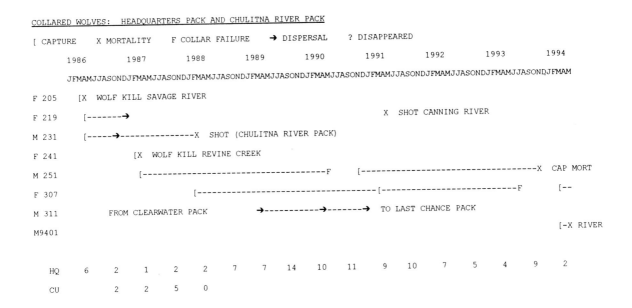

```
COLLARED WOLVES:  HEADQUARTERS PACK AND CHULITNA RIVER PACK

[ CAPTURE     X MORTALITY    F COLLAR FAILURE    → DISPERSAL    ? DISAPPEARED

      1986          1987          1988          1989          1990          1991          1992          1993          1994

      JFMAMJJASONDJFMAMJJASONDJFMAMJJASONDJFMAMJJASONDJFMAMJJASONDJFMAMJJASONDJFMAMJJASONDJFMAMJJASONDJFMAM

F 205    [X  WOLF KILL SAVAGE RIVER

F 219    [------->                                              X   SHOT CANNING RIVER

M 231    [----->--------------X   SHOT (CHULITNA RIVER PACK)

F 241         [X   WOLF KILL REVINE CREEK

M 251            [---------------------------------F    [---------------------------------X  CAP MORT

F 307               [------------------------------[-------------------------F    [--

M 311      FROM CLEARWATER PACK        →-----------→-------→  TO LAST CHANCE PACK

M9401                                                                              [-X RIVER


      HQ    6    2    1    2    2    7    7   14   10   11    9   10    7    5    4    9    2

      CU         2    2    5    0
```

COLLARED WOLVES:  LAST CHANCE PACK

[ CAPTURE     X MORTALITY     F COLLAR FAILURE    ➔ DISPERSAL    ? DISAPPEARED

```
        1986         1987         1988         1989         1990         1991         1992         1993         1994
    JFMAMJJASONDJFMAMJJASONDJFMAMJJASONDJFMAMJJASONDJFMAMJJASONDJFMAMJJASONDJFMAMJJASONDJFMAMJJASONDJFMAM
M 311              FROM CLEARWATER, HEADQUARTERS PACKS            ➔---X   CAPTURE MORTALITY LAST CHANCE CREEK
M 415                                                      [------------➔ X   ROAD KILL RICHARDSON HWY
F 425                                                      [---------------------X   WOLF KILL COAL CR
                                                                   4
```

COLLARED WOLVES: CLEARWATER PACK AND PIRATE CREEK PACK

[ CAPTURE     X MORTALITY     F COLLAR FAILURE    ➔ DISPERSAL    ? DISAPPEARED

```
        1986         1987         1988         1989         1990         1991         1992         1993         1994
    JFMAMJJASONDJFMAMJJASONDJFMAMJJASONDJFMAMJJASONDJFMAMJJASONDJFMAMJJASONDJFMAMJJASONDJFMAMJJASONDJFMAM
F 213    [--------➔              X   TRAPPED DOT LAKE
M 223    [-----------------------------X   WOLF KILL ALDER CREEK
F 151    [---------➔            X   SHOT STYX RIVER
F 227        [-----------------------------X   WOLF KILL CLEARWATER CREEK
M 250          [-----F   TO PIRATE CREEK PACK
F 339             [------------X   DIED STARVATION, ULCERS (PIRATE CREEK PACK)
M 311                [---------➔   TO HEADQUARTERS, LAST CHANCE PACKS
F 361                    [--------?
M 363                [--------X   DIED MOOSE CREEK UNKNOWN CAUSES


CW      5    6    3    6    4    4    2    8    0
PC                          2    9    0
```

COLLARED WOLVES:  EAST FORK PACK

[ CAPTURE     X MORTALITY     F COLLAR FAILURE    ➔ DISPERSAL    ? DISAPPEARED

```
        1986         1987         1988         1989         1990         1991         1992         1993         1994
    JFMAMJJASONDJFMAMJJASONDJFMAMJJASONDJFMAMJJASONDJFMAMJJASONDJFMAMJJASONDJFMAMJJASONDJFMAMJJASONDJFMAM
M 215    [--➔                        X   TRAPPED TANADA LAKE
F 217    [-------------------------------------------[------➔   X   WOLF KILL LITTLE MOOSE CREEK
M 221    [--------------?
M 239      [-➔ ➔---➔              X   SHOT WOOD RIVER
M 5051            [--------------------------------[---------------------┬-X   TRAP TEKLANIKA R
M 395                              [-➔      X   SHOT MULCHATNA RIVER
F1080                                  [------X   DIED NATURAL CAUSES SUSHANA R
F 467                                      [----------------------------
M 469                                      [----➔   X   MORT TOTATLANIKA R
M 513                                           [-------------
        11    9    6    8    7    19   18   27   24   29   18   16   11   15   10   9    6
```

COLLARED WOLVES: ALMA LAKES PACK

[ CAPTURE     X MORTALITY     F COLLAR FAILURE     → DISPERSAL     ? DISAPPEARED

```
       1986          1987          1988          1989          1990          1991          1992          1993          1994
     JFMAMJJASONDJFMAMJJASONDJFMAMJJASONDJFMAMJJASONDJFMAMJJASONDJFMAMJJASONDJFMAMJJASONDJFMAMJJASONDJFMAM

M 229      [-------?

F 233      [--→   X SHOT LAKE MINCHUMINA

           4      3
```

COLLARED WOLVES:  SUSHANA PAIR AND TOTEK HILLS PACK

[ CAPTURE     X MORTALITY     F COLLAR FAILURE     → DISPERSAL     ? DISAPPEARED

```
       1986          1987          1988          1989          1990          1991          1992          1993          1994
     JFMAMJJASONDJFMAMJJASONDJFMAMJJASONDJFMAMJJASONDJFMAMJJASONDJFMAMJJASONDJFMAMJJASONDJFMAMJJASONDJFMAM

F 235           [--X   WOLF KILL/DROWNED, LOWER TEKLANIKA CANYON

M 237           [--→-----------------------------------                                                    X SNARE

     SU      2    0

     TO              15          7          12                              10
```

COLLARED WOLVES:  WINDY CREEK PACK

[ CAPTURE     X MORTALITY     F COLLAR FAILURE     → DISPERSAL     ? DISAPPEARED

```
       1986          1987          1988          1989          1990          1991          1992          1993          1994
     JFMAMJJASONDJFMAMJJASONDJFMAMJJASONDJFMAMJJASONDJFMAMJJASONDJFMAMJJASONDJFMAMJJASONDJFMAMJJASONDJFMAM

M 243           [------------?

M 245           [-----------------------------------[-------?

F 377                               [---------------F

F 413                                               [?

                 6    8    Ċ    5    5    8    8    17
```

COLLARED WOLVES:  MCLEOD LAKE PACK

```
[ CAPTURE    X MORTALITY    F COLLAR FAILURE (INCLUDES CHEWED-OFF COLLARS)   → DISPERSAL   ? DISAPPEARED

        1986         1987         1988         1989         1990         1991         1992         1993         1994
    JFMAMJJASONDJFMAMJJASONDJFMAMJJASONDJFMAMJJASONDJFMAMJJASONDJFMAMJJASONDJFMAMJJASONDJFMAMJJASONDJFMAM

M 253                  [------------------F                  [--------------------------------X MORT UNK

M 255             [----?

M 792                    [-----------X  MORTALITY, HEART VALVE INFECTION

F 309                         [----------------------------X  MORT, PROLAPSED DISC, STARVATION

F 365                                      [------?

F 367                                  [-----------------------→  TO MCLEOD WEST PACK

F 409                                          [-----------→  TO MCLEOD WEST PACK

F 453                                                  [-----→  TO MCLEOD WEST PACK

F 465                                                  [----------------------X  UNK

F 471                                                  [--------?

F 473                                                  [--------------------X  UNK

F 481                                                  [→  DISPERSED NORTHEAST

F 483                                                  [--F         [----F LOST COLLAR 2X

M 485                                                  [--F

F 487                                                  [-------------------F [--

M 489                                                  [--→  TO UPPER SUSITNA RIVER

F 491                                                  [-X  KILLED BY WOLVES

F 497                                                  [-------------------F [--

M 519                                                          [------F LOST COLLAR

F 521                                                          [-------F LOST COLLAR

F 523                                                          [--------F

M 525                                                          [--------X  UNK CAUSE

                      4    7    7    12    8    12    10    20    15    13    13    13    11    15    11
```

COLLARED WOLVES:  MCLEOD LAKE WEST PACK

```
[ CAPTURE    X MORTALITY    F COLLAR FAILURE   → DISPERSAL   ? DISAPPEARED

        1986         1987         1988         1989         1990         1991         1992         1993         1994
    JFMAMJJASONDJFMAMJJASONDJFMAMJJASONDJFMAMJJASONDJFMAMJJASONDJFMAMJJASONDJFMAMJJASONDJFMAMJJASONDJFMAM

F 367                                                  →----------?

F 409                                                  →--------X  MORT UNK NATURAL CAUSES

F 453                                                      →----------

                                                      7    11    11    17
```

193

COLLARED WOLVES:  BIRCH CREEK PACK, BIRCH NORTH PACK.

[ CAPTURE     X MORTALITY     F COLLAR FAILURE     → DISPERSAL     ? DISAPPEARED

```
      1986        1987        1988        1989        1990        1991        1992        1993        1994

      JFMAMJJASONDJFMAMJJASONDJFMAMJJASONDJFMAMJJASONDJFMAMJJASONDJFMAMJJASONDJFMAMJJASONDJFMAMJJASONDJFMAM
```

BIRCH CREEK:

M  257              [--F   COLLAR CHEWED OFF

F  263              [--------------?

M  301                   [-------[-----------------→----------------→            X   SNARED MINTO

F  345                       [-F   COLLAR CHEWED OFF

F  347                       [-------F   COLLAR CHEWED OFF, TO BIRCH NORTH PACK

F  369                          [--------------------→    TO BIRCH NORTH PACK

F  371                           [------------------------------X   KILLED BY WOLVES

M  449                                   [---X   MORT, UNKNOWN NATURAL CAUSES

```
                    7    11    11    23    22    15    16    16     9     6
```

BIRCH NORTH:

F  369                   FROM BIRCH CREEK PACK      →-X   KILLED BY WOLVES

F  347                   FROM BIRCH CREEK PACK      →  [-----------X   SNARED

F  431                   FROM BIRCH CREEK PACK      [X   SHOT

```
                                                    6     5
```


COLLARED WOLVES:  BEARPAW PACK

[ CAPTURE     X MORTALITY     F COLLAR FAILURE     → DISPERSAL     ? DISAPPEARED

```
      1986        1987        1988        1989        1990        1991        1992        1993        1994

      JFMAMJJASONDJFMAMJJASONDJFMAMJJASONDJFMAMJJASONDJFMAMJJASONDJFMAMJJASONDJFMAMJJASONDJFMAMJJASONDJFMAM
```

M 259              [-------X  WOLF KILL LOWER MOOSE CREEK

F 261              [---------X  WOLF KILL BEARPAW RIVER

F 313                 [X  WOLF KILL LOWER BEAR CREEK

```
                5    10     4     1     0
```


COLLARED WOLVES:  EWE CREEK PACK

[ CAPTURE     X MORTALITY     F COLLAR FAILURE     → DISPERSAL     ? DISAPPEARED

```
      1986        1987        1988        1989        1990        1991        1992        1993        1994

      JFMAMJJASONDJFMAMJJASONDJFMAMJJASONDJFMAMJJASONDJFMAMJJASONDJFMAMJJASONDJFMAMJJASONDJFMAMJJASONDJFMAM
```

M  980              [--[-----X   SNARED JUST OUTSIDE PARK BOUNDARY

F  330                [-[--→--→    DISPERSED EAST

F  341                  [----X   TRAPPED CRIPPLE CREEK

F  343                  [----------------------------------------------------?  COLLAR FAIL?

M  381                    [--→     X   SHOT NEAR UPPER SUSITNA RIVER

F  383                   [-------X   KILLED BY WOLVES MOODY CREEK

M  405                        [-----------------------------------F

```
                6         8     5     5     4     3     2     4     3     3     5     3     2
```

# APPENDIX 3

COLLARED WOLVES:  MCKINLEY RIVER PACK, CHILCHUKABENA PACK

[ CAPTURE     X MORTALITY     F COLLAR FAILURE     → DISPERSAL     ? DISAPPEARED

| 1986 | 1987 | 1988 | 1989 | 1990 | 1991 | 1992 | 1993 | 1994 |

JFMAMJJASONDJFMAMJJASONDJFMAMJJASONDJFMAMJJASONDJFMAMJJASONDJFMAMJJASONDJFMAMJJASONDJFMAMJJASONDJFMAM

MCKINLEY RIVER PACK:

M  315                              [------------→  TO CHITSIA MOUNTAIN PACK

F  321                              [--------------→  TO FORAKER PACK

M  379                                   [→    X   SNARED CHENA HOT SPRINGS ROAD

F  401                                        [--------------------------------------F

M  407                                   [-----→  TO CHILCHUKABENA PACK

M  397                 FROM STAMPEDE PACK      →----------------------F  LOST COLLAR   [--

F  451                                               [-----------X  SHOT MOOSE CREEK

M  533                                                       [----------[--

                    10    10    10    8     8     8    10     5     9     8     7     3     3     3


CHILCHUKABENA PACK:

M  407                 FROM MCKINLEY RIVER PACK      →---------------X  KILLED BY WOLVES

F  439                                          [------------------X   MORT UNKN NAT CAUSES

                                              3     6     3     7     0


COLLARED WOLVES:  CHITSIA MOUNTAIN PACK

[ CAPTURE     X MORTALITY     F COLLAR FAILURE     → DISPERSAL     ? DISAPPEARED

| 1986 | 1987 | 1988 | 1989 | 1990 | 1991 | 1992 | 1993 | 1994 |

JFMAMJJASONDJFMAMJJASONDJFMAMJJASONDJFMAMJJASONDJFMAMJJASONDJFMAMJJASONDJFMAMJJASONDJFMAMJJASONDJFMAM

F  359                              [-----------------------------------------------------------

M  315         FROM MCKINLEY R PACK  →---------------------------------------F

M  379         FROM MCKINLEY R PACK  →→    X   SHOT CHENA HOT SPRINGS ROAD

M  461                                               [---X WOLF KILL KANTISHNA RIVER

F  463                                               [----------------------------

                     4     4     4     8     8    12     7     9     6     8     4

195

COLLARED WOLVES:  FORAKER PACK, SLIPPERY CREEK PACK

[ CAPTURE    X MORTALITY    F COLLAR FAILURE    ➜ DISPERSAL    ? DISAPPEARED

```
        1986        1987        1988        1989        1990        1991        1992        1993        1994
     JFMAMJJASONDJFMAMJJASONDJFMAMJJASONDJFMAMJJASONDJFMAMJJASONDJFMAMJJASONDJFMAMJJASONDJFMAMJJASONDJFMAM
```

FORAKER PACK:

F  321    FROM MCKINLEY R PACK    ➜-------------------------X  MORT FROM UNKNOWN NATURAL CAUSES

F  387                                      [---------------------X   KILLED BY WOLVES

M  385                        FROM HIGHPOWER PACK    ➜--------------------X   TRAP, PRESERVE

M  441                                                  [➜   TO SLIPPERY CREEK PACK

F  493                                                        [-------------------------

M  517                                                              [--------------

```
                          2       7       7       9       4       8       3       7       6       6       7
```

SLIPPERY CREEK PACK:

M  441                              FROM FORAKER PACK    ➜--------------X  MORT UNK NAT CAUSES

F  495                                                  [--------X  KILLED BY WOLVES

```
                                                2       5       3       1       0
```

COLLARED WOLVES:  HIGHPOWER PACK

[ CAPTURE    X MORTALITY    F COLLAR FAILURE    ➜ DISPERSAL    ? DISAPPEARED

```
        1986        1987        1988        1989        1990        1991        1992        1993        1994
     JFMAMJJASONDJFMAMJJASONDJFMAMJJASONDJFMAMJJASONDJFMAMJJASONDJFMAMJJASONDJFMAMJJASONDJFMAMJJASONDJFMAM
```

M  325              [----------------------------------[------------------    X UNK NAT CAUSE

F  337              [-➜--------------------    X  MORT UNKNOWN NATURAL CAUSES

M  357          [--X   KILLED BY WOLVES TELIDA MOUNTAINS

M  385                        [---------------➜   TO FORAKER PACK

```
             5       8       7      10      10      12       8      11       8      10
```

COLLARED WOLVES:  CASTLE ROCKS PACK

[ CAPTURE    X MORTALITY    F COLLAR FAILURE    ➜ DISPERSAL    ? DISAPPEARED

```
        1986        1987        1988        1989        1990        1991        1992        1993        1994
     JFMAMJJASONDJFMAMJJASONDJFMAMJJASONDJFMAMJJASONDJFMAMJJASONDJFMAMJJASONDJFMAMJJASONDJFMAMJJASONDJFMAM
```

F  333              [--------X  KILLED BY WOLVES

M  335              [--------X  KILLED BY WOLVES

```
             2       8       0
```

COLLARED WOLVES:  STAMPEDE PACK

[ CAPTURE     X MORTALITY     F COLLAR FAILURE     → DISPERSAL     ? DISAPPEARED

    1986        1987        1988        1989        1990        1991        1992        1993        1994

JFMAMJJASONDJFMAMJJASONDJFMAMJJASONDJFMAMJJASONDJFMAMJJASONDJFMAMJJASONDJFMAMJJASONDJFMAMJJASONDJFMAM

F  349                           [--------------X  KILLED IN AN AVALANCHE

M  351                           [----------F[--X  KILLED IN AN AVALANCHE

M  397                                 [-→  TO MCKINLEY RIVER PACK

F  399                                 [-----X  SHOT ALONG PARKS HIGHWAY

F  427                                      [--------X  SNARED, TOKLAT SPRINGS

M  429                                      [---------→ X  MORT UNK NAT CAUSES

M  437                   FROM LITTLE BEAR PACK     →-→  X  KILLED BY HUMANS, FERRY

M  455                                      [--→-F         [--------------

F  475                                      [------------------------

                2     7     7    10     7     4     3     2     3     2     2     3     3


COLLARED WOLVES:  SWIFT FORK PACK, TONZONA PACK

[ CAPTURE     X MORTALITY     F COLLAR FAILURE     → DISPERSAL     ? DISAPPEARED

    1986        1987        1988        1989        1990        1991        1992        1993        1994

JFMAMJJASONDJFMAMJJASONDJFMAMJJASONDJFMAMJJASONDJFMAMJJASONDJFMAMJJASONDJFMAMJJASONDJFMAMJJASONDJFMAM

SWIFT FORK PACK:

M  353                             [-----X  MORTALITY, UNKNOWN NATURAL CAUSES

F  355                             [----X  KILLED BY WOLVES

                           2

TONZONA PACK:

F  443                                      [--------X  SHOT, PINGSTON CREEK

F  445                                      [--------X  SHOT, PINGSTON CREEK

                                     5     5

COLLARED WOLVES:  LITTLE BEAR PACK

[ CAPTURE     X MORTALITY     F COLLAR FAILURE     → DISPERSAL     ? DISAPPEARED

```
          1986        1987        1988        1989        1990        1991        1992        1993        1994
      JFMAMJJASONDJFMAMJJASONDJFMAMJJASONDJFMAMJJASONDJFMAMJJASONDJFMAMJJASONDJFMAMJJASONDJFMAMJJASONDJFMAM

M  373                              [-------------------X  KILLED BY WOLVES, SUSHANA RIVER

M  375                              [---------------------?

F  391                                                [-X  DROWNED, CLEARWATER FORK OF TOKLAT RIVER

F  433                                                             [------------→  DISP SW WITH 10 OTHERS

F  435                                                             [------------→  DISPERSED SW    X  SHOT

M  437                                                         [-→  TO STAMPEDE, FERRY PACKS

F  457                                                                 [------→  DISPERSED SW ALONE

M  459                                                                 [-----→  DISP SW WITH 10 OTHERS

F  503                                                             [------?

F  507                                                             [--------------------

F  541                                                                         [------?

                    2       7       7      12       7        13      23      14      12      12      12      13
```

COLLARED WOLVES:  YANERT PACK, REINDEER HILLS PACK

[ CAPTURE     X MORTALITY     F COLLAR FAILURE     → DISPERSAL     ? DISAPPEARED

```
          1986        1987        1988        1989        1990        1991        1992        1993        1994
      JFMAMJJASONDJFMAMJJASONDJFMAMJJASONDJFMAMJJASONDJFMAMJJASONDJFMAMJJASONDJFMAMJJASONDJFMAMJJASONDJFMAM
```

YANERT PACK:

```
M  417                                                         [-?

M  419                                                         [-----------------------    X TRAP

                   20       7       5       6      18      17      27
```

REINDEER HILLS PACK:

```
M  421                                                         [---------X  SHOT BRUSKASNA CREEK

F  423                                                         [----------------------X  SHOT SEATTLE CR

                                                                9                       7       6
```

APPENDIX 3

COLLARED WOLVES:  TURTLE HILL PACK

[ CAPTURE     X MORTALITY     F COLLAR FAILURE     → DISPERSAL     ? DISAPPEARED

```
         1986         1987         1988         1989         1990         1991         1992         1993         1994
     JFMAMJJASONDJFMAMJJASONDJFMAMJJASONDJFMAMJJASONDJFMAMJJASONDJFMAMJJASONDJFMAMJJASONDJFMAMJJASONDJFMAM

M 4520                                                                              [---------------------?

M  505                                                                             [-X  KILLED BY WOLVES

F  527                                                                              [-----------?

F  529                                                                              [------X WOLF KILL

M  531                                                                              [→        X SHOT TANGLE L

F  535                                                                              [-------------

F  537                                                                              [-------------
                                                                          3        8        7        7        6
```

COLLARED WOLVES:  SAVAGE PACK

[ CAPTURE     X MORTALITY     F COLLAR FAILURE     → DISPERSAL     ? DISAPPEARED

```
         1986         1987         1988         1989         1990         1991         1992         1993         1994
     JFMAMJJASONDJFMAMJJASONDJFMAMJJASONDJFMAMJJASONDJFMAMJJASONDJFMAMJJASONDJFMAMJJASONDJFMAMJJASONDJFMAM

F  501                                                                              [-------------------

M  509                                                                              [---→ NE   X MORT?
```

COLLARED WOLVES:  THOROFARE PACK, JENNY CREEK PACK

[ CAPTURE     X MORTALITY     F COLLAR FAILURE     → DISPERSAL     ? DISAPPEARED

```
         1986         1987         1988         1989         1990         1991         1992         1993         1994
     JFMAMJJASONDJFMAMJJASONDJFMAMJJASONDJFMAMJJASONDJFMAMJJASONDJFMAMJJASONDJFMAMJJASONDJFMAMJJASONDJFMAM
```

THOROFARE PACK:

```
F  499                                                                              [------------------?

M  515                                                                                [--------X AVALANCHE
                                                                          1        2        2        7        0
```

JENNY CREEK PACK:

```
M  539                                                                                [---X AVALANCHE

M  543                                                                                [ NOT COLLARED

M  545                                                                                [    [--
                                                                                   2        6
```

199

COLLARED WOLVES: LONERS

[ CAPTURE     X MORTALITY     F COLLAR FAILURE     ➔ DISPERSAL     ? DISAPPEARED

|      | 1986 | 1987 | 1988 | 1989 | 1990 | 1991 | 1992 | 1993 | 1994 |
|------|------|------|------|------|------|------|------|------|------|

JFMAMJJASONDJFMAMJJASONDJFMAMJJASONDJFMAMJJASONDJFMAMJJASONDJFMAMJJASONDJFMAMJJASONDJFMAMJJASONDJFMAM

M  389                                                    [-----➔

M  411                                                         [-----------X SNARED

M  447                                                      [-➔

M  547                                                                                        [-

# Scientific Names of Birds and Mammals Mentioned in the Text

bear, black *(Ursus americanus)*

bear, grizzly *(Ursus arctos)*

beaver *(Castor canadensis)*

caribou *(Rangifer tarandus)*

coyote *(Canis latrans)*

Dall sheep *(Ovis dalli)*

eagle, golden *(Aquila chrysaetos)*

fox, red *(Vulpes vulpes)*

ground squirrel *(Citellus parryii)*

lynx *(Felis lynx)*

marmot *(Marmota caligata)*

moose *(Alces alces)*

saiga antelope *(Saiga tartarica)*

snowshoe hare *(Lepus americanus)*

white-tailed deer *(Odocoileus virginianus)*

wolf *(Canis lupus)*

wolverine *(Gulo gulo)*

# Literature Cited

Adams, C. C. 1925. The conservation of predatory mammals. *J. Mammal.* 6:83–96.

Adams, L. G., and B. W. Dale. 1998. Timing and synchrony of parturition in Alaskan caribou. *J. Mammal.* In press.

Adams, L. G., B. W. Dale, and L. D. Mech. 1995. Wolf predation on caribou calves in Denali National Park, Alaska. Pages 245–60 in L. N. Carbyn, S. H. Fritts, and D. R. Seip, eds., *Ecology and conservation of wolves in a changing world.* Canadian Circumpolar Institute, Edmonton, Alberta, Can.

Adams, L. G., B. W. Dale, and B. Shults. 1989. *Population status and calf mortality of the Denali caribou herd, Denali National Park and Preserve, Alaska: 1984–1988.* U.S. Natl. Park Serv. Nat. Resour. Rept. AR-89/13.

Adams, L. G., F. G. Singer, and B. W. Dale. 1995. Caribou calf mortality in Denali National Park, Alaska. *J. Wildl. Mgt.* 59:584–94.

Alaska's wolves, how to manage for the 90's. Supplement to *Alaska's Wildlife*, Jan.–Feb. 1992.

Albright, H. 1931. The National Park Service's policy on predatory animals. *J. Mammal.* 12:185–86.

Allen, D. L. 1979. *Wolves of Minong: Their vital role in a wild community.* Houghton Mifflin Company, Boston.

Ayres, L. D. 1986. The movement patterns and foraging ecology of Dall sheep in the Noatak National Preserve Alaska. Master's thesis, Univ. of California, Berkeley.

Bailey, T. N., E. E. Bangs, and R. O. Peterson. 1995. Exposure of wolves to canine parvovirus and distemper on the Kenai National Wildlife Refuge, Kenai Peninsula, Alaska, 1976–1988. Pages 441–46 in L. N. Carbyn, S. H. Fritts, and D. R. Seip, eds., *Ecology and conservation of wolves in a changing world.* Canadian Circumpolar Institute, Edmonton, Alberta, Can.

Ballard, W. B., L. A. Ayres, K. E. Roney, and T. H. Spraker. 1991. Immobilization of gray wolves with a mixture of tiletamine hydrochloride and zolazepam hydrochloride. *J. Wildl. Mgt.* 55:71–74.

Ballard, W. B., R. Farnell, and R. O. Stephenson. 1983. Long distance movement by gray wolves, *Canis lupus. Can. Field Nat.* 97:333.

Ballard, W. B., T. H. Spraker, and K. P. Taylor. 1981. Causes of neonatal moose calf mortality in southcentral Alaska. *J. Wildl. Mgt.* 45:335–42.

Ballard, W. B., J. S. Whitman, and C. L. Gardner. 1987. Ecology of an exploited wolf population in southcentral Alaska. *Wildl. Monogr.* 98.

Bekoff, M., and L. D. Mech. 1984. Simulation analyses of space use: Home range estimates, variability, and sample size. *Behav. Res. Meth. and Instrumentation Comput.* 16:32–37.

Bergerud, A. T. 1964. A field method to determine annual parturition rates for Newfoundland caribou. *J. Wildl. Mgt.* 28:477–80.

———. 1971. The population dynamics of Newfoundland caribou. *Wildl. Monogr.* 25.

———. 1973. Movements and rutting behavior of caribou (*Rangifer tarandus*) at Mount Alberta, Quebec. *Can. Field Nat.* 87:357–69.

———. 1980. A review of the population dynamics of caribou and wild reindeer in North America. Pages 556–81 in E. Reimers, E. Gaare, and S. Skjenneberg, eds., *Proc. 2nd Int. Reindeer/Caribou Symp.*

———. 1983. The natural population control of caribou. Pages 14–61 in F. L. Bunnel, D. S. Eastman, and J. M. Peek, eds., *Symposium on Natural Regulation of Wildlife Populations*, Proc. No. 14, For. Wildl. and Range Expt. Sta., Univ. of Idaho, Moscow.

———. 1985. Antipredator strategies of caribou: Dispersion along shorelines. *Can. J. Zool.* 63:1324–29.

Bergerud, A. T., and W. B. Ballard. 1988. Wolf predation on caribou: The Nelchina herd case history, a different interpretation. *J. Wildl. Mgt.* 52:344–57.

Bergerud, A. T., H. E. Butler, and D. R. Miller. 1984. Antipredator tactics of calving caribou: Dispersion in mountains. *Can. J. Zool.* 62:1566–75.

Bergerud, A. T., R. Ferguson, and H. E. Butler. 1990. Spring migration and dispersion of woodland caribou at calving. *Anim. Behav.* 39:360–68.

Bergerud, A. T., and R. E. Page. 1987. Displacement and dispersion of parturient caribou at calving as antipredator tactics. *Can. J. Zool.* 65:1597–1606.

Bjorge, R. R., and J. R. Gunson. 1989. Wolf population characteristics and prey relationships near Simonette river, Alberta. *Can. Field Nat.* 103:327–34.

Boertje, R. D. 1981. Nutritional ecology of the Denali caribou herd. Master's thesis, Univ. of Alaska, Fairbanks.

———. 1984. Seasonal diets of the Denali caribou herd, Alaska. *Arctic* 37:161–65.

Boertje, R. D., W. C. Gasaway, D. V. Grangaard, and D. G. Kelleyhouse. 1988. Predation on moose and caribou by radio-collared grizzly bears in east central Alaska. *Can. J. Zool.* 66:2492–99.

Boertje, R. D., and R. O. Stephenson. 1992. Effects of ungulate availability on wolf reproductive potential in Alaska. *Can. J. Zool.* 70:2441–43.

Boertje, R. D, P. Valkenburg, and M. E. McNay. 1996. Increases in moose, caribou, and wolves following wolf control in Alaska. *J. Wildl. Mgt.* 60:474–89.

Boyd, D. K., L. B. Secrest, and D. H. Pletscher. 1992. A wolf, *Canis lupus*, killed in an avalanche in southwestern Alberta. *Can. Field Nat.* 106:526.

Bresler, D. E., G. Ellison, and S. Zamenhof. 1975. Learning deficits in rats with malnourished grandmothers. *Developmental Psychobiology* 8:315–23.

Brown, W. E. 1991. *A history of the Denali–Mount McKinley region, Alaska: Historic resource study of Denali National Park and Preserve.* Natl. Park Serv., South West Reg. Office.

Brown, W. K., J. Huot, P. Lamothe, S. Luttich, M. Pare, B. St. Martin, and J. B. Theberge. 1986. The distribution and movement patterns of four woodland caribou herds in Quebec. *Proc. 4th Int. Reindeer/Caribou Symp.*: 43–49.

Bunnell, F. L., and N. A. Olsen. 1976. Weights and growth of Dall sheep in Kluane Park Reserve, Yukon Territory. *Can. Field Nat.* 90:157–62.

Burkholder, B. L. 1959. Movements and behavior of a wolf pack in Alaska. *J. Wildl. Mgt.* 23:1–11.

Burles, D., and M. Hoefs. 1984. Winter mortality of Dall sheep in Kluane National Park. *Can. Field Nat.* 98:479–84.

Carbyn, L. N. 1974. Wolf population fluctuations in Jasper National Park, Alberta, Canada. *Biol. Conserv.* 6:94–101.

———. 1981. Territory displacement in a wolf population with abundant prey. *J. Mammal.* 62:193–95.

Carbyn, L. N., S. M. Oosenbrug, and D. W. Anions. 1993. *Wolves, bison and the dynamics related to the Peace-Athabasca Delta in Canada's Wood Buffalo National Park.* Art Design Printing Inc., Edmonton, Alberta, Can.

Clarkson, P. L., and I. S. Liepins. 1991. *Inuvialuit wildlife studies: Western Arctic wolf research project progress report, April 1989–January 1991.* Govt. Northwest Territ., Dept. of Renewable Resour.

Clutton-Brock, T. H., F. E. Guinness, and S. D. Albon. 1982. *Red deer: Behavior and ecology of two sexes.* Univ. of Chicago Press, Chicago.

Cowan, I. M. 1947. The timber wolf in the Rocky Mountain national parks of Canada. *Can. J. Res.* 25:139–74.

Crisler, L. 1956. Observations of wolves hunting caribou. *J. Mammal.* 37:337–46.

Dale, B. W., L. G. Adams, and R. T. Bowyer. 1994. Functional response of wolves preying on barren-ground caribou in a multiple-prey ecosystem. *J. Anim. Ecol.* 63:644–52.

———. 1995. Winter wolf predation in a multiple ungulate system, Gates of the Arctic National Park, AK. Pages 223–30 in L. N. Carbyn, S. H. Fritts, and D. R. Seip, eds., *Ecology and conservation of wolves in a changing world.* Canadian Circumpolar Institute, Edmonton, Alberta, Can.

Dalle-Molle, J. 1987. *Denali National Park Moose Trend*

*Survey 1987.* Natural Resource Survey and Inventory Report AR-87-11.

Dalle-Molle, J., and J. VanHorn. 1985. *Wolf survey 1985, Denali National Park and Preserve.* U.S. Natl. Park Service Surv. and Inv. Rept. AR-85/11.

Darwin, C. 1859. *On the origin of species by means of natural selection, or the preservation of favoured races in the struggle for life.* John Murray, London.

Darling, L. M. 1987. Habitat use by grizzly bear family groups in interior Alaska. *Int. Conf. Bear Res. Manage.* 7:169–78.

Dauphine, T. C., Jr. 1971. Physical variables as an index to condition in barren-ground caribou. *Trans. Northeastern Fish and Wildl. Conf.*: 91–108.

———. 1976. *Biology of the Kaminuriak population of barren-ground caribou, part 4: Growth, reproduction, and energy reserves.* Can. Wildl. Serv. Rept. Series 38.

Dauphine, T. C., Jr., and R. L. McClure. 1974. Synchronous mating in barren-ground caribou. *J. Wildl. Mgt.* 38:54–66.

Davis, J. L., and P. Valkenburg. 1991. A review of caribou population dynamics in Alaska emphasizing limiting factors, theory and management implications. *Proc. 4th North Amer. Caribou Workshop*: 184–207.

Davis, J. L., P. Valkenburg, and S. J. Harbo. 1979. *Refinement of the aerial photo-direct count-extrapolation caribou census technique.* Alaska Dept. Fish and Game Fed. Aid in Wildl. Restor. Final Rept.

Davis, J. L., P. Valkenburg, and H. V. Reynolds. 1980. Population dynamics of Alaska's western arctic caribou herd. *Proc. 2nd Int. Reindeer/Caribou Symp.*: 595–604.

Dawkins, R. 1976. *The selfish gene.* Oxford University Press, Oxford.

Dean, F. C. 1987. Brown bear density, Denali National Park, Alaska, and sighting efficiency adjustment. *Int. Conf. Bear Res. and Manage.* 7:37–43.

Dean, F. C., L. M. Darling, and A. G. Lierhaus. 1986. Observations of intraspecific killing by brown bears, *Ursus arctos. Can. Field Nat.* 100:208–11.

DelGiudice, G. D., L. D. Mech, and U. S. Seal. 1990. Effects of winter undernutrition on body composition and physiological profiles of white-tailed deer. *J. Wildl. Mgt.* 54:539–50.

Doerr, J. G., and R. A. Dieterich. 1979. Mandibular lesions in the western arctic caribou herd of Alaska. *J. Wildl. Diseases* 15:309–18.

Eberhardt, L. L., and K. W. Pitcher. 1992. A further analysis of the Nelchina caribou and wolf data. *Wildl. Soc. Bull.* 20:385–95.

Edmonds, E. J. 1988. Population status, distribution, and movements of woodland caribou in west central Alberta. *Can. J. Zool.* 66:817–26.

Eide, S. H., and W. B. Ballard. 1982. Apparent case of surplus killing of caribou by gray wolves. *Can. Field Nat.* 96:87–88.

Errington, P. L. 1967. *Of predation and life.* Iowa State Univ. Press, Ames.

Farnell, R., and J. McDonald. 1988. The influences of wolf predation on caribou mortality in Yukon's Finlayson caribou herd. *Proc. 3rd North American Caribou Workshop*: 52–70.

Feldhamer, G. A., T. P. Kilbane, and D. W. Sharp. 1989. Cumulative effect of winter on acorn yield and deer body weight. *J. Wildl. Mgt.* 53:292–95.

Franzmann, A. W., and P. D. Arneson. 1976. Marrow fat in Alaskan moose femurs in relation to mortality factors. *J. Wildl. Mgt.* 40:336–39.

Franzmann, A. W., R. E. LeResche, R. A. Rausch, and J. L. Oldemeyer. 1978. Alaskan moose measurements and weights and measurement-weight relationships. *Can. J. Zool.* 56:298–306.

Fritts, S. H. 1983. Record dispersal by a wolf from Minnesota. *J. Mammal.* 64:166–67.

Fritts, S. H., and L. D. Mech. 1981. Dynamics, movements, and feeding ecology of a newly protected wolf population in northwestern Minnesota. *Wildl. Monogr.* 80.

Froberg, S. O., L. A. Carlson, and L. G. Ekelund. 1971. Local lipid stores and exercise. *Adv. Exp. Med. Biol.* 11:307–13.

Fuller, T. K. 1989. Population dynamics of wolves in north-central Minnesota. *Wildl. Monogr.* 105.

Fuller, T. K., and L. B. Keith. 1980. Wolf population dynamics and prey relationships in northeastern Alberta. *J. Wildl. Mgt.* 44:583–602.

———. 1981. Woodland caribou population dynamics in northeastern Alberta. *J. Wildl. Mgt.* 45:197–213.

Gasaway, W. C., R. D. Boertje, D. V. Grangaard, D. G. Kelleyhouse, R. O. Stephenson, and D. G. Larsen. 1992. The role of predation in limiting moose at low densities in Alaska and Yukon and implications for conservation. *Wildl. Monogr.* 120.

Gasaway, W. C., and J. W. Coady. 1974. Review of energy requirements and rumen fermentation in moose and other ruminants. *Nat. Can.* 101:227–62.

Gasaway, W. C., R. O. Stephenson, J. L. Davis, P. E. K. Shepard, and O. E. Burris. 1983. Interrelationships of wolves, prey, and man in interior Alaska. *Wildl. Monogr.* 84.

Geist, V. 1971. *Mountain sheep: A study in behavior and evolution.* Univ. of Chicago Press, Chicago.

———. 1974. On the relationship of social evolution and ecology of ungulates. *Amer. Zoologist* 14:205–20.

Gese, E. M., and L. D. Mech. 1991. Dispersal of wolves (*Canis lupus*) in northeastern Minnesota, 1969–1989. *Can. J. Zool.* 69:2946–55.

Grinnell, J., and T. Storer. 1916. Animal life as an asset of national parks. *Science* 44:375–80.

Haber, G. C. 1977. Socio-ecological dynamics of wolves and prey in a subarctic ecosystem. Ph.D. diss., Univ. of British Columbia, Vancouver, Can.

Haber, G. C. 1996. Biological, conservation, and ethical implications of exploiting wolves. *Conserv. Biol.* 19:1068–81.

Harbo, S. J., and F. C. Dean Jr. 1983. Historical and current perspectives on wolf management in Alaska. Pages 51–64 in L. N. Carbyn ed., *Wolves in Canada and Alaska: Their status, biology, and management.* Can. Wildl. Service Rept. Series 45.

Harrington, F. H., and L. D. Mech. 1979. Wolf howling and its role in territory maintenance. *Behaviour* 68:207–49.

Harrington, F. H., P. C. Paquet, J. Ryon, and J. C. Fentress. 1982. Monogamy in wolves: A review of the evidence. Pages 209–22 in F. H. Harrington and P. C. Paquet, eds., *Wolves of the world: Perspectives of behavior, ecology, and conservation.* Noyes Publications, Park Ridge, N.J.

Hayes, R. D. 1995. Numerical and functional responses of wolves, and regulation of moose in the Yukon. Master's thesis, Simon Fraser Univ., Burnaby, British Columbia, Can.

Hayes, R. D., and A. Baer. 1992. Brown bear, *Ursus arctos,* preying upon gray wolf, *Canis lupus,* pups at wolf den. *Can. Field Nat.* 106:381–82.

Hayes, R. D., A. M. Baer, and D. G. Larsen. 1991. *Population dynamics and prey relationships of an exploited and recovering wolf population in the southern Yukon.* Yukon F & W Branch, Dept. of Renewable Resources, Final Report TR-91-1.

Hayes, R. D., and J. R. Gunson. 1995. Status and management of wolves in Canada. Pages 21–34 in L. N. Carbyn, S. H. Fritts, and D. R. Seip, eds., *Ecology and conservation of wolves in a changing world.* Canadian Circumpolar Institute, Edmonton, Alberta, Can.

Hechtel, J. L. 1991. *Population dynamics of black bear populations.* Fort Wainwright, Alaska, Final Report to the U.S. Army.

Hillis, T. L. 1990. *The demography of the tundra wolf, Canis lupus, in the Keewatin District, Northwest Territories.* Dept. of Biology, Laurentian University, Sudbury, Ontario, Can.

Holand, O. 1992. Fat indices versus ingesta-free body fat in European roe deer. *J. Wildl. Mgt.* 56:241–45.

Holt, R. D. 1977. Predation, apparent competition, and the structure of prey communities. *Theor. Pop. Biol.* 12:197–229.

Hoskinson, R. L., and L. D. Mech. 1976. White-tailed deer migration and its role in wolf predation. *J. Wildl. Mgt.* 40:429–41.

Hovell, F. D. DeB., E. R. Orskov, D. J. Kyle, and N. A. Macleod. 1987. Undernutrition in sheep. Nitrogen repletion by N-depleted sheep. *Br. J. Nutr.* 57:77–78.

Howard, W. E. 1960. Innate and environmental dispersal of individual vertebrates. *Amer. Midl. Nat.* 63:152–61.

Hultman, E., and L. H. Nilsson. 1971. Liver glycogen in man, effect of different diets and muscular exercise. *Adv. Exp. Med. Biol.* 11:143–51.

Huot, J., and F. Goudreault. 1985. Evaluation of several indices for predicting total body fat of caribou. *Proc. 2nd N. Amer. Caribou Workshop*: 157–75.

Huxley, J. S. 1934. A natural experiment on the territorial instinct. *British Birds* 27 (10):270–77.

Johnson, M., D. H. Pletscher, and D. K. Boyd. 1994. Serologic investigations of canine parvovirus and canine distemper in relation to wolf pup mortalities. *J. Wildl. Diseases* 30:270–73.

Jordan, P. A., P. C. Shelton, and D. L. Allen. 1967. Numbers, turnover, and social structure of the Isle Royale wolf population. *Amer. Zoologist* 7:233–52.

Joslin, P. W. B. 1967. Movements and home sites of timber wolves in Algonquin Park. *Amer. Zoologist* 7:279–88.

Keith, L. B. 1983. Population dynamics of wolves. Pages 66–77 in L. N. Carbyn, ed., *Wolves in Canada and Alaska: Their status, biology, and management.* Can. Wildl. Service Rept. Series 45.

Kelsall, J. P. 1957. Continued barren-ground caribou studies. *Can. Wildl. Serv. Manage. Bull.* series 1, no. 12.

———. 1968. The migratory barren-ground caribou of Canada. Can. Wildl. Service Monogr. Series, no. 3.

Kennedy, P. K., M. L. Kennedy, P. L. Clarkson, and I. S. Liepins. 1991. Genetic variability in natural populations of the gray wolf. *Can. J. Zool.* 69:1183–88.

Klein, D. R., and R. G. White, eds., 1978. *Parameters of caribou population ecology in Alaska: Proceedings of a symposium and workshop*. Biol. Papers Univ. of Alaska Spec. Rept. 3, Fairbanks.

Kreeger, T. J. 1996. *Handbook of wildlife chemical immobilization*. International Wildl. Vet. Serv., Laramie, Wyo.

Kreeger, T. J., A. M. Fagella, U. S. Seal, L. D. Mech, M. Callahan, and B. Hall. 1987. Cardiovascular and behavioral responses of gray wolves to ketamine hydrochloride-xylazine hydrochloride immobilization and antagonism by yohimbine hydrochloride. *J. Wildl. Dis.* 23:463–70.

Kruuk, H. 1972. Surplus killing by carnivores. *J. Zool. Soc. London* 166:233–44.

Kunkel, K. E., and L. D. Mech. 1994. Wolf and bear predation on white-tailed deer fawns in northeastern Minnesota. *Can. J. Zool.* 72:1557–65.

Lack, D. 1954. *The natural regulation of animal numbers*. Clarendon Press, Oxford.

Landis, John. 1996. Unpublished 16 mm. footage. Gardner, Mont.

Lehman, N. E., P. Clarkson, L. D. Mech, T. J. Meier, and R. K. Wayne. 1992. A study of the genetic relationships within and among wolf packs using DNA fingerprinting and mitochondrial DNA. *Behav. Ecol. and Sociobiology* 30:83–94.

Leibholz, J. 1970. The effect of starvation and low nitrogen intakes on the concentration of free amino acids in the blood plasma and on the nitrogen metabolism in sheep. *Aust. J. Agric. Res.* 21:723–34.

Loftus, A. 1967. Tom Gibson—Meat hunter. *Alaskan Sportsman* 33 (8):20–22.

Mautz, W. W. 1978. Nutrition and carrying capacity. Pages 321–48 in J. L. Schmidt and D. L. Gilbert, eds., *Big game of North America: Ecology and management*. Stackpole Books, Harrisburg, Pa.

McCullough, D. R., and D. E. Ullrey. 1983. Proximate mineral and gross energy composition of white-tailed deer. *J. Wildl. Mgt.* 47:430–41.

McLaren, B. E., and R. O. Peterson. 1994. Wolves, moose, and tree rings on Isle Royale. *Science* 266:1555–58.

McRoberts, R. E., L. D. Mech, and R. O. Peterson. 1995. The cumulative effect of a consecutive winters' snow depth on moose and deer populations: A defence. *J. Anim. Ecol.* 64:131–35.

Mech, L. D. 1966a. *The wolves of Isle Royale*. U.S. National Park Service, Fauna of the National Parks Series, no. 7. Washington, D.C.

———. 1966b. Hunting behavior of timber wolves in Minnesota. *J. Mammal.* 47:347–48.

———. 1970. *The Wolf: The Ecology and behavior of an endangered species*. Doubleday Publishing Co., New York.

———. 1973. *Wolf numbers in the Superior National Forest of Minnesota*. USDA, Forest Service Res. Paper NC-97.

———. 1974a. Mammalian species: *Canis lupus*. The American Society of Mammalogists 37:1–6.

———. 1974b. Current techniques in the study of elusive wilderness carnivores. *Proc. XIth Int. Cong. Game Biol.*: 315–22.

———. 1977a. Population trend and winter deer consumption in a Minnesota wolf pack. Pages 55–79 in R. L. Phillips and C. Jonkel, eds., *Proc. 1975 Predator Symp.* Montana For. and Cons. Exp. Sta., Missoula.

———. 1977b. Productivity, mortality and population trend of wolves in northeastern Minnesota. *J. Mammal.* 58:559–74.

———. 1977c. Wolf-pack buffer zones as prey reservoirs. *Science* 198:320–21.

———. 1979. Making the most of radio-tracking. Pages 85–95 in C. J. Amlaner and D. W. MacDonald, eds., *A handbook on biotelemetry and radio tracking*. Pergamon Press, Oxford.

———. 1983. *A handbook of animal radio-tracking*. Univ. of Minnesota Press, Minneapolis.

———. 1986. *Wolf population in the central Superior National Forest, 1967–1985*. USDA, Forest Service Res. Paper NC-270.

———. 1987. Age, season, distance, direction, and social aspects of wolf dispersal from a Minnesota pack. Pages 55–74 in B. D. Chepko-Sade and Z. Halpin, eds., *Mammalian dispersal patterns*. Univ. of Chicago Press, Chicago.

———. 1988a. *The arctic wolf: Living with the pack*. Voyageur Press, Stillwater, Minn.

———. 1988b. Longevity in wild wolves. *J. Mammal.* 69:197–98.

———. 1990. Snow as a driving force in a wolf-deer system. *Trans. 19th Int. Union of Game Biol. Congr.*: 562 (abstract).

———. 1991. *The way of the wolf*. Voyageur Press, Stillwater, Minn.

———. 1993. Resistance of young wolf pups to inclement weather. *J. Mammal.* 74:485–86.

———. 1994a. Buffer zones of territories of gray wolves as regions of intraspecific strife. *J. Mammal.* 75:199–202.

———. 1994b. Regular and homeward travel speeds of arctic wolves. *J. Mammal.* 75:741–42.

———. 1995a. A ten-year history of the demography and productivity of an arctic wolf pack. *Arctic* 48:329–32.

———. 1995b. Summer movements and behavior of an arctic wolf, *Canis lupus*, pack without pups. *Can. Field Nat.* 109:473–75.

———. 1995c. What do we know about wolves and what more do we need to learn? Pages 537–45 in L. N. Carbyn, S. H. Fritts, and D. R. Seip, eds., *Ecology and conservation of wolves in a changing world.* Canadian Circumpolar Institute, Edmonton, Alberta, Can.

Mech, L. D., and G. D. DelGiudice. 1985. Limitations of the marrow-fat technique as an indicator of body condition. *Wildl. Soc. Bull.* 13:204–6.

Mech, L. D., and L. D. Frenzel Jr. 1971. *Ecological studies of the timber wolf in northeastern Minnesota.* USDA, Forest Service Res. Paper NC-52.

Mech, L. D., and S. M. Goyal. 1995. Effects of canine parvovirus on gray wolves in Minnesota. *J. Wildl. Mgt.* 59:565–70.

Mech, L. D., S. M. Goyal, C. N. Bota, and U. S. Seal. 1986. Canine parvovirus infection in wolves (*Canis lupus*) from Minnesota. *J. Wildl. Diseases* 22:104–6.

Mech, L. D., and H. H. Hertel. 1983. An eight year demography of a Minnesota wolf pack. *Acta Zool. Fenn.* 174:249–50.

Mech, L. D., and P. D. Karns. 1977. *Role of the wolf in a deer decline in the Superior National Forest.* USDA, Forest Service Res. Paper NC-148.

Mech, L. D., and R. E. McRoberts. 1990a. Relationship between age and mass among female white-tailed deer during winter and spring. *J. Mammal.* 71:686–89.

———. 1990b. Survival of white-tailed deer fawns in relation to maternal age. *J. Mammal.* 71:465–67.

Mech, L. D., R. E. McRoberts, R. O. Peterson, and R. E. Page. 1987. Relationship of deer and moose populations to previous winters' snow. *J. Anim. Ecol.* 56:615–27.

Mech, L. D., T. J. Meier, J. W. Burch, and L. G. Adams. 1995. Patterns of prey selection by wolves in Denali National Park, Alaska. Pages 231–44 in L. N. Carbyn, S. H. Fritts, and D. R. Seip, eds., *Ecology and conservation of wolves in a changing world.* Canadian Circumpolar Institute, Edmonton, Alberta, Can.

Mech, L. D., T. J. Meier, and U. S. Seal. 1993. Wolf nipple measurements as indices of age and breeding status. *Amer. Midl. Nat.* 129:266–71.

Mech, L. D., and M. E. Nelson. 1990a. Evidence of prey-caused mortality in three wolves. *Amer. Midl. Nat.* 123:207–8.

———. 1990b. Non-family wolf, (*Canis lupus*), packs. *Can. Field Nat.* 104:482–83.

Mech, L. D., M. E. Nelson, and R. E. McRoberts. 1991. Effects of maternal and grandmaternal nutrition on deer mass and vulnerability to wolf predation. *J. Mammal.* 72:146–51.

Mech, L. D., M. K. Phillips, D. W. Smith, and T. J. Kreeger. 1996. Denning behaviour of non-gravid wolves, *Canis lupus. Can. Field Nat.* 110:343–45.

Mech, L. D., and U. S. Seal. 1987. Premature reproductive activity in wild wolves. *J. Mammal.* 68:871–73.

Mech, L. D., U. S. Seal, and S. M. Arthur. 1984. Recuperation of a severely debilitated wolf. *J. Wildl. Diseases* 20:166–68.

Medjo, D. C., and L. D. Mech. 1976. Reproductive activity in nine and ten month old wolves. *J. Mammal.* 57:406–8.

Meier, T. J. 1987. *1986 aerial moose census—Denali National Park and Preserve.* U.S. Natl. Park Serv. Nat. Resour. Rept. AR-87/10.

Meier, T. J., J. W. Burch, L. D. Mech, and L. G. Adams. 1995. Pack structure and genetic relatedness among wolf packs in a naturally-regulated population. Pages 293–302 in L. N. Carbyn, S. H. Fritts, and D. R. Seip, eds., *Ecology and conservation of wolves in a changing world.* Canadian Circumpolar Institute, Edmonton, Alberta, Can.

Meier, T. J., J. A. Keay, J. C. Van Horn, and J. W. Burch. 1991. *1991 aerial moose survey—Denali National Park and Preserve.* U.S. Natl. Park Serv. Rept. AR-91/06.

Messier, F. 1985. Solitary living and extra-territorial movements of wolves in relation to social status and prey abundance. *Can. J. Zool.* 63:239–45.

———. 1991. The significance of limiting and regulating factors on the demography of moose and white-tailed deer. *J. Anim. Ecol.* 60:377–93.

———. 1995. Is there evidence for cumulative effect of snow on moose and deer populations? *J. Anim. Ecol.* 64:136–40.

Miller, F. L. 1995. Status of wolves on the Canadian Arctic Islands. Pages 35–42 in L. N. Carbyn, S. H. Fritts, and D. R. Seip, eds., *Ecology and conservation of wolves in a changing world.* Canadian Circumpolar Institute, Edmonton, Alberta, Can.

Miller, F. L., and E. Broughton. 1974. *Calf mortality on the calving grounds of Klaminuriak caribou, during 1970.* Can. Wildl. Service Rept. Series 26.

Miller, F. L., E. Broughton, and A. Gunn. 1988. *Mortality of migratory barren-ground caribou on the calving grounds of the Beverly herd, Northwest Territories, 1981–1983.* Can. Wildl. Service Occas. Paper 66.

Miller, F. L., A. Gunn, and E. Broughton. 1985. Surplus killing as exemplified by wolf predation on newborn caribou. *Can. J. Zool.* 63:295–300.

———. 1988. Utilization of carcasses of newborn caribou killed by wolves. *Proc. 3rd N. Amer. Caribou Workshop*: 73–87.

Miquelle, D. G., J. M. Peek, and V. Van Ballenberghe. 1992. Sexual segregation in Alaskan moose. *Wildl. Monogr.* 122.

Murie, A. 1944. *The wolves of Mount McKinley.* U.S. National Park Service, Fauna of the National Parks Series, no. 5. Washington, D.C.

———. 1981. *The grizzlies of Mount McKinley.* U.S. National Park Service Sci. Monogr. Series, no. 14. Washington, D.C.

Murie, O. J. 1935. *Alaska-Yukon caribou.* USDA Bur. Biol. Surv. N. Amer. Fauna Series, no. 4. Washington, D.C.

Neiland, K. A. 1970. Weight of dried marrow fat as indicators of fat in caribou femurs. *J. Wildl. Mgt.* 34:904–7.

Nelson, M. E., and L. D. Mech. 1981. Deer social organization and wolf predation in northwestern Minnesota. *Wildl. Monogr.* 77.

Nelson, M. E., and L. D. Mech. 1986a. *Deer population in the central Superior National Forest, 1967–1985.* USDA, Forest Service Res. Paper NC-271.

———. 1986b. Relationship between snow depth and gray wolf predation on white-tailed deer. *J. Wildl. Mgt.* 50:471–74.

Nelson, T. A., and A. Woolf. 1987. Mortality of white-tailed deer fawns in southern Illinois. *J. Wildl. Mgt.* 51:326–29.

Nichols, L., Jr. 1978. Dall's sheep. Pages 173–89 in J. L. Schmidt and D. L. Gilbert, eds., *Big game of North America: Ecology and management.* Stackpole Books, Harrisburg, Pa.

Olson, S. F. 1938a. Organization and range of the pack. *Ecology* 19:168–70.

———. 1938b. A study in predatory relationship with particular reference to the wolf. *Sci. Monthly* 46:323–36.

Ozoga, J. J., and L. J. Verme. 1982. Physical and reproductive characteristics of a supplementally-fed white-tailed deer herd. *J. Wildl. Mgt.* 46:281–301.

———. 1986. Relation of maternal age to fawn-rearing success in white-tailed deer. *J. Wildl. Mgt.* 50:480–86.

Packard, J. M., and L. D. Mech. 1980. Population regulation in wolves. Pages 135–50 in M. N. Cohen, R. S. Malphasse, and H. G. Klein, eds., *Biosocial mechanisms of population regulation.* Yale Univ. Press, New Haven, Conn.

———. 1983. Population regulation in wolves. Pages 151–73 in F. L. Bunnell, D. S. Eastman, and J. M. Peek, eds., *Symp. on natural regulation of wildlife populations.* Proc. No. 14, For. Wildl. and Range Exp. Stn., Univ. of Idaho, Moscow.

Page, R. E. 1985. Early caribou calf mortality in northwestern British Columbia. Master's thesis, Univ. of Victoria, British Columbia, Can.

Paquay, R., R. Debaere, and A. Lousse. 1972. The capacity of the mature cow to lose and recover nitrogen and the significance of protein reserves. *Br. J. Nutr.* 27:27–37.

Parker, G. R., and S. Luttich. 1986. Characteristics of the wolf (*Canis lupus labradorius* Goldman) in northern Quebec and Labrador. *Arctic* 39:145–49.

Peace River Films. 1974. *Following the Tundra Wolf.*

Peters, R. P., and L. D. Mech. 1975. Scent marking in wolves: A field study. *Amer. Scient.* 63:628–37.

Peterson, R. O. 1977. *Wolf ecology and prey relationships on Isle Royale.* U.S. National Park Service Sci. Mon. Series, no. 11.

———. 1988. Increased osteoarthritis in moose from Isle Royale. *J. Wildl. Diseases* 24:461–66.

———. 1995. *The wolves of Isle Royale: A broken balance.* Willow Creek Press, Minocqua, Wis.

Peterson, R. O., and D. L. Allen. 1974. Snow conditions as a parameter in moose-wolf relationships. *Naturaliste Canadien* 101:481–92.

Peterson, R. O., and R. E. Page. 1988. The rise and fall of the Isle Royale wolves. *J. Mammal.* 69:89–99.

Peterson, R. O., N. J. Thomas, and J. M. Thurber, J. A. Vucetich, and T. A. Waite. 1998. Population limitation and the wolves of Isle Royale, 1987–1995. *J. Mammal.* 79.

Peterson, R. O., J. D. Woolington, and T. N. Bailey. 1984. Wolves of Kenai Peninsula, Alaska. *Wildl. Monogr.* 88.

Pimlott, D. H. 1959. Reproduction and productivity of Newfoundland moose. *J. Wildl. Mgt.* 23:381–401.

Pimlott, D. H., J. A. Shannon, and G. B. Kolenosky. 1969. *The ecology of the timber wolf in Algonquin Provincial Park, Ontario.* Ont. Dep. Lands and For. Res. Rept. (Wildl.). 87.

Pimm, S. L. 1991. *The balance of nature? Ecological issues in the conservation of a species and communities.* Univ. of Chicago Press, Chicago.

Potvin, F. 1988. Wolf movements and population dynamics in Papineau-Labelle Reserve, Quebec. *Can. J. Zool.* 66:1266–73.

Queller, D. C., and K. F. Goodnight. 1989. Estimating relatedness using genetic markers. *Evolution* 43:258–75.

Rausch, R. A. 1967. Some aspects of the population ecology of wolves, Alaska. *Amer. Zoologist* 7:253–65.

Rausch, R. A., and R. A. Hinman. 1977. Wolf management in Alaska—exercise in futility? Pages 147–56 in R. L. Phillips and C. Jonkel, eds., *Proc. 1975 Predator Symp.* Montana For. and Cons. Exp. Sta., Missoula.

Rawson, T. M. 1994. Alaska's first wolf controversy: Predator and prey in Mount McKinley National Park, 1930–1953. Ph.D. diss., Univ. of Alaska, Fairbanks.

Ream, R. R., M. W. Fairchild, D. K. Boyd, and D. H. Pletscher. 1991. Population dynamics and home range changes in a colonizing wolf population. Pages 349–66 in R. B. Keiter and M. S. Boyce, eds., *The greater Yellowstone ecosystem: Redefining America's wilderness heritage.* Yale Univ. Press, New Haven, Conn.

Reynolds, H., and J. L. Hechtel. 1983. *Population structure, reproductive biology, and movement patterns of grizzly bears in northcentral Alaska Range.* Alaska Dep. Fish and Game. Fed Aid in Wildl. Restor. Final Rept., Juneau.

Risenhoover, K. L. 1989. Composition and quality of moose winter diets in interior Alaska. *J. Wildl. Mgt.* 53:568–77.

Rogers, L. L., L. D. Mech, D. K. Dawson, J. M. Peek, and M. Korb. 1980. Deer distribution in relation to wolf pack territory edges. *J. Wildl. Mgt.* 44:253–58.

Rothman, R. J., and L. D. Mech. 1979. Scent-marking in lone wolves and newly formed pairs. *Anim. Behav.* 27:750–60.

Roy, M. S., E. Geffen, D. Smith, E. A. Ostrander, and R. K. Wayne. 1994. Patterns of differentiation and hybridization in North American wolf-like canids. MOI Biol. Evol. II:553–70.

Rutberg, A. T. 1987. Adaptive hypotheses of birth synchrony in ruminants: An interspecific test. *Amer. Nat.* 130:692–710.

Sadleir, R. M. F. S. 1969. *The ecology and reproduction in wild and domestic mammals.* Methuen, London.

Scarff, J. E. 1972. The politics of wolf control: An interdisciplinary evolution of public policies, political institutions, and political science analyses and decision-making models. Honor's thesis, Stanford Univ., Calif.

Schlegal, M. 1976. *Factors affecting calf elk survival in northcentral Idaho.* W. Assoc. of State Game and Fish Commissioners. 56:342–55.

Schmidt, P. A., and L. D. Mech. 1997. Wolf pack size and food acquisition. *Amer. Nat.* 150 (4):513–17.

Schwartz, C. C., and A. W. Franzman. 1991. Interrelationship of black bears to moose and forest succession in the northern coniferous forests. *Wildl. Monogr.* 113.

Seal, U. S., and L. D. Mech. 1983. Blood indicators of seasonal metabolic patterns in captive adult wolves. *J. Wildl. Mgt.* 47:704–15.

Seal, U. S., L. D. Mech, and V. Van Ballenberghe. 1975. Blood analyses of wolf pups and their ecological and metabolic interpretation. *J. Mammal.* 56:64–75.

Seip, D. R. 1991. Predation and caribou populations. *Proc. 5th N. Amer. Caribou Workshop*: 46–52.

Sheldon, C. 1930. *The wilderness of Denali: Explorations of a hunter-naturalist in northern Alaska.* Charles Scribner's Sons, New York.

Shields, W. M. 1983. Genetic considerations in the management of the wolf and other large vertebrates: An alternative view. Pages 90–92 in L. N. Carbyn, ed., *Wolves in Canada and Alaska: Their status, biology, and management.* Can. Wildl. Service Rept. Series 45.

Singer, F. J. 1986. History of caribou and wolves in Denali National Park and Preserve-appendices. U.S. Natl. Park. Serv. Res/Resour. Mgt. Rept. AR-11, Anchorage, Alaska.

Singer, F. J., J. Dalle-Molle, and J. Van Horn. 1981. *Dall sheep count, 1981.* unpubl. rept., U.S. Natl. Park Service.

Skogland, T. 1990. Density-dependence in a fluctuating wild reindeer herd: Maternal vs offspring effects. *Oecologia* 84:442–50.

Skoog, R. O. 1968. Ecology of the caribou (*Rangifer tarandus granti*) in Alaska. Ph.D. diss. Univ. of California, Berkeley.

Smith, D., T. J. Meier, E. Geffen, L. D. Mech, J. W. Burch, L. G. Adams, and R. K. Wayne. 1997. Is incest common in gray wolf packs? *Behav. Ecol.* 8:384–91.

Smith, E. L., R. L. Hill, I. R. Lehman, R. J. Lefkowitz, P. Handler, and A. White. 1983. *Principles of biochemistry. Part 2. General aspects.* 7th ed. McGraw Hill, New York.

Smith, M. E. 1994. Black bear denning ecology and habitat selection in interior Alaska. Master's thesis. Univ. of Alaska, Fairbanks.

Sokolov, V. E., A. S. Severtsov, and A. V. Shubkina. 1990. Modelling of the selective behavior of the predator towards prey: The use of borzois for catching saigas. *Zool. J.* 69:126–27.

Stenlund, M. H. 1955. *A field study of the timber wolf* (Canis lupus) *in the Superior National Forest, Minnesota.* Minn. Dept. Cons. Tech. Bull. 4.

Stephan, J. K., B. Chow, L. A. Frohman, and B. F. Chow. 1971. Relationship of growth hormone to the growth retardation associated with maternal dietary restriction. *J. Nutr.* 101:1453–58.

Stephenson, R. O., W. B. Ballard, C. A. Smith, and K. Richardson. 1995. Wolf biology and management in Alaska, 1981–1992. Pages 43–54 in L. N. Carbyn, S. H. Fritts, and D. R. Seip, eds., *Ecology and conservation of wolves in a changing world.* Canadian Circumpolar Institute, Edmonton, Alberta, Can.

Stephenson, R. O., and D. James. 1982. Wolf movements and food habits in northwest Alaska. Pages 26–42 in F. H. Harrington and P. C. Paquet, eds., *Wolves of the world: Perspectives of behavior, ecology, and conservation.* Noyes Publications, Park Ridge, N.J.

Stephenson, R. O., and L. J. Johnson. 1972. *Wolf report.* Alaska Dept. Fish and Game Fed. Aid in Wildl. Restoration Proj. Rept., Proj. W-17-13. vol. X.

Stephenson, T. R. 1995. Nutritional ecology of moose and vegetation succession on the Copper River Delta, Alaska. Ph.D. diss., Univ. of Idaho, Moscow.

Sumanik, R. S. 1987. Wolf ecology in the Kluane region, Yukon Territory. Master's thesis. Mich. Tech. Univ., Houghton.

Taylor, D. L., J. Dalle-Molle, and J. Van Horn. 1987. *Survey of Dall sheep, Denali National Park and Preserve—1987.* U.S. Natl. Park Serv. Nat. Resour. Rept. AR-88/13.

Thiel, R. P., and S. H. Fritts. 1983. Chewing-removal of radio collars by gray wolves in Wisconsin. *J. Wildl. Mgt.* 47:851–52.

Thomas, D. C. 1982. The relationship between fertility and fat reserves of Peary caribou. *Can. J. Zool.* 60:597–602.

Thurber, J. M., and R. O. Peterson. 1993. Effects of population density and pack size on the foraging ecology of gray wolves. *J. Mammal.* 74:879–89.

Torbit, S. C., L. H. Carpenter, D. M. Swift, and A. W. Alldredge. 1985. Differential loss of fat and protein by mule deer during winter. *J. Wildl. Mgt.* 49:80–85.

Treisman, M. 1975. Predation and evolution of gregariousness. I. Models for concealment and evasion. *Anim. Behav.* 23:779–800.

Troyer, W. 1977. *Population movement studies of the McKinley caribou herd.* U.S. National Park Serv. Nat. Res. Prog. Rept. AR-76/01, Anchorage, Alaska.

———. 1978. *Population and movement studies of the McKinley caribou herd.* U.S. Natl. Park Serv. Surv. and Inv. Rept. AR-77/03.

Valkenburg, P., D. A. Anderson, J. L. Davis, and D. J. Reed. 1985. Evaluation of an aerial photocensus technique for caribou based on radio-telemetry. *Proc. 2nd North Amer. Caribou Workshop:* 287–99.

Valkenburg, P., and J. L. Davis. 1988. *Status, movements, range use patterns, and limiting factors of the Fortymile caribou herd.* Alaska Dept. Fish and Game Fed. Aid in Wildl. Restoration. Rept.

Van Ballenberghe, V. 1983a. Extraterritorial movements and dispersal of wolves in southcentral Alaska. *J. Mammal.* 64:168–71.

———. 1983b. Two litters raised in one year by a wolf pack. *J. Mammal.* 64:171–72.

———. 1985. Wolf predation on caribou: The Nelchina Herd Case history. *J. Wildl. Mgt.* 49:711–20.

Van Ballenberghe, V., and A. W. Erickson. 1973. A wolf pack kills another wolf. *Amer. Wildl. Nat. Resour. Confer.* 39:313–20.

Van Ballenberghe, V., A. W. Erickson, and D. Byman. 1975. Ecology of the timber wolf in northeastern Minnesota. *Wildl. Monogr.* 43.

Van Ballenberghe, V., and L. D. Mech. 1975. Weights, growth, and survival of timber wolf pups in Minnesota. *J. Mammal.* 56:44–63.

Verme, L. J. 1962. Mortality of white-tailed deer fawns in relation to nutrition. *Natl. Deer Disease Symp. Proc.:* 15–38.

———. 1963. Effect of nutrition on growth of white-tailed deer fawns. *Trans. N. Amer. Wildl. Confer.:* 431–43

Voigt, D. R., G. B. Kolenosky, and D. H. Pimlott. 1976. Changes in summer foods of wolves in central Ontario. *J. Wildl. Mgt.* 40:636–68.

Walker, T. 1992. *Denali journal: A thoughtful look at wildlife in Alaska's majestic national park.* Stackpole, Harrisburg, Pa.

Watkins, B. E., J. H. Witham, D. E. Ullrey, D. J. Watkins, and J. M. Jones. 1991. Body composition and condition evaluation of white-tailed deer fawns. *J. Wildl. Mgt.* 55:39–51.

Wayne, R. K., D. A. Gilbert, D. Lehman, K. Hansen,

A. Eisenhawer, D. Girman, L. D. Mech, P. J. P. Gogan, U. S. Seal, and R. J. Krumenaker. 1991. Conservation genetics of the endangered Isle Royale gray wolf. *Conserv. Biol.* 5:41–51.

Weaver, J. L., C. Arvidson, and P. Wood. 1992. Two wolves, *Canis lupus*, killed by a moose, *Alces alces,* in Jasper National Park, Alberta. *Can. Field Nat.* 106:126–27.

Whitten, K. R., G. W. Garner, F. J. Mauer, and R. B. Harris. 1992. Productivity and early calf survival in the Porcupine caribou herd. *J. Wildl. Mgt.* 56:201–12.

Wilson, E. O. 1975. *Sociobiology*. Belknap Press, Cambridge, Mass.

Wolfe, M. L. 1969. Age determination in moose from cementum layers of molar teeth. *J. Wildl. Mgt.* 33:428–31.

Wolfe, M. L., and D. L. Allen. 1973. Continued studies of the status, socialization and relationships of Isle Royale wolves, 1967–70. *J. Mammal.* 54:611–35.

Woolpy, J. H., and I. Eckstrand. 1979. Wolf pack genetics, a computer-simulation with theory. Pages 206–24 in E. Klinghammer, ed., *The behavior and ecology of wolves*. Garland STPM Press, New York.

Wydeven, A. P., R. N. Schultz, and R. P. Theil. 1995. Monitoring of a gray wolf (*Canis lupus*) population in Wisconsin, 1979–1991. Pages 147–56 in L. N. Carbyn, S. H. Fritts, and D. R. Seip, eds., *Ecology and conservation of wolves in a changing world*. Canadian Circumpolar Institute, Edmonton, Alberta, Can.

Young, S. P., and E. A. Goldman. 1944. *The wolves of North America: Part two*. General Publishing Company, Toronto, Ontario, Can.

Zamenhof, S., and E. Van Marthens. 1977. The effects of chronic undernutrition on rat brain development. *Federation Proc.* 36:1108.

———. 1978. The effects of chronic undernutrition over generations on rat development. *J. Nutr.* 108:1719–23.

Zamenhof, S., E. Van Marthens, and L. Grauel. 1971. DNA (cell number) in neonatal brain: Second generation (F2) alteration by maternal (F0) dietary protein restriction. *Science* 172:850–51.

Zarnke, R. L., and W. B. Ballard. 1987. Serologic survey for selected microbial pathogens of wolves in Alaska. *J. Wildl. Diseases* 23:77–85.

Zeman, F. J. 1967. Effect on the young rat of maternal protein restriction. *J. Nutrition* 93:167–73.

# *Index*

*L. David Mech* has been a wildlife research biologist studying wolves for the U.S. Department of the Interior since 1970, and an adjunct professor at the University of Minnesota since 1979. He has published numerous articles about wolves and other wildlife and five books about wolves, including *The Wolf: Ecology and Behavior of an Endangered Species* and *The Arctic Wolf: Living with the Pack,* both of which have sold over 100,000 copies.

*Layne G. Adams* was a wildlife research biologist for the National Park Service in Alaska from 1985 to 1993, until U.S. Department of the Interior research was consolidated into the U.S. Geological Survey. He has studied mountain goats, grizzly bears, caribou, raptors, and wolves and has published numerous articles about them.

*Thomas J. Meier* is a wildlife biologist who has studied wolves since 1976. After working in Minnesota and Wisconsin, he moved to Alaska in 1986 to conduct fieldwork for the Denali wolf project along with John Burch. Meier has published several articles about wolves, and he is working toward a Ph.D. at the University of Minnesota on the relationship between wolf pack spacing and wolf genetics.

*John W. Burch* studied wolves in Minnesota from 1980 to 1985 and was hired as a wildlife biologist in Alaska to help carry out fieldwork for the Denali wolf project. Burch is studying wolves in Yukon Charley Rivers National Preserve for the U.S. National Park Service. He has authored several articles about wolves and is working toward a master's degree at the University of Alaska on computer analysis of wolf location data.

*Bruce W. Dale* conducted research with the U.S. National Park Service in Alaska from 1984 to 1995 on wolves, moose, and caribou and has published several articles about these species. He is currently a wildlife biologist for the Alaska Department of Fish and Game.